A Life at the Crossroads

A Life at the Crossroads

An Autobiography

MICHAEL L. COOPER-WHITE

RESOURCE *Publications* · Eugene, Oregon

A LIFE AT THE CROSSROADS
An Autobiography

Copyright © 2024 Michael L. Cooper-White. All rights reserved. Except for brief quotations in critical publications or reviews, no part of this book may be reproduced in any manner without prior written permission from the publisher. Write: Permissions, Wipf and Stock Publishers, 199 W. 8th Ave., Suite 3, Eugene, OR 97401.

Resource Publications
An Imprint of Wipf and Stock Publishers
199 W. 8th Ave., Suite 3
Eugene, OR 97401

www.wipfandstock.com

PAPERBACK ISBN: 978-1-6667-8988-1
HARDCOVER ISBN: 978-1-6667-8989-8
EBOOK ISBN: 978-1-6667-8990-4

VERSION NUMBER 01/03/24

Dedicated to my family, who make life joyful,
friends and colleagues who made it possible,
and to those yet to come, so they understand.

Thus says the Lord: Stand at the crossroads and look, and ask for the ancient paths, where the good way lies; and walk in it and find rest for your souls.

—Jeremiah 6:16

Does not wisdom call and understanding raise her voice?
On the heights, beside the way at the crossroads she takes her stand.

—Proverbs 8:1–2

Two roads diverged in a wood, and I—I took the one less traveled by,
And that has made all the difference.

—Robert Frost

We have to get used to the idea that at the most important crossroads in our life there are no signs.

—Ernest Hemingway

We stand at the crossroads, each minute, each hour, each day, making choices.

—Benjamin Franklin

If you are going down a road and don't like what's in front of you, and look behind you and don't like what you see, get off the road. Create a new path!

—Maya Angelou

Bearing witness at the crossroads of history and hope, the Lutheran Theological Seminary at Gettysburg proclaims Jesus Christ to a restless world by preparing our students for faithful discipleship.

—Vision statement of former Gettysburg Seminary

Contents

Prologue: Looking Through the Crossroads Prism | ix
Acknowledgements | xv
Introduction: Not Just the Facts, but "What Does This Mean?" | xvii

1   Roots in Germany and the American Midwest | 1
2   Growing Up in the 1950's and 60's | 20
3   Moving East and from Law to Gospel | 52
4   Chile: A Life-Changing Pilgrimage | 66
5   Back to the U.S. and Final Year of Seminary | 84
6   The Angelica Years: Farm Boy Becomes City Shepherd | 91
7   Coalition and Synodical Ministry: A Dozen Years of *Syzygy* | 112
8   Serving a New Church and Unity-Challenged Synod | 127
9   The Chicago Years: Living in the Whole Church | 141
10   Gettysburg Seminary: My Early Years on the Ridge | 159
11   Seminary in an Era of Historic Transformation | 189
12   Gettysburg's Surprising Final Chapter | 208
13   Endgame: Historic Seminary's Last President | 236
14   An Active Retirement | 246

End Word: Summing It All Up (Thus Far!) | 260

Prologue: Looking Through the Crossroads Prism

It had been a long, sweltering hot day in the remote "repoblación" (repopulated village) of Panchimilama in the Department of La Paz south of El Salvador's capital city. We had accompanied Salvadoran Bishop Medardo Gomez and a small entourage of others making a pastoral visit to the fragile, fearful community of a few hundred brave repatriated Salvadorans. Years before, Panchimilama had been decimated by Salvador's brutal armed forces, who were systematically destroying hundreds of similar communities under the guise of "rooting out the communists." Those who survived the massacre scattered in all directions, with many joining thousands of their compatriots across the border at refugee camps in Honduras. With the support of the Salvadoran Lutheran Church and human rights organizations, the word went out in 1987 that Panchimilama's residents could return and rebuild their lives.

By the time our small delegation arrived in early1988, the courageous people of Panchimilama had made good progress. Despite living in abject poverty, with few jobs and scarce resources available to them, they had organized a school, formed a community council, and founded a mission church.

After an arduous minivan journey over a "road" that hardly merited the name, we were dropped off and made the rest of the journey to the hidden enclave on foot. My spouse Pamela and I will never forget the image of the bishop galloping down into a steep ravine, kept from falling again and again by a walking stick that, unlike the "croziers" carried by many bishops in liturgical processions, actually had a practical purpose!

As things often go in El Salvador and other places in Latin America, "time" is a fluid concept. The worship service doesn't necessarily begin at a fixed hour, but rather when the people are gathered. Desperate for contact with any friendly outsiders, the local residents couldn't get enough of our time, especially that of the renowned and revered bishop. Following the assassination of Roman Catholic Archbishop Oscar Romero in 1980, Bishop Gomez became for many Salvadorans, including non-Lutherans, his unofficial successor. More than most of the Catholic bishops, Gomez was recognized as a fearless champion of human rights who would go toe-to-toe with Salvadoran military and civic leaders when necessary. Medardo had been arrested and interrogated, and briefly left the country for a time after receiving multiple death threats.

So, while the day's planning by church officials insisted on getting us out of the village and back to San Salvador before dark, things didn't go as planned. Not only did we leave the village later than expected, but when we arrived at the designated rendezvous point, the promised van was not there. With darkness descending rapidly on a moonless evening, our transport finally arrived, and we began the journey homeward. As we proceeded, we suddenly spotted a couple of teenage soldiers coming out onto the road with their machine guns poised. "Son los militares," ("They're military soldiers") our driver blurted out anxiously.

As we came to a halt, the young soldiers demanded we get out of the vehicle. We found ourselves looking down the barrels of their ominous automatic weapons. As they began their interrogation, they kept clicking the safeties off and on, signaling their readiness to gun us down at any instant. Without exchanging a word or glance, Pam and I instinctively moved to flank the bishop. Each putting an arm around his shoulders, we felt Medardo trembling as we identified ourselves as U.S. citizens accompanying the bishop on a Christian pastoral visit.

For several years, U.S. church leaders and others committed to human rights had formed small delegations to accompany Salvadoran church leaders. It was widely known that the Salvadoran armed forces depended heavily on U.S. financial support for the civil war against the country's own citizens. Public outcries followed the murder of four American women missionaries in 1980, and other atrocities that befell U.S. citizens. Salvadoran government and military officials understood that acts of violence against American citizens could jeopardize their U.S. aid. Accordingly, "accompaniment" by North Americans afforded a measure of protection to vulnerable Salvadoran church leaders accused of being "communist supporters."[1]

Three years before, in January of 1985, I had joined three others in a delegation Pam organized and led. During that month-long sojourn, our small delegation provided similar support for Baptist church leaders, accompanying them at church services and on all their travels to the countryside, and at important meetings. While that mission had its hairy moments, we had never felt as vulnerable and likely to be killed as at that tiny crossroads near Panchimilama.

Getting out of the van, I clicked on a small mini-Dictaphone I carried in my pocket. I thought to myself, "If we're shot, maybe it will be recorded, and someone will know what truly happened and how we died." As our interrogation proceeded, one of the soldiers began rifling through our possessions, demanding, "Let me see your communist propaganda." We kept repeating we had on board only Bibles and Christian pamphlets. It appeared the soldier might be illiterate as he kept staring at materials with a puzzled look on his face. After a few moments of further harassment, which seemed an eternity at the time, the youthful soldiers gruffly said that while they still had suspicions we were free to go.

Crossroads Moments

Three and a half decades after that nighttime incident at a nondescript intersection in the depths of Salvador's outback, it remains a vivid memory as one of the "crossroads moments" of my life. While not the first time I had stood "in the shadow of death," as the Psalmist describes such life-threatening occasions, that encounter in the Salvadoran province of La Paz (which means "Peace") has shaped my vocational and personal journey. In ways I cannot fully describe, over time it has become a kind of prism through which the years both before and after are seen with greater clarity and richer colors.

As noted, those precarious moments after our visit to Panchimilama were not the first time Pam and I chose to place ourselves in harm's way in El Salvador. Also, a dozen years before, I had spent an entire year in another Latin American war zone, at one point sheltering in my home an

---

1. Such "protection" and the safety of U.S. citizens accompanying Salvadorans facing persecution had its limits, of course. Less than a year after our visit to Panchimilama, the beleaguered village suffered a grenade attack, in which two American Lutherans were among those sustaining serious shrapnel wounds.

individual who was on the most-wanted list of Chile's brutal secret death squads. During that year, too, I had the incredible privilege of working alongside some of the world's most valiant and courageous Christian leaders, including Lutheran Bishop Helmut Frenz and his successor, my internship supervisor Esteban Schaller.

At times when I have been discouraged and tempted to wallow in self-pity, I recalled the bravery displayed over decades by Bishops Frenz, Schaller, Gomez, and so many other courageous leaders around the world. While not insubstantial, my challenges have paled in comparison to theirs. These saints of our time, who also include a host of "ordinary folks" with whom I have rubbed shoulders, have been my inspiration, especially in times of challenging professional seasons and personal crises.

Looking back over five decades since I began my journey on a pathway of church leadership, I am amazed at the opportunities and privileges I have been afforded. My ministries have taken me from coast to coast in this country, along with occasional forays into Latin America. When I enrolled in seminary in the fall of 1972, I imagined myself serving an entire career as pastor in a local congregation. After an initial parish call of five years, I have never again engaged in full-time parish ministry. Each place I served came as a surprise. As I so often counseled seminarians anxious about where they might end up to "be open to surprises," my calls came from unexpected directions and posed challenges for which I sometimes felt inadequately prepared and ill-equipped. Had anyone suggested in the mid-1970's when I was ordained a Lutheran pastor, that this farm boy's journey would include inner city ministry in Los Angeles, the nation's second largest city, directing an urban coalition in the San Francisco Bay area for a decade, serving as a regional and national church executive, and then a seminary president I would have said, "That's not going to happen." But all those things did happen!

That pattern of being surprised has continued now in what are called my "retirement" years. For over five years I was a part-time journalist contributing several times a week to our local daily newspaper, *The Gettysburg Times*. Adjunct teaching for Union Theological Seminary in New York City and the Eastern Mennonite University, plus serving Brite Divinity School in Fort Worth, Texas as interim president, have given me the opportunity to keep a foot in academia. While I had planned to continue flying and some flight instructing, learning to fly gliders and being a tow pilot hauling other motorless crafts into the air were surprises I had not envisioned on my retirement bucket list.

While there are a few regrets and some painful memories, my overarching feeling is one of gratitude. Above all, I am grateful for a loving family, and a wide circle of friends and former colleagues. It is for them I write, to express that gratitude and share stories of our planned and chance meetings at a number of life's crossroads.

Acknowledgements

As noted, the people who have had an impact on my life number in the hundreds. I can offer only a few glimpses into the stories of a small circle of family, friends, and coworkers. If in any way I have misrepresented their actions or attitudes, I sincerely apologize. To all who have been mentors, colleagues, and companions on my journey, I express profound gratitude. Foremost, of course, are the members of my family, both living and those who have completed their sojourn on earth. To them this book is dedicated, with thanks for recalling events that make up our collective stories, and for their unwavering love and encouragement.

While much in the book flows from the wells of my memory, I have also relied heavily on historical documents accumulated and preserved over the years. Where there were gaps in memory or paper trails, I consulted a number of former colleagues for clarification of details. Meriting special note are Pastors Eric Shafer and John Spangler. Our frequent conversations inevitably turn to events of the past, when I served with Eric in ELCA churchwide leadership posts, and with John at Gettysburg Seminary.

The good folks at Wipf and Stock publishers have been kind and helpful at every turn, and I thank them for including the book in the Resources line.

Above all, I owe a debt of gratitude to the person who has been my life partner now for almost four decades. Among her many gifts, Pamela Cooper-White is an internationally recognized professor, scholar, and acclaimed writer. In addition to signaling where my recollection of certain shared events may have been incomplete or inaccurate, she offered her editorial expertise in reviewing every sentence. While my final product may still lack fluidity or lucidity at some points, incorporating her hundreds of editorial suggestions and corrections improved it immeasurably. I am blessed beyond measure by her love!

Introduction:
Not Just the Facts, but
"What Does This Mean?"

OUT ON THE EASTERN edge of the great prairie flatlands in western Minnesota, two narrow gravel roads intersect five miles northwest of a tiny rural village. Of the millions of crossroads on the planet, it is among the more remote and unremarkable. Only recently, that remote rural locale was assigned a street address, and a green signpost designates it as 270th Avenue and 330th Street, Wendell, MN 56590.

In the dead of winter, howling winds rush in from the west. There on "the flats," those frigid winds rage unimpeded. For hundreds of miles westward, no hills or obstructions tame them as they gain momentum and whip up gale-force blizzards. Come summer on the prairie, thunderstorms build mountain-sized cumulonimbus clouds on blistering hot afternoons. Rainstorms' impressiveness is outdone only when some of those dark clouds start swirling around like water swishing down a drain. They can generate tornados as impressive and destructive as any on the planet.

At that little crossroads in that remote prairie spot, a visitor passing by today sees only prairie grasses, short scrub trees, and a small shallow lake. It is a popular stopover and refueling site for migrating waterfowl in springtime and fall. A farmstead at that forlorn crossroads, known for a generation as "the Cooper place," is no more. The landscape has returned to the way it appeared for eons before it was interrupted by human occupancy for a few decades. Only the crossroads remain to mark the memories and signal a history of "civilization." All signs are gone that a family once lived on that acreage in an old frame house, that an award-winning small dairy operation was housed in a typical 1950's barn, or that lush vegetable and flower gardens were tended lovingly by the lady of the land.

Where tractors roamed the fields and prepared them for planting, now only gophers ply their trade when the earth wakes up in springtime. Where on hot summer evenings a few decades ago the sounds of machines running late into the night echoed off the walls of the buildings, now there is only the soft whooshing of nocturnal prairie winds. Where two teenagers and their little brother walked down a driveway to catch the big orange bus by the mailbox on brisk autumn days, no one sets foot these days. The mailbox is long gone. A bus passes by no more. The schools in town, to which the bus delivered the threesome, have gone the way of consolidation in a neighboring community.

One of those teenagers died decades ago in her 50's, and the other is an octogenarian. Little brother has retired. He now finds time to write these reflections. He finds the imagery of a crossroads fitting to the task. There have been many along the way. The best part of the journey has been sharing it with those who traveled with me. Most memorable among the many crossroads have been those intersections at which I was introduced to those who mean most to me. Family members, of course, top the list. An ever-expanding circle of friends enlivened the many roads traveled thus far. Coworkers, who number in the hundreds, were met, and later bid farewell at a dozen workplace stopovers along the way.

By the grace of God, mine remains an unfinished journey as I now find myself in my eighth decade. Whether I am blessed with many more years or only a few, I have the sense that the most significant chapters of my life have been written—at least in terms of my professional contributions. Perhaps my children or others will write a final addendum when I move along into the larger life of God. But it is time to record personal memories, and also preserve some elements of Lutheran church history and particularly its most historic American seminary, of which I was privileged to serve as the twelfth and last president. From one perspective, any autobiography can be viewed as intrinsically egotistical. All who presume to record their life stories do so with the conviction that they matter. I do believe that every life matters, and I wish that every person who has ever lived could have had the resources and luxury of time which now enable me to do this work. If pressed further on the matter of why I have taken on this challenging task of creating a memoir or autobiography, I respond on two levels, personal and professional. I believe those closest to me—my wife, children and grandchildren, and a small circle of

INTRODUCTION: NOT JUST THE FACTS, BUT "WHAT DOES THIS MEAN?" xix

intimate friends—will appreciate a record of their roots and our shared experiences. If the maxim is true that we cannot know who we are if we don't understand from whence we have come, this book will make at least modest contributions to my progeny's grasp of their roots.

On a personal level, I do confess to a yearning that I think is a universal human one: I want to be remembered! In my mind's eye I imagine days long after my cremains have been absorbed back into the soil in which they are placed after my death. Perhaps a great grandchild will come across this book and, if only for a passing moment, catch a few glimpses into my life and that of others whose lives are chronicled herein. Before continuing in her or his busy day, after reading a few pages, that yet-unborn great grandchild will conclude, "Their lives did indeed matter."

Professionally, as my full-time working life neared its end some years ago, I began to reflect on the reality that I have been privileged to serve as an ordained minister of the Lutheran church during a significant period of its history in the United States and globally. Of course, all times are "historic" in their own unique ways. But the decades of my lifetime have coincided with some of the most dramatic events and movements in national and world Lutheranism, as well as the broader ecumenical and interfaith communities.

In the case of some of those developments, I was but an observer, at least at the initial breakthrough moments. In 1970, for example, our branch of U.S. Lutheranism made the monumental decision to change one word in the constitution. Those who could serve as ordained ministers changed from "men" to "persons." The decision to ordain women surely was among the most significant in 20th century Lutheranism.

At other moments, I was fortunate to play a small part in some historic events. I was among the pioneers developing Hispanic or Latino[2] outreach ministry in my first call to a bilingual parish in Los Angeles. In my years as a bishop's associate, the decades-long struggle to embrace and include the LGBTQ[3] community was at its zenith. Serving in the

---

2. Terms used to describe persons of Spanish and Latin American heritage have been in flux and continue to be debated within the communities of such persons. Currently, while *Latinx* and *Latine* have been introduced as gender neutral options, surveys show their acceptance by only a small minority of the persons described. Since Latino and Hispanic continue to seem preferred, I will use them interchangeably.

3. Similarly in flux are abbreviations for various groups often commonly described as "sexual minorities." I will use throughout the book LGBTQ, which includes lesbians, gays, bisexual, transgender, and "queer" persons.

San Francisco Bay area meant that we were at the epicenter. My ability to have some influence in that decades-long struggle continued while I served in the Evangelical Lutheran Church in America's Office of the Presiding Bishop. During those years also, we forged the ELCA's historic full communion ecumenical partnerships with the Episcopal Church and churches of the Reformed tradition.

My opportunity to help shape the future of our church included the unique role of heading the ELCA's most historic seminary during the school's final years. As events unfolded, I ended up being the last president of the Lutheran Theological Seminary at Gettysburg. I led the school in consolidating with its sister seminary in Philadelphia, an effort that had been attempted a half-dozen times before without success. I trust my recollections about the merger process and creation of United Lutheran Seminary (ULS) will be of value to students and future historians of American Lutheranism, particularly the broad sweep of Lutheran theological education in the early twenty-first century.

One of the most painful periods for me personally came after my retirement as I watched the birth pangs unfold during the initial years at United Lutheran Seminary. I viewed those events with a unique background, knowledge of players, and grasp of dynamics that only a long-term former president possesses. Somewhat reluctantly, I followed the urging of several confidantes and have written an extensive document preserving the early ULS history and my assessment of those distressing events. But this book is not the place for that chronicle, which resides in sealed archives, to be released at some future time for historical researchers. Herein I will share only a few brief reflections on watching the meltdown of a venture many of us worked so hard to launch.

A Crossroads Prism Approach

As work on this chronicle of my life has proceeded, I have found it helpful to read others' autobiographies and memoirs. Every author approaches the telling of their life story in a unique way. Some autobiographies seek to deliver what Detective Joe Friday, the star character in one of early television's most popular programs, *Dragnet*, was believed (inaccurately) to demand of a witness: "Just the facts, ma'am." Such primarily factual accounts provide objective data about a person's life and events experienced. Others write memoirs, which are weighted heavily toward subjective meaning-making. Beyond setting forth "just the facts," these writers offer their interpretation and render assessments of their own and others' lives and accomplishments.

In this chronological survey of my life thus far, I have sought to achieve a blend of telling stories, presenting factual accounts based upon memory, personal interviews, and preserved documents, while also engaging in meaning-making. Although the latter is primarily for my own reflection and meditation, I hope it may be of some value to others. This approach might be thought of as viewing events through the "crossroads" prism. That is, at many points in the book, as I set forth a chronology of events, I go on to draw from them my own learnings and reflections.

Another way of describing my method would be to regard it as thoroughly in keeping with the Lutheran catechetical tradition in which I was marinated from childhood. In his small catechism, Martin Luther proceeded by setting forth key tenets of the Christian faith—from scripture, the creeds and Lord's Prayer in particular. After each pithy excerpt of "what we are taught" from these spiritual fonts of wisdom, Luther in Socratic fashion poses the question for rumination and discussion: "What does this mean"? I hope my reflections might spark readers' musings on your own meaningful lives.

— 1 —

Roots in Germany and the American Midwest

As is the case for all Americans of European heritage, members of the Biss-Cooper family into which I was born were descendants of immigrants. In my case, three of my four grandparents immigrated to this country from Germany in the late nineteenth century. The fourth, my paternal grandmother, Bessie Bosma, was a second-generation European American.

My maternal grandfather, Joachim Eduard Biss, was born to Christian Ferdinand Biss and Elise Dorothea Freick Biss on April 3, 1879, in the village of Vadersdorf ("father's town") on the island of Fehmarn in the Baltic Sea. This charming island equidistant between the German mainland and Denmark is described as follows by another with ties to Fehmarn:

> The tiny island of Fehmarn is situated in the Baltic Sea between Germany and Denmark. Its strategic position between mainland Europe and Scandinavia meant that its history at times has been turbulent. Originally settled by Slavs in the eighth century, the twelfth century saw a wave of Christianization and Germanization sweep the area. German has been spoken from this time. Although there have been strong links both geographically and politically with Denmark, only a few leading citizens would have spoken Danish. Certainly, our ancestors would have been German speaking. Fehmarn is flat and small island of only 100 square miles, with a population today of 14,000. The capital

Burg, established in the early thirteenth century, contains half the island's population.

The last century has seen a thirty percent increase in Fehmarn's population. This, however, occurred entirely within the city of Burg. This stagnant population growth means that the forty villages scattered throughout the island have been able to retain much of their character from previous centuries. In these villages, already established by the early 1600's, little development has occurred in the past fifty years and approximately thirty-five percent of the homes still standing are from pre-1850. Each possesses common features: a village pond, cobbled streets, huge brick barns and clusters of trees. A number of these villages are coastal, and the Island also boasts a small fishing fleet. Between the villages, fields under cultivation and pastures for grazing exist much as they have for centuries.[1]

In the spring of 2019, my daughter Macrina and I visited Fehmarn and stayed at a guesthouse in the tiny village of Sulsdorf, where records indicate some of our ancestors were born. During our two-day sojourn on the island, we rode in taxis and walked along roads and trails that "Grandpa Biss" likely traversed in his youth before leaving Fehmarn forever at age 15. Records indicate he boarded a ship in Hamburg and sailed to New York in company of his older brother and an aunt and uncle. The reasons for their coming to the U.S. in 1895 are unknown. While economic conditions in Germany had improved in the late 19th century, Denmark continued to struggle, and remote Fehmarn likely lacked opportunities for aspiring young people like Joachim.

Fehmarn island is a tranquil pastoral place where we could imagine young Joachim (he went by Edward after immigrating) spending his childhood and youth. Archival records we were able to retrieve at the Fehmarn *Rathaus* or City Hall indicate that Joachim was the son of a shoemaker. Given the tiny clientele such a merchant would have had in a remote village, we surmised that Christian Ferdinand Biss (Grandpa's father) likely was a farmer or laborer as well. Grandpa's mother died when he was two, and one can imagine a sad-hearted little boy, though I never recall him speaking of his childhood or hearing reports about it from my mother or her siblings.

---

1. Harders, Kenneth, *Rauert of Fehmarn*, with permission of the author, who also credits Julie Rauert Swane of Australia. http://www.peterunbehauen.de/familie/history.html

Prior generations of Bisses can be traced on Fehmarn as far back as Hans Hinrich Biß, who was born in 1716 not far from the island on German's mainland in northern Schleswig-Holstein. Discovering that the birthplace of a number of Bisses is listed as the village of Bisdorf (also spelled Bißdorf) led us to speculate that either the place was named for our ancestors, or they adopted the Biß name from the town.

On the last morning of our stay, I took a taxi to Bisdorf where the driver stopped at the home of a retired teacher he regarded as the local historian. Fortunately, she spoke enough English to disabuse me of this false assumption. She explained that in the 12th century when Fehmarn was under the sway of Denmark, a bishop besought a village he might call his own (perhaps for a fee?) So, Bisdorf was granted by the king and named "bishop's town," my ancestors who came several centuries later having nothing to do with the matter! I also learned from the kindly retired teacher that the last known Biss in the area had died just a couple of years before our visit. While sketchy, as are most such records, the archival material provided by a gruff but efficient official at the Burg-Fehmarn Rathaus (courthouse) listed the occupations of the male members of the Biss clan going back to the 1700's as "workers" or "laborers." One was listed as having been a wheel maker.

Following his arrival in the U.S., Grandpa Biss initially resided in southern Minnesota (Rock County). According to family memories, like so many of that era, his immigration was sponsored by a patron for whom young Edward then worked at no salary for seven years. He and my grandmother moved to Delaware Township in Grant County in 1914 and farmed there until retirement in 1943, when they moved into the town of Elbow Lake. Grandpa Biss died at age 83 on September 17, 1962, at the Community Memorial Hospital in Elbow Lake.

My maternal grandmother, Emma Wilhelmine Sophie Marie Oldenburg, was also from northern Germany. She was born on January 14, 1888, in Friedrichshagen, Mecklenburg-Vorpommern (also listed as Mecklenburg-Schwerin) to eighteen-year-old Wilhelmine Marie Dorothea Oldenburg. While some records show her father as Friedrich Georg Johann Möller, the fact her name is listed as Oldenburg suggests her birth was prior to Wilhelmine's marriage to Friedrich. She had two sisters and one brother, all born to her mother and Möller about a decade after Emma.

My grandmother boarded the SS Pennsylvania in Hamburg in 1909. She is recorded in the 1910 U.S. census as living in Springwater, Minnesota, where the rest of her family resided. Emma and Edward Biss married on June 23, 1911, in Rock County, Minnesota. They had nine children in 22 years, of which my mother, Alice Florence Mabel, was child number eight. The first four Biss children were boys, followed by five girls. Grandma Biss died on May 3, 1976, also at the Community Memorial Hospital, at the age of eighty-eight. She was buried next to her husband in the Union Cemetery, where my parents' cremains are also interred.

As is true in many if not most extended relationships, there was a "family secret" that only came to light in my adult years. As a child I knew my Mom had eight siblings, but at family gatherings only seven others ever appeared. The eighth, my oldest uncle Walter, lived locally, but he and his family never joined with the rest of the clan. I also recall overhearing some hushed conversations around the time of my grandfather's death about how this eldest uncle was "left out of Grandpa's will." My cousins and I would come to learn that Grandma Biss became pregnant and gave birth prior to her marriage to Edward. The uncle's last name initially was hers (Oldenburg), but after their marriage Grandpa Biss formally adopted my uncle Walter. While such occurrences go without mention in most social circles today, in the early part of the twentieth century they were widely regarded as scandalous, especially among pious God-fearing folk who attended church on even an irregular basis. I was glad to finally have an explanation for the strange circumstances regarding the semi-estranged uncle and his family.

From humble immigrant origins, "Edward" and Emma followed the pattern of millions in attaining a solid middle-class existence in 20th century America. They acquired substantial acreage in west-central Minnesota's rich farmland. With the help of their children, the Bisses gleaned much of their food from huge gardens, milked a herd of cows, butchered their own cattle and in almost every regard were self-sufficient and "lived off the land." My mother often told of Grandpa's frugality and Grandma's prowess in the kitchen to set a table day after day for a large family.

While visits with Grandpa and Grandma were always cordial, I did not have the kind of warm relationship with grandparents enjoyed by many of my peers. Perhaps this was due in part to the ethos of the time in which many first- and second-generation immigrants had a somewhat stern and serious demeanor. It may also stem from the simple reality that my grandparents had so many offspring and grandchildren that they simply could not lavish us with gifts and attention in the way that is more common today.

And on the Cooper Side . . .

My paternal grandfather, Jacob Cooper, was born April 20, 1871, in Osthrieslanst, Germany, the son of Gurina (or Gunnia) Shuver and John Cooper. Young Jacob immigrated to the U.S. and arrived in Iowa in 1891. My grandmother, Bessie Bosma, was born January 12, 1880, in Kamrar, Iowa to Herman Bosma and Aldertja Koop Ricks. Aldertja's first husband, Ed Ricks, had died in 1872, after which she was remarried to Bosma. Official court records from Winnebago County, Iowa, cite her name as "Alice Cope," which may have been the Americanized version of Koop she adopted upon immigrating.

Jacob and Bessie were married on May 11, 1899. Bessie's obituary stated that the marriage took place at Buffalo Center, Iowa, but official Winnebago County records indicate they were married "at the Court House in Forest City" by a district court judge. By 1904 they had moved to North Ottawa Township in western Grant County Minnesota where they farmed on what her obituary referred to as "the Schneider farm." The Coopers had a total of 13 children in 25 years, one of whom was either stillborn or died shortly after birth.

Sadly, following the birth of my youngest uncle Edward, Grandma Cooper developed complications and died within days on February 11, 1926. Her obituary in the *Grant County Herald* described her as "a loving mother, strongly attached to her family and will be sadly missed in her home. She was a Christian woman and was ready to go home to her Savior. She had made her peace with God and had nothing to fear as death approached."

Grandpa Cooper died the next year at age fifty-six, on February 4, 1927, under tragic and mysterious circumstances. Following a funeral at the Church of God, he was buried next to Bessie in the Hereford Cemetery near Wendell, Minnesota. A story in the *Grant County Herald* newspaper, indicates that "he was found dead in the road in Charlesville Friday evening." The lengthy *Herald* story states that "Jake Cooper met his death accidentally by a car driven by Ernest Lee of Fergus Falls, a coroner's jury of six decided Monday morning following an inquest." It goes on to indicate that "Cooper's body was found in a pool of blood" where the accident was presumed to have occurred. At the coroner's hearing, however, Lee testified "that he had struck a man with his car about a mile and a half north of Charlesville." Lee apparently fled the scene, but "returned to the place a day or two later and found a small pool of blood there." Lee contended that Cooper was not alone and speculated that his companion, "whose identity was not revealed had taken Cooper's body, placed it in a truck, hauled it to Charlesville and there abandoned it in the street."

Witnesses who had helped my grandfather get his car out of a ditch a short time before "both testified that Cooper was drunk." A quart bottle found in his car contained liquid "that smelled like 'moon' of a most virulent type." Lee testified further that Grandpa and another man were standing in the road, that Cooper was waving his hands and Lee "thought it was a holdup and stepped on the gas. He attempted to avoid the man but was unable to do so." My grandfather's leg and back were broken, and his skull crushed in the horrible incident. The night was foggy and while Lee knew Grandpa Cooper well, he said he did not recognize him. The *Herald* article states, "Cooper had planned an auction sale for February 17," which would suggest he planned to cease farming. It concludes, "A background of moonshine in the whole affair has helped smother facts."

Orphan Bennie Finds His Way

My father, Bendt "Bennie" Cooper (born February 26, 1915) was the eighth of twelve living children born to Jacob and Bessie. To his own and others' amazement, he was the last of his siblings to survive as he lived to the age of 100. While Bennie spoke infrequently of his earliest memories, they were ones of a hardscrabble childhood and youth marked by austerity and loneliness, but also a measure of special closeness with at least one of his brothers, Jake. That the large family lived austerely is suggested by Dad's recollections of seldom having his own shoes and school lunches consisting of a piece of bread smeared with lard. Farm kids in the early 1900's were expected to grow up and assume adult responsibilities at a young age. Dad recalled that by age nine he and Jake were put in charge of a team of horses, and on their own one fall season, the two youngsters harvested enough corn to fill nine silos.

Dad never spoke much of his parents, but I could always sense a deep sadness about them, which he carried throughout his life. He recalled that his older brothers escaped from the farm home as often as they could, due to strife with their alcoholic father. After his father's death, the siblings were scattered in multiple directions. For a year or so, Bennie lived on a farm (still the Schneider farm?) with his oldest brother, Herman, who was in his late teens. Dad reported that Herman, eager for social engagement, would sometimes be gone for several days, leaving young Ben to milk cows and tend to other chores on his own.

Then a neighboring farm couple, Ole and Lillian Amundsen, invited Bennie to live and work at their place. While never formally adopting him (as occurred with a younger brother Pete who was adopted by the Kube family), the Amundsens became a surrogate family for young Bennie. They were the closest my siblings and I had to paternal grandparents, and I recall fondly our occasional visits in their home. While Dad was grateful for their welcoming him into their home (and especially the kindness extended him by "Lill"), he also spoke of the hard work (at no pay during the school year) demanded by Ole. Young Bennie was seldom granted freedom to venture beyond the farm and country school he attended sporadically in winter months when his farm chores were somewhat lessened.

Despite his family's financial austerity, Dad's mother's estate parceled out a modest amount to each of her children. By the time the estate was finally settled, in the fall of 1929, young Bennie had finished the eighth grade and planned to attend the West Central School of Agriculture in Morris, Minnesota to gain the equivalent of a high school education. His portion of the inheritance was about $600, which would be his ticket to advance his education. Receiving his check on the last Friday in October, the teenager wisely determined to bank his inheritance lest he be tempted to spend it frivolously. He took the check to the bank that very day. The bank did not reopen the following Monday morning, and never opened again. It was one of the thousands of financial institutions devastated on "black Friday" when the stock market crashed, setting off the Great Depression of the 1930's.

Once again penniless, Ben Cooper was not to be deterred in forging ahead with his plans to attend school at Morris. As he told the story, he simply showed up at the beginning of the term and told school officials he would work to earn his way. And did he ever work! One or more summers, he shoveled gravel to help build the "quad" of what has evolved into the Morris campus of the great University of Minnesota. Winter nights found him shoveling coal into the giant furnaces of the central heating plant that served the entire campus. When he graduated from Morris in the spring of 1934, one classmate penned the following in his yearbook, "I guess you will be in trim for the next world after all the coal you shoveled this winter." Another friend wrote, "When you were the fireman, we could always tell by how much heat was on in what kind of humor you were."

A yearbook photo of Bennie and three other members of "The Advanced Class" (a fourth year at West Central was optional and Bennie elected to attend) bears the following commentary: "Grouped on the steps of the Dining Hall are four individuals who are among the most congenial people of whom our class can boast. Prominent among them is Bennie Cooper. Good-natured Bennie is everyone's friend." Bennie served as treasurer of the Advanced Class and played football as a lineman. The "Aggies" were scoreless in losing their first four games of 1934 but fought to a 13:13 tie against counterparts from the ag school in Crookston for my father's final appearance on the gridiron. Reminiscing about his football career, he would explain to us that, apart from Crookston, the other teams were from colleges or other post-high school institutions, whereas the students at Morris were mostly teenagers outclassed and outweighed by the opposing teams. "They almost killed us," he would quip, as he recalled those days wearing a leather helmet as the only protective equipment.

Following his graduation from the school at Morris, Bennie continued working for the Amundsons and was briefly in the Civilian Conservation Corps in late 1936. The CCC fielded three million young Americans in Franklin Delano Roosevelt's "New Deal" effort to provide meaningful work and complete multiple public works projects. Bennie helped create some of what are now outstanding federal and state parklands in northern Minnesota. His honorable discharge from the CCC listed his character as "excellent" and cited the reason for his leaving the Corps as being "ineligible for reselection for one year."

While the story has been disputed by my oldest uncle's children, Dad insisted that his earnings of $25 per month (which CCC camp enrollees were required to send home for a savings account) were spent by his brother Herman, who was destitute at the time and had a family to feed. By whatever means the loss of his meager savings occurred, it appears that upon his release from the CCC, Dad once again found himself penniless and unemployed.

Young Alice Also from Large Farm Family

In their yearbook jottings, many of his classmates at the "ag school" commented on Bennie's good humor, and a few of his female friends wrote tributes to Bennie's prowess on the dance floor. That attribute was among the attractions felt by a fifteen-year-old named Alice who Bennie met at a dance in the fall of 1937. In her later years, my Mom confessed to falling head over heels in love at first sight. "He was simply the most beautiful man I had ever seen; he just took my breath away the night I met him!" she exclaimed of the handsome fellow to whom she was married for seventy-five years.

Born January 10, 1922, Alice Florence Mabel Biss was second-to-youngest in a family of nine children. She described her childhood as generally happy, though her parents were somewhat stern and, with such a large family and farm to tend, always working. Mom was especially close to her sisters, all of whom doted on the youngest, Helen, born ten years after Alice. As did my father, she stayed in touch with her siblings throughout their lives.

In describing her childhood and adolescence, Mom recalled her parents' resourcefulness and the work ethic that enabled them to provide for their nine children. Virtually all their food was grown or raised on the farm. She described how her father would butcher a steer and use every part of the critter in some fashion: "Waste not, want not" was obviously an apt descriptor for the *modus operandi* on the Biss farm. While by no means wealthy, the Bisses prospered through their hard work, and Mom was spared the kind of hand-to-mouth economic uncertainty that young Bennie experienced. Typical of immigrants in that era, the Bisses strove to become Americanized. So, Mom grew up speaking only English, though her parents would lapse into German when they didn't want the kids to know what they were talking about!

Alice learned to drive a Model T Ford when Grandpa Biss insisted she do so in her early teens. No one in the family could be spared from farm work to transport her to the country Lutheran church near Barrett where she had to appear for confirmation instruction. These weekly sessions with the pastor were also referred to as "reading for the minister." As she described her "driver's training," one day her father simply boosted her into the driver's seat, gave her a brief orientation to the levers and pedals, and sent her off on her own. She got out on the road and saw a herd of cattle but did not know how to stop. Grandpa Biss yelled "step on the brake," which she did and killed the motor. After a few tries she got the hang of driving and kept doing so well into her 80's, when her two sons insisted that the time had come to give up her car. She was still upset with us about that when she died at ninety-two!

Typical of youngsters in the mid-1930's, Alice's formal education concluded with her graduation from the eighth grade in 1936. She was confirmed at Zion Evangelical Lutheran Church in Barrett, Minnesota, on July 11, 1937. Still in her mid-teens, she "hired out" as a teenage live-in nanny and housekeeper for farm families. She said she typically earned $2.50 per week plus room and board. Alice recalled one situation in which her "living quarters" consisted of a thin mattress on boards spread out over a bathtub. So, while Alice was only in her mid-teens when she and Bennie realized they were desperately in love and simply had to get married, she had a level of maturity unlike that of most teenagers then or now.

The Young Couple Start Their Life Together

Following a whirlwind courtship after that first encounter at a dance, that "beautiful man" and his awestruck female companion were determined to marry. As they told the story, in Minnesota marriage of a minor could only occur with the concurrence of the individual's parents. Knowing that the Bisses would never approve of Alice's marriage at the tender age of 16, they determined to cross the border into South Dakota and elope. As I recall the version of the story Mom and Dad told us, South Dakota had no minimum age matrimonial law at the time, so Mom's being a minor would not have been an impediment. However, Macrina's genealogical research discovered that the Grant County South Dakota Division of Vital Statistics recorded Bennie's age as twenty-three and Alice's as twenty-one in their official Record of Marriage!

After securing a marriage license, accompanied by Dad's brother, Jake, and Mom's best friend, Gladys Olson, the young couple presented themselves to the Rev. F. Wessler in Milbank, South Dakota. Following a few moments of "pre-marital counseling," the Lutheran minister tied the knot and signed their marriage certificate on July 30, 1938. Bennie recalled giving the good reverend an honorarium of $10, which was a handsome sum in that era. Concerned that we children might replicate their hasty passion-driven elopement, when we could pry the story out of them, Bennie and Alice always wagged their fingers and admonished Bernice, David and me, "Do as we say and not as we did!"

A brief honeymoon to the Detroit Lakes, Minnesota area would await the fall after harvest, when Bennie could finally get away from his duties at the Amundson farm for a few days. Alice's asthma condition worsened while on the trip, and Bennie went in frantic search of a doctor. "I thought I was going to lose her right there," he would recall decades later in telling the story of how he desperately sought medical aid to relieve his young bride's respiratory distress.

In the early days of their marriage, Bennie continued working for the Amundsons and Alice returned to her tasks at another farm, which meant many nights apart. Soon growing tired of this "commuter marriage" lifestyle, they left those jobs and jointly "hired out" to a bachelor farmer near Barrett, where Bennie did farm chores and Alice served as cook and housekeeper. When their new employer, George Slovsve, married shortly thereafter, it became apparent his new wife did not want to share the household. Once again, the Coopers relocated to nearby Brewsterville. Bennie worked briefly with the Works Progress Administration (WPA) and was then unemployed until the couple was hired by another farmer, Paul Nelson, for a combined annual salary of $475. Employment with the Nelsons also included housing. But Mom and Dad would recall how that ramshackle house on the prairie was so poorly insulated that a cup of water left at either child's bedside in the evening would be frozen solid by morning. Additional perks of the couple's job included one quart of milk per day and a weekly dozen eggs.

During their first year of marriage, the Coopers managed to purchase a washing machine, a set of tires for their car, and saved enough to cover the doctor's fee and other expenses surrounding the birth of their first child. Bernice Adele was born July 12, 1939, in Elbow Lake at a midwife's home. Shortly over a year after Bernice's birth, Alice and Bennie were blessed by a second child, David Leslie, born at home on November 8, 1940, amidst an early winter snowstorm. Fortunately, the blizzard did not prevent the doctor from arriving in time to assist with the delivery.

The young family endured many hardships in their early years together. Living at what by any standards would be regarded today as poverty level, they were still better off than millions of their fellow citizens who endured the worst years of the Great Depression. Being among the younger children in both of their large families, they held no expectations of new or fancy clothes since they were used to receiving hand-me-downs (though Alice was proud to get new dresses for her confirmation and eighth grade graduations). When clothes became worn or frayed, Alice simply sewed patches and darned socks. They grew most of their own food on the farm, with Alice canning and storing up huge quantities of fruits and vegetables.

Rather than complain or express anger at their deprivation during those early years of their marriage, I recall Mom's and Dad's recollection of that initial phase of their family life as being one of gratitude. They regarded the Nelsons as benevolent employers who made every effort to offer support and encouragement. While impossible now to determine, I have a hunch the Nelsons offered the Coopers employment as a measure of compassion and may have stretched their own resources to help provide the newlyweds a pathway out of poverty.

Bennie and Alice also struggled to reestablish a harmonious relationship with her parents, who had been quite distraught at the young couple's hasty marriage. I recall hearing two different versions of what finally broke the ice and enabled Grandpa Biss to again start speaking with his daughter and son-in-law. Dad spoke of a period early in their first year of marriage when things got so dire he had to humble himself and ask his in-laws for a small loan. According to his recollection, that was the moment my grandfather opened his wallet and heart and accepted Dad into the family. While perhaps not contradictory, Mom's story of Edward Biss's heart-melting revolves around the birth of their first child. As she told it, the moment she laid tiny Bernice into her father's arms he beamed and fell in love with both the new baby and her parents!

In 1941, the Coopers moved near Norcross, Minnesota where they rented a farm for the first time. Unfortunately, it was an extremely wet year with poor crops, so Bennie also worked on the railroad as a laborer. In ensuing years, they rented in sequence three other farms southwest of the town of Wendell. While there seemed to be promise of better fortunes in the post-Depression years, hard luck continued to plague the couple as hailstorms totally destroyed developing bumper crops on more than one occasion.

Stories from Their Early Years

In preparation for celebrating Mom's and Dad's sixty-fifth anniversary in 2003, we asked them to recall particularly memorable incidents from their early years together. The first attests Alice's lifelong grit and gumption (and when needed physical strength, her small stature notwithstanding!).

Literally Putting Out a Fire

One afternoon Bennie was out haying at his brother John Cooper's farm. Alice had put David and Bernice to bed for their naps and went out into the garden to weed and hoe. The sky became increasingly ominous, until Alice realized it was almost too dark to see, and a storm was coming fast. She went into the house, planning to wash the dishes while the children were still napping. It got so dark she went to the door to see what the weather was doing and determine if she needed to take the children to the basement. With wet hands from the dishwater, she grasped the doorknob. At that very moment, lightning struck the barn. Her hand became frozen to the doorknob by the shock she received from the electric charge that surrounded the whole farmstead. She felt effects from the shock in her arm, back and neck for several days afterward.

Finally able to relax her hand and let go of the doorknob, Alice ventured outside and saw that the lightning had struck the back of the barn and started a fire. Calves in the barn were in danger of being burned alive, so Alice braced herself and detached a feed trough nailed on with spikes, which barricaded the door. She shooed the cattle outside, and also quickly removed critically needed farm implements like horse harnesses, a cream separator, pitchforks, and a shovel. She then put the children in the car and drove to a neighbor's farm to phone the fire department. Enroute, she had to power the car through a mud hole.

Fortunately, Bennie had recently scattered green alfalfa all around the barn, so it didn't burn quickly. After some time, the volunteer firefighters arrived, but they didn't know how to use their brand-new fire truck. The firemen began extinguishing the fire by hand with buckets, and eventually, after reading their instruction manual, were also able to use the truck's hose to finish the job. Bennie finally arrived home to find Alice in command of the entire operation. After it was all wrapped up, Alice fed everyone fresh cake, cookies, and coffee.

Thirsty Horses and Unrelenting Water Pumping

One summer night it was so hot, and the mosquitoes were so bad, sleep eluded the young couple. For unknown reasons, their landlord's horses kept circling the house as close as they could get to the building. Hour after hour, Bennie and Alice lay awake hearing the horses' tails switching against the siding. The greater burden of having their fenced-in yard serve as the corral was that Alice had to pump water for the thirsty horses. Finally, the owner put up a windmill, and Alice was relieved of the laborious pumping. But within a few weeks a fierce windstorm blew up one night, and down went the new windmill. Alice returned to the drudgery of pumping and pumping. Telling the story a half century afterward, she concluded, "You never saw critters drink so much water!"

Cooper Kids Survive Perilous Adventures

Since I was a decade younger than my siblings, I knew of their childhood events only through stories told by them and our parents. One story about each seemed to be told more often than all the others. David was about three years old when he disappeared one balmy summer afternoon. Beginning by checking the cattle's watering tanks in fears that he might have drowned, the Coopers searched frantically for some time before discovering that little Dave had crawled under a corn storage bin and promptly fallen fast asleep!

The story about Bernice's younger years I recall being recounted most frequently similarly took place in the farmyard. Racing around in the barn's haymow one afternoon during haying season, when the big door on the second story level stood open, our sister apparently got going so fast she couldn't stop and fell out the door onto a hay wagon some fifteen feet below. While unharmed, she tumbled precariously close to an upturned pitchfork!

At Last, A Farm of Their Own

By 1948, with a loan extended by Grandpa and Grandma Biss, the Coopers were finally in a position to purchase a 175-acre farm five miles northwest of Wendell for $10,500. They later acquired an adjacent additional twenty-five acres, and some years rented another eighty. As was common at the time, the farm operation included milk cows, pigs, and chickens in addition to growing crops of oats, wheat, barley, corn, and soybeans. Most of the crops produced were consumed by the dairy and beef cattle, but some grain was also sold most years. Their hard work and frugality enabled the Coopers to repay Grandpa Biss and retire the entire mortgage within just a few years.

As with so many of their generation, that ethos of frugality in which both Bennie and Alice were raised persisted throughout their years of farming. A commitment to be the best stewards of garden produce and farmyard creatures was a marker of Mom's and Dad's lifestyle on our farm in Grant County's Stony Brook township. By the dozens of jars and deep-freeze bags, Alice preserved fruits and vegetables grown in our expansive garden, which graced our tables throughout the year. We Cooper kids grew up drinking Grade A whole milk dipped directly from the bulk tank filled from the udders of our cows, and eating beef from livestock born and raised on our own farm. Long before "farm to table" became a watchword in the finest urban restaurants, we simply could not imagine another means by which human beings were fed.

In an era when it was uncommon for women with children to work outside the home, and particularly so in the case of a farm family, my mom's adventurous spirit and desire to make a bit of "spending money" on her own resulted in a succession of part-time jobs in town. As a young lad, I recall visiting her in the dark "candling room" of a local egg business where she stood for hours checking each egg for imperfections. For several years, she worked as a clerk in the sole grocery store in our hometown of Wendell. The couple who owned the store came to trust Alice highly and her responsibilities grew to the point she was sometimes alone running the store on Friday nights or Saturdays. I was always proud to visit Mom at "the store." Later, she joined the cleaning crew at a nursing home in Fergus Falls.

Bennie and Alice continued farming until the late 1970's, though the milk cows were sold not long after I entered college, when Dad wanted to be free of the daily grind of doing all the chores on his own. Finally, they sold their acreage to a neighboring farmer and the farmstead to a young couple who wanted to live in a rural setting. Within days after selling all the farm equipment and many of their household furnishings at an auction on April 7, 1977, they loaded up their remaining possessions in a U-Haul truck and headed south to Arizona.

During their later years on the farm, Mom and Dad had purchased sight unseen a lot in the new community of Prescott Valley from a developer peddling Arizona homesites throughout the upper Midwest. Arriving in their new town about seventy miles north of Phoenix, Bennie and Alice lived in an apartment for a few months as their brick rancher home was being built. During their early retirement years, Dad worked part-time in carpentry and Mom joined a friend in occasional house cleaning.

They became active members in a start-up Missouri Synod mission congregation, Emmanuel Lutheran Church.

With growing frustrations at the way Prescott Valley was developing, after a few years they sold their home and built another new residence at the Prescott Country Club a few miles away. Their final Arizona home was in Prescott city where they moved after my brother Dave and his new wife Diane also moved to Prescott in retirement. Dave's and Diane's constant care and assistance with all aspects of their lives enabled Mom and Dad to remain in their own home much longer than would have been possible otherwise. Finally, as they needed a higher level of constant care for their safety and wellbeing, they moved into an assisted living facility.

Upon Dave's and Diane's decision to relocate "back east" to Virginia (due to having several young grandchildren on the eastern seaboard), Mom and Dad were game to move also. I scouted options for their care, and they moved into the Robinwood Assisted Living facility in Hagerstown, Maryland in late summer of 2010. That location was midway between Gettysburg and Dave's and Diane's new home in Winchester, Virginia. It was so good having my folks less than an hour away from Gettysburg for the last years of their lives. About a year later, Pamela's folks, Tom and Connie White, also moved to Robinwood and we enjoyed frequent visits with all four, who became fast friends and ate together during meals in the dining room.

Good and Faithful Citizens

That Bennie and Alice sought out a Lutheran minister to perform their marriage in South Dakota is symbolic of their faith commitment. As noted above, Alice was confirmed at age 15 through the rigorous Lutheran process of "reading for the minister," typically a minimal two-year period of study, memorization of Luther's small catechism, and exposure to scripture. I recall no recounting by Bennie of a similar religious formation. In fact, his orphaned status and family dissolution resulted in there being no record of his being baptized. Accordingly, shortly after their marriage Bennie was baptized and joined the Lutheran church by adult confirmation.

Upon buying their own farm and moving to Stony Brook township, the Coopers became active members of Rock Prairie Lutheran Church. Mom joined the "Ladies Aid" and women's circles, and also taught Sunday

School for a number of years. Due to being tethered to a dairy herd, Dad was less active beyond regular Sunday worship attendance. And both struggled in their early years at the parish to feel fully accepted. Virtually all the other members were of Norwegian descent and perpetuated the highly Scandinavian flavor of congregational life. While the worship services were in English, fellowship times often found their peers reverting to Norwegian, which, of course, Ben and Alice could not understand.

In rural communities at the time, the wide range of civic organizations we have in society today did not exist. But I do recall Dad's service with a community board that made critical decisions regarding farmers who were on the verge of bankruptcy and needed a helping hand. And Mom was involved in the Parent-Teacher Association (PTA) and Band Boosters of our school.

My Dad and Mom, Bennie and Alice Cooper

A Debt of Gratitude

By any measure, ours was a loving home marked by the values of hard work, respect for others, faith, and a dogged determination to persist in times of adversity. I lacked for nothing by way of material goods as my parents had achieved a modest middle-class lifestyle by the time I came along. At the same time, I learned stewardship principles at an early age as Bennie and Alice avoided excessive and unnecessary spending, though they did buy two brand new cars during my adolescence.

In the course of my vocational life as a pastor, church executive and seminary president, there were seasons of great intensity and heavy workload. Whenever I would start feeling a bit sorry for myself, I would be reminded of the incredible and unrelenting faithfulness required of my dairy farmer parents. Twice a day, seven days a week, month after month, year by year Dad arose at or before dawn to milk the cows, only to do it all over again about nine hours after he finished. And in addition to preparing three full meals daily, plus delivering hearty "lunches" to the field in summertime, Mom managed the household, stewarded huge vegetable and flower gardens, helped out in twice-daily milk room cleanups, and worked part-time in town as well! I recall only a handful of times when Mom and Dad were able to take a week-long vacation trip after Dave and I were old enough in turn to manage the farm chores on our own for a few days. Due to the nature of a farm family's vocation, we simply were never able to take family vacations. Even a day of fishing or a picnic with our extended family was inevitably cut short as Dad and I had to head home around 5:00 p.m. for the evening milking.

While I failed to fully appreciate it in my growing up years, the grit required on my parents' part was extraordinary. If he woke up feeling ill, Dad went down to the barn anyway. If a piece of equipment broke while haying or harvesting grain, he figured out a way to fix it. When a cow had difficulty delivering a calf, he had to serve as the resident veterinarian. Similarly, Mom would rise to any occasion and take on tasks a given day required, including offering meals to unexpected friends and relatives who might just drop by the farm while "out visiting" on a Sunday afternoon.

So, in my own life when the tough times came, I did my chores! I tried to maintain a healthy balance in life and certainly had freedoms my parents did not. But especially during the early years of ministry when days off frequently got swept away by a pastoral emergency or need to work ahead on sermons, class preparations, or administrative duties, I was able to muster the energy and will to work long hours.

Over the course of four decades of ministry in a series of intense contexts, it was also inevitable there were many challenging times. Some of those, of course, were of my own creation. Other conflicts were generated by other people's unreasonableness or even irrationality. When I was the target of what in polite company can only be called "crap," I could remind myself of farm skills mastered during boyhood. In the diary I kept up through much of my last semester of high school, I wrote the following on Saturday, March 23, 1968: "I got up at 8:00 and pitched manure all day!"

— 2 —

Growing Up in the 1950's and 60's

"The fifties." Many cultural historians regard the 1950's as a pivotal decade in U.S. and world history. Victorious in World War II, by mid-century the United States was building a head of steam in economics, technology, education, transportation, and popular culture. The millions of veterans had come home to find jobs, start businesses, marry, have children, and fuel an economic engine that was fast becoming the marvel of the globe.

The decade over which war hero Dwight D. Eisenhower presided in the White House saw prosperity expand like wildfire. The average cost of a new home at $8,450 (less than three times the average worker's annual wages) was within reach of millions of young families, and suburbs surrounding major cities were popping up like dandelions in springtime. A new car cost about $1,500 and filling its gas tank required less than a $5 bill with gasoline averaging eighteen cents per gallon. Looking back from the end of the second decade of the twenty-first century, some nostalgic old-timers view "the fifties" as an idyllic time in which life was simple, crime was low, children respected their elders (and their teachers), churches were burgeoning, and "America" was rapidly becoming the leader of the free world.

August 30, 1950 was a Wednesday. According to the weather history for Minneapolis, it was an unusually mild Minnesota August day, with temperatures only in the seventies. In the final stages of her last pregnancy, Alice Cooper had been growing increasingly uncomfortable as the days of August crawled toward September. While surely sensitive to his wife's condition and her desire for a timely delivery, her husband Bennie nevertheless hoped the birthing process would be delayed until the grain harvest was finished. He got his way and hauled the last loads of wheat and oats to the granary on the little dairy farm in Stony Brook township of west central Minnesota's Grant County just hours before Alice said it was time to go to the hospital.

Youngest of three children born to Bennie and Alice, I was the only one whose birth took place in a hospital. Eleven and ten years older respectively, sister Bernice and brother David were both born in homes. As already noted, Dave's birth was particularly memorable in that it occurred during an early winter snowstorm in November, when the attending doctor had to fight blizzard conditions in order to arrive at Mom's bedside by delivery time.

By the time I entered the world, hospital births had become the norm even in our rural community out on the western edge of Minnesota's lake country. So, Dad drove Mom to the Lake Region Hospital in Fergus Falls. Joining Alice on the maternity ward that late August was Marlys Jeppson, whose son Joel took a bit longer to arrive and was born August thirty-first. The few hours that separated our births were to determine our fates two decades later when Joel and I joined the hundreds of thousands of young men included in the first Vietnam war era draft lottery. (More about that in a later chapter.) Starting first grade six years after we shared the hospital nursery, Joel and I became close friends, and were co-captains of our championship high football team our senior year. Our friendship continues to this day, and I recently rode back seat with the former Navy and airline pilot as Joel looped and rolled his personal single engine airplane!

Coming along ten and eleven years respectively after brother David's and sister Bernice's births inevitably raised at some point the question, "So was I an 'accident' or result of my parents' poor family planning"? On the few occasions I would hint at that possibility, our parents were quick to assure me that was not the case. Since Mom was still in her late teens when the other two were born, in her later twenties she and Dad decided they simply were not ready to be empty nesters in just a few years. Also factoring in their decision to have a third child was the fact that by the late 1940's they had been enabled to rise above the poverty-level economic state in which they spent the first dozen years of their marriage. Mom recalled, "We wanted to have another child in an era where everything wasn't quite as much a struggle."

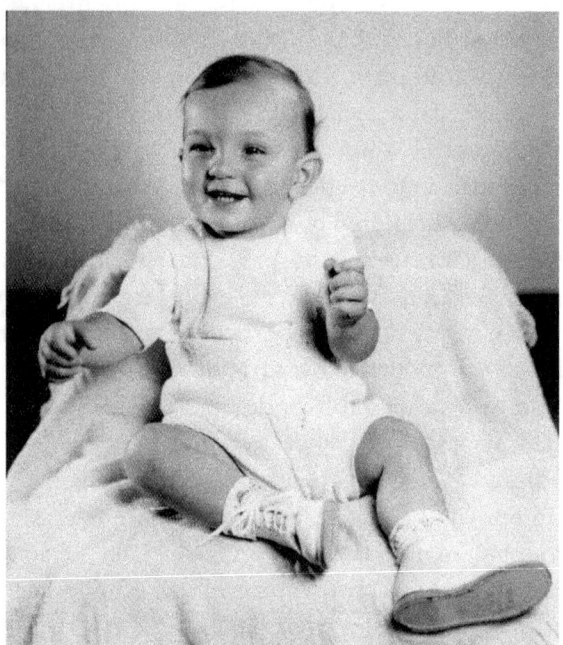

My baby photo

Any details about one's history as a baby and toddler, of course, can only be based on secondhand reports by family members and others who were close to the scene. As I recall her telling, Mom found nothing particularly remarkable about baby Michael's development. Both she and Dad would tell me in my adult years that my eleven-year-old sister Bernice was ecstatic to have a new baby brother. While a bit disappointed the parents did not accept her preferred name for the newborn (Stephen), Bernice never seemed to hold it against them or me! In fact, she later expressed gratitude that since the name was not taken for me, she could affix it to her own son, my nephew Stephen Lee Anderson.

The story I heard most often about my toddler years was that of falling off a chair at age two and incurring a strangulation hernia as a result. My parents rushed me to the doctor's office, who quickly diagnosed the gravity of the situation and insisted they proceed at once to surgery in the hospital some twenty miles away. Since Dad had jumped in the car in his "barn clothes," he was embarrassed at his attire and wanted to stop off at home and change. "Your child's life is in danger, and I will say again you *are* going directly to the hospital," was the gist of Doc Parson's insistent response. While I have no conscious memory of that traumatic event at such a young age, my therapist wife thinks some deep recollection of operating room lights explains my strong aversion to bright overhead ceiling lighting.

A decade later, another high-speed drive to the same hospital occurred when once again my life hung in the balance. As my abdominal pains grew worse, Mom and Dad concluded my distress was more than the flu or reaction to something I had eaten. In the wee hours of the morning, they drove the fifteen miles to Fergus Falls with me groaning in pain in the back seat of our 1961 Rambler automobile. By the time on-call doctors arrived, my appendix had burst, leading to a series of medical procedures that failed to alleviate the damage caused by poisonous fluids seeping throughout my abdominal cavity. My condition deteriorated to the point where our pastor made a late-night hospital call that I can only imagine may have been "commendation of the dying" or last rites. Fortunately, a relatively new drug, Terramycin, was administered as a last-ditch medical intervention, and it succeeded in knocking out the infection.

Within a few months, I was back on the football field with a clean bill of health and a typical teenager's sense of invulnerability. But the experience had a profound effect on me emotionally as well as physically. At a young age, I had stared death in the face and became aware of life's fragility. In those days of excruciating pain and suffering, when I knew there was a good possibility I would never grow up, my mother and I had deep conversations about faith. I felt confident that I was in God's hands and experienced a measure of peace with whatever the outcome would be. A particularly poignant moment came when a little two-year-old girl in the room across the hall from mine died of spinal meningitis. Observing her parents' anguish, I felt for my own family should I also end up not going home from the hospital. The whole experience made me a more serious kid, and I think imbued a sense of urgency to "make a difference in the world."

My relief that these health challenges caused by the ruptured appendix were behind me was short-lived. After a few months, it became apparent that there were lingering effects from the abdominal surgeries that followed the post-op development of peritonitis. Scar tissue from the operations would cause bowel obstructions that brought on the same gut-wrenching pain, especially on occasions when I would overeat. I lived in constant fear that one day the obstructions would not be released of their own accord. Three years later, at age fifteen, another surgery was required to remedy the situation. That time around, the repair seemed to be permanently successful and the anxiety I had lived with in my early teenage years was left behind—I hoped forever. That was not to be the case.

Boyhood on the Farm

Some might describe mine as among the seeming idyllic childhoods experienced by millions of us in the "baby boomer generation." Although there was some typical teenage drinking, back then we did not face the threats posed by drugs and crime today, including in rural and small-town communities. I doubt there was a murder in our county in decades, and I recall hearing of only a handful of petty thefts during all the years I was growing up. The greatest perils faced by those of all ages were automobile crashes and farm accidents (and the ever-present threat of nuclear war). I grew up knowing several farmers missing fingers that were caught in machines, absent the kind of shields and other protections that would not come about until OSHA and other government regulators came into being decades later. The cars and trucks in which we all learned to drive and rode on occasion at reckless speeds on poorly maintained country roads, especially dangerous under harsh winter conditions, had no seat belts, let alone airbags and other safety features now standard in all vehicles. Apart from those hazards, life in rural Minnesota was relatively safe and tranquil.

My first eighteen years were lived out in our old farmhouse, which my parents were frequently upgrading and modernizing as time and money allowed. The original house had been added onto in several stages, and for some unknown reason the floors in the additions were never at the same level as the original structure. Until I became more familiar with other people's houses, it didn't seem strange or unusual to step up an inch going from kitchen to living room. Over the years, as rooms were remodeled, additional flooring was added in the lower rooms, and I think by the time renovations were finished our house had seamless transitions from room to room like most homes. The leveling of the floors seems somehow symbolic of the Coopers' progress toward a "normal" middle-class lifestyle.

During my elementary school years, before a bathroom and furnace were installed, Saturday night baths were in a big round rub in front of the oil burning stove in the living room. I don't recall all the details, but the fact that the living room had no doors must have meant there were simply unwritten rules that we respected one another's privacy and stayed out while another family member was bathing. The lack of a bathroom meant trips to an outhouse in the warmer months and use of a built-in commode on the second floor during winter. Again, that "facility" was in full view in the public hallway, so there must have been ways of signaling it was occupied and others should not come out of their rooms. By the time I was in the second or third grade we had a modern bathroom, which included space for another marvelous new invention especially valued by my mother—an electric clothes dryer. Prior to its arrival, I can recall Mom hanging clothes outside almost year-round. There were times in winter when she would bring a pair of jeans in from the clothesline and stand it in a corner to thaw out!

In that poorly insulated old farmhouse, heated only by the living room oil burner, winter nights in my upstairs bedroom could be quite chilly. There was a heat register that allowed the upward flow of heat from the living room. An added advantage of that arrangement was that by lying on the floor to get warm, with my ear to the register, I could hear quite well my parents' and their friends' or relatives' conversations after I was tucked into bed. At an early age I learned there were some very interesting things adults talked about after the kids were sent off to bed!

Our home was modestly furnished, but as their income gradually improved Mom and Dad bought some new pieces of furniture. When my bedroom was remodeled, it included a built-in desk and bookshelf, which gave it an office-like quality conducive for homework in a quiet place far removed from the television and other distractions. Ever since, it has always been important for me to have a home office of some fashion, even though prior to retirement I have always had workplace offices.

Another furniture-related recollection speaks to an area in which I have sometimes wished my parents would have made a different decision. As a young child, I remember an upright piano that stood unused in our dining room. Both Bernice and David had begun piano lessons, but soon lost interest and abandoned musical instruction. For reasons never explained to me, before I even had the chance to give it a try, they sold the piano! My instrumental musical opportunities, therefore, were limited to options available at school, and I chose to play the saxophone, beginning lessons with our school band director, Gordon Peterson, in the fifth grade. I mastered the instrument to the degree I was chosen section leader my senior year, played in a newly formed stage or jazz band as well as the concert band, and won awards for excellent performance in regional high school competitions.

While boyhood on the farm was in many ways a sheltered life, it was anything but dull or boring. Since the school bus stopped at our driveway at 7:15 each morning, about the time my Dad went down to the barn to start the morning milking, I was exempt from morning chores. But every evening, after an hour of freedom following my homecoming on the bus, around 5:30 I headed to the barn. For the next two-plus hours I helped with the feeding and milking until Dad and I got back to the house for supper around 8 p.m. It was only after that, when most of my classmates were watching television or getting ready for bed, that I could begin my homework. During my high school years, the light in my room was often on until midnight or later as I wrestled with chemistry and physics or scratched my head to solve differential equations.

The intensity of farm work increased substantially during the spring and summer months, especially after Dave left home for a short stint in the Army and to pursue higher education. In springtime, the hours for homework or recreation (spare in general) were even more limited as Dad would often need me on a tractor doing fieldwork until darkness fell. During the summers I was a full-time unpaid hired hand, often working in the fields ten to twelve hours daily, especially during haying and harvesting seasons. While I sometimes bemoaned the amount of work required, a huge plus was its effect in terms of physical fitness, which greatly enhanced my athletic abilities. By my senior year of high school, I was a well-muscled 180-pound fullback and middle linebacker (yes, I weighed about thirty pounds more back then than I do now, and the added pounds were mostly muscle!) for our championship football team.

The hard-earned physical strength and agility that came from work on the farm undoubtedly contributed to a growing sense of self-confidence and perhaps even a measure of courage. In those days, the whole notion of "cyber bullying" was unthinkable, but we had our share of the old-fashioned kind—boys who intimidated their peers by brute strength and antagonistic personalities. The terror of our grade school class was a boy named Ricky. Bigger than the rest of us, he got his way by threatening to beat us up—and sometimes doing so for no apparent reason other than to be a bully. For months I silently endured Ricky's harassment and intimidation, until one evening down in the barn I tearfully blurted out my frustrations to my father. In his quiet way, Dad looked me in the eye and said simply, "Michael, my boy, I don't think you have to take this anymore. I think you're really stronger than him." Suffice it say, the next time Ricky came after me I stood my ground, and the nature of the relationship got readjusted! Along life's journey, as I have encountered bullies (usually of the verbal type who by demeanor or position seek to intimidate), I have remembered Dad's encouragement and stood up to them.

Typical of the socialized gender expectations of that era (which still persists widely today), my mother and sister were the nurturers, and Dad and brother Dave were a bit more emotionally distant. I don't mean to suggest they were less loving and supportive, but merely that at the time I experienced all the men in our immediate and extended family as more stoic and less demonstrative as compared to the women. That fact, coupled with the reality that all my grade school and Sunday School teachers were female, may have contributed to my being comfortable around strong women in leadership roles. I believe that served me well in my professional career as one who came of age in ministry in the era when a growing number of colleagues are women.

During my latter years as Gettysburg Seminary president, mine was the only office on our wing inhabited by a man. Some of the female colleagues with whom I was blessed to serve may have differing perspectives, but I hope I was able to avoid the degree of overt sexism exhibited by many males of my generation. Along the way, I have attempted to be an ally and confront prejudices that created barriers for women in ministry and other arenas. My marriage to a well-known feminist and champion for women's rights has helped keep me honest and forced confrontation with lingering vestiges of sexism and unconscious bias so ingrained in men of my generation.

While "the fifties" were years of relative tranquility and growing prosperity for white middle-class Americans, "the sixties" emerged in our national life as a time of turbulent societal and cultural upheaval. The changes in our farm household mirrored those going on in millions of homes around the country, with the coming of a small black-and-white television, then a "hi-fi" record player followed a few years later by a more sophisticated stereo sound system and our first color television. On these revolutionary technological wonders, we listened to the radical new music coming from the likes of Elvis Presley, Bobby Vee, and that upstart British quartet that had all America abuzz—the Beatles. I remember as a boy puzzling as I heard words describing new inventions like "tv trays" (Why would we need one since the television already had its own stand?),

and new-fangled devices like a "barbeque grill" (What was wrong with our perfectly good electric oven to cook meat?). The introduction of some new menu items was quite stunning as well, bringing to our table such delights as Tang orange drink, Cheese Whiz spread, and "pizza pies."

Our old crank-activated wall telephone was replaced by one that sat on a desk and had a rotary dial to make calls. The party line shared by a half-dozen farm families in our neighborhood would be replaced by a private line. While that alleviated the need to wait until our neighbors finished their conversations, and afforded a previously unknown measure of privacy, it cut us off from knowing as much about our neighbors' business as had previously been the case!

As did most boys and girls growing up in rural America, I began helping with farmyard and field chores at a young age. Barnyard chores like feeding livestock and drawing well water with a hand pump are among my earliest memories. While such engagement by a youngster would be discouraged as being unsafe in many circles today, it was simply the norm in that era. Before I entered elementary school, I drove a tractor slowly in the hayfield between rows of hay bales as Dad and Dave loaded them onto a wagon. The John Deere "B" had a hand clutch, and since I wasn't yet strong enough to disengage it when we had to stop, one of my elders would run up and pull the lever backward. Another early driving experience came on a day when Dad and I were checking electric fences in the cow pasture. While I remained in the pickup, he walked on ahead a quarter mile or so, scouting for a short that had disabled the fence that kept our cattle within their proper confines. Suddenly, he motioned with his arms for me to drive the pickup to where he was taking a rest. Having watched him use the clutch to shift and so on, I got that old Chevy pickup started, into a lower gear and off we went. I seemed adept enough that Dad kept me at the wheel when we returned to the farmyard where my mother about fainted when she saw who was driving! I was too short to look over the steering wheel, so I simply did the obvious and peered through it to see where we were going.

While work was a given, life on the farm was hardly all drudgery. Although time for recreation was sparse for busy farm families, especially in the summer months, my dad occasionally took us fishing at nearby lakes on a Sunday afternoon. We gathered with some of our aunts, uncles, and cousins for picnics on holidays like the 4th of July, always waiting exactly one hour after lunch before swimming in the lake (the then-standard to avoid "cramps" that could cause drowning). I also accompanied

Dad ice fishing in a little portable shack he co-owned with our neighbor and friend Morris Baasen. Peering down through a hole chopped in the foot-thick ice for hours wasn't the most exciting activity for a young lad perhaps, but the camaraderie with the men who swapped yarns and gossip brings back warm memories from those frigid winter afternoons.

Weddings of family members or neighbors were grand opportunities for celebrations, and the younger crowd relished "decorating the car" in which the newlyweds would escape to their honeymoon. What may sound like a benign and harmless activity going on outside while the reception proceeded (almost always in the basement of the church where the wedding took place) could end up going "over the top" sometimes. Such was the case, for example, during a reception in our church fellowship hall following my sister Bernice's marriage. We car "decorators" put limburger cheese on the exhaust manifold, jacked up the car's rear axle so it would go nowhere when put in gear, smothered frogs and placed a few in the couple's suitcases, and thereby created a smelly mess for the new couple that got worse and worse as the miles wore on. Payback usually came down the road, as in my wedding to my high school sweetheart when we exited the church to find my 1965 Ford Galaxy filled to the roof with straw from somebody's haymow!

Our farmstead in Stony Brook Township, Grant County

A Large Extended Family Expanded My Horizons

With Dad's and Mom's large casts of siblings (nineteen in total), the roster of first cousins grew to a total of seventy-two In one case, Dad's brother Eddie married Mom's sister Helen, so we regarded their three daughters, Karen, Kathy, and Cheryl as our "double cousins." In various combinations, depending on which family members were gathered on a given occasion, we kids played some of the typical childhood standards like hide-and-seek (with endless possibilities on large farmsteads where barns and other buildings were fair game for hiding places). Both summer and winter family reunions found us engaged in outdoor activities like ball games, lake swimming or ice skating and building snow forts. And long winter evenings or snowy Sunday afternoons afforded ample time for board games like Monopoly, Clue, Sorry, and Parcheesi. An added bonus for us kids was listening to the inevitable shouting matches that broke out among our dads and uncles as they played the popular card game of Whist!

The majority of my parents' siblings had also married into farming families, so most of our visits were to nearby relatives whose lives mirrored our own. But a couple of my uncles broke out of the mold and were city-dwellers. Most notable were Uncle Ed and Aunt Helen, mentioned above, who lived in a suburb of Minneapolis. While relatively rare, our visits to their home opened my eyes to urban realities that seemed a million rather than less than two hundred miles from our small farm in west central Minnesota. Eddie was a Twin Cities Metropolitan Transit driver who knew the entire metro area like the back of his hand and seemed fearless navigating the streets in any quarter of those great cities. On a couple of occasions, I was permitted to ride along with him for a portion of his duty shift. I recall being amazed that he knew many of his riders by name, and they greeted him warmly as well as they boarded the bus bound for work, shopping or perhaps to visit friends across town. Those ride-alongs were my first real exposure to racial diversity, as the only African American I ever recall encountering in our entire rural county was a foster son of the local Lutheran Church Missouri Synod minister.

Another horizon- and worldview-expanding development was my sister's marriage to Ron Anderson, an Air Force sergeant whose orders took them overseas early in their life together. Close to Bernice, who by virtue of being eleven years my senior was almost a second mother, I remember being both excited and sad upon learning that she and husband Ron would be stationed in Great Britain for a three-year tour of duty. Upon their return, the Anderson family included my niece Patti and nephew Stephen. Within a few years Ron would again be deployed; this time his family could not accompany him, as he was among the thousands of U.S. soldiers sent to far-away Vietnam. While Ron and Bernice maintained an almost-daily correspondence of private letters, he would also occasionally have access to a tape recorder on which he spoke at length about his wartime experiences loading bombs on U.S. aircraft, and his impressions of the local people and conditions in Southeast Asia. Two subsequent tours in Vietnam affected Ron in ways we were only to discover years later when he was finally ready to speak of some of more painful dimensions of his wartime service. While we will never know for sure, his death at a relatively young age (mid-60's) may have been at least partially due to the stresses endured during those years far from family in a war zone.

A few cousins and neighbors further stretched my view of the world as they returned and shared stories from their international service in the fledgling Peace Corps. My cousin Judy and her husband, for example, served a stint in the Philippines, and a neighbor returned to regale us with stories from his time in the Southeast Asian island of Borneo. My own first international travel occurred when our high school band was invited to offer a round of concerts in Winnipeg, Canada. I was slowly beginning to break out of a restricted and insular mindset.

School and Church Anchored My Adolescence

Having a big brother and older sister gave me a measure of security when it was time for little Michael to head off to school. Most rural communities in those days had no kindergarten, so my foray into the world of public education began with first grade just a couple of days after I turned six in the late summer of 1956. I remember being excited to start school at the Wendell Elementary school in our hometown five miles from our farm.

Our tiny hometown, Wendell, Minnesota

Dave and Bernice accompanied me as we headed down our driveway each morning to await the big orange school bus that stopped along the gravel township road. I recall getting carsick (or more accurately "bus-sick") on a few occasions and being comforted (and cleaned up!) by my big sister. Bus rides with her lasted only that one year as she completed high school in the spring of 1957, as did brother Dave a year later. Bernice went off to beautician's school in "the cities" following her graduation, and Dave entered the army shortly after high school. So, beginning with the third grade, my life took on more the daily tenor of an "only child" in many respects. I always looked forward to homecomings of my sister and brother, and soon their spouses and then my nieces and nephews as well. And I recall my sadness each time a weekend visit ended, and they headed back to their own homes quite distant from the farm.

As mentioned in the previous chapter, after more than a decade of working for other farmers as a "hired man-and-wife," Bennie and Alice were at last able to afford a down payment on a small farm they would call home for nearly thirty years. In the late 1940's, they moved to Stony Brook township in the northernmost part of Grant County near the little town of Wendell (population of about 250). There they joined the local country parish, Rock Prairie Lutheran Church of rural Fergus Falls. While hard to imagine now, to some degree the Coopers "integrated" that small congregation as our German-heritage family were among the first non-Norwegians. Mom told stories of coming home from the Ladies Aid society meetings and weeping because she felt like a real outsider. As time went by, however, they seemed warmly embraced in the congregation, though to my knowledge neither was ever invited to serve on the parish council or in other major leadership roles.

As was the case for most Midwesterners in the middle of the twentieth century, life revolved around work, school, and church. Among my cherished artifacts from my childhood is a series of "perfect attendance" pins marking years of uninterrupted participation in Rock's Prairie's weekly Sunday School classes. As a teenager I joined, and ultimately became president of the congregation's "Luther League" youth group. By contrast with today's church youth activities, our monthly meetings almost invariably consisted of a "program" that seemed more geared for Rock Prairie's adult members than for us kids.

One of the things we young folks appreciated about Rock Prairie, however, was that Sunday worship was held only every other week. The congregation shared a pastor with another nearby Lutheran church, but the two were only three miles apart, so the minister readily could have led weekly worship at both. But everybody seemed fairly content with the arrangement until a new minister arrived in the mid-1960's and insisted on weekly worship at both sites. By the time Pastor Harold Underdahl came, I was already accustomed to weekly services since I had joined the parish choir, which graced the Sunday services at both churches. Some services got longer on average also, since the new pastor also moved the congregations to celebrate communion monthly, whereas the pattern had been only quarterly under previous leadership.

Unimaginable in today's pluralistic and more secular cultural milieu, the ethos of that time in rural America was such that it was nearly unthinkable for someone to be "unchurched." And in our heavily Scandinavian-heritage cultural context, not to be Lutheran placed one in a very small minority, though I do recall three of my twenty grade school classmates going to a local Presbyterian's home for our biweekly "religious release time" from school. This was a common arrangement in mid-century whereby public schools recessed for a couple of hours so virtually all students could receive religious instruction in their own denominations at nearby churches or other off-site locales. Later, in junior and senior high school, there were a handful of Roman Catholic classmates, and I was invited by one to be her date at the annual girls-ask-boys Sweetheart Ball.

While being church-focused was, thus, normative for most families in that time and place, my own religious development did not feel forced or oppressive in ways I have heard others of my generation describe. The appendicitis and subsequent events that nearly ended my life at a young age prompted some early wrestling with my own mortality and the "great questions" of life's meaning. I found inspiration particularly in the church's hymnody and would often sing some of my favorites while working alone in the barn or driving tractor out in the fields. I remember being impressed on a couple of occasions when a "foreign missionary" visited our church, thinking it could be interesting to work overseas at some point. When I was hospitalized for an additional abdominal surgery at age fifteen, Pastor Underdahl stood at the foot of my bed and read the famous passage from Romans 10: "And how shall they hear without a preacher"? That incident, together with encouragement from a parishioner named Edwin Thunselle ("Michael, you read[1] real good; you should think of becoming a pastor") first planted the seeds that would later germinate in my decision to enter seminary.

---

1. The use of "read" among those in our community was equivalent to "speak," "study," or "preach." "Reading for the minister" meant studying with the pastor in preparation for confirmation. As I recall the background for Mr. Thunselle's encouraging comment, I had made a brief presentation on some youth event at Sunday worship and he was impressed with my public speaking ability.

My confirmation picture (left front) in 1963

Even more formative in many ways than church-centered activities were my secondary school experiences. Minnesota's public schools in that era ranked academically among the finest in the nation, and we were blessed by some outstanding teachers who obviously found joy in their chosen vocation and invested themselves deeply in us students. The Elbow Lake High School I attended was marked by high percentages of graduates going on to college and prestigious careers. For a small school, with graduates numbering in the 50's or 60's in that era, we were also blessed with an extraordinary menu of high-caliber extracurricular activities. Many "Golden Eagle" athletes (only boys were offered organized teams back then in our school) went on to college sports. One of our football stars, Richard Enderle, a bruising 250-pound running back whom I had to tackle in practices, went on to be a starting lineman in the NFL.

Our high school concert band held the Minnesota state record for outstanding contest performances during a period of over thirty years, competing annually in the highest category against bands from the huge metropolitan schools. We also won many awards in ensemble and individual performance competitions. Our saxophone quartet gained superior ratings, and I received the superior rating for baritone saxophone performances each year in senior high. Our director formed a stage (swing and jazz) band during my senior high years, in which I thoroughly enjoyed playing lead alto saxophone. In the spring and summer months, the same players who made up the concert band donned our heavy, hot wool uniforms and became the Elbow Lake marching band, performing annually in parades both locally and in nearby communities. One year we were afforded the high honor of being chosen to march in the Minneapolis Aquatennial parade. Some years after I graduated the Elbow marching band would go to the Rose Bowl Parade in Pasadena. Our widely acclaimed band director, Gordon Peterson, asked me to play bass drum in the marching band, and then my senior year he appointed me drum major, leading the band in all our parades.

I was fortunate that schoolwork, while challenging, was never overwhelming, and I could manage the increasing levels of homework required as we moved through junior and senior high schools. During my elementary and early junior high days, I was content with above-average performance and grades. Somewhere mid-year in the eighth grade, things changed. I still remember my mother's eyes getting big as she opened the report card after one six-week period and saw all A's! From then on, I was a "straight-A" student, and ended up being valedictorian of our high school class. Over fifty years later, I still recall there simply coming a time when I became convinced I could do better with a bit more studying. My resolve was reinforced by our farmhouse being under kitchen renovation. After supper, I escaped the slightly chaotic scene by heading upstairs to study in my room rather than lingering downstairs watching television.

In my studies, I enjoyed virtually all subjects except history. I recall in grade school being particularly puzzled at my good friend Don Lilleboe's fascination with the Civil War. "How can anybody be so taken up studying that boring stuff about a bunch of guys dressed in blue and gray meeting up to kill each other in a place called Gettysburg where that lanky guy named Lincoln gave a pretty good speech"? The irony of that boyhood attitude did not escape me decades later when I became president of the school for which Gettysburg's world-famous Seminary Ridge is named!

Throughout my secondary and college education, I found myself interested both in the humanities and what are now called STEM subjects (science, technology, engineering, and mathematics). In the latter, I gravitated especially toward physics and considered it as a potential college major and possible launching pad for a career in engineering. Given my interest in aviation, mathematics (particularly geometry) seemed to have immediate practical applications, and I enjoyed solving complex problems and equations. Since I was college-bound, where a foreign language would be required, and Spanish was the only one offered in our high school, I learned the basics of its grammar and rudimentary vocabulary. That happenstance was also to shape the course of my life in ways I could not have imagined as I sat in class with our teacher Myrtle Stensland. While, as her name belies, Spanish was not Stensland's native tongue, she was an inspirational teacher with a deep love for the language and Hispanic cultures. One of my classmates, Karen Ellingson, went on to earn a Ph.D. in Spanish, followed by law school, which enabled her to become a prominent Twin Cities bilingual immigration attorney.

During my high school years, I took advantage of many of the extracurricular activities mentioned above. I was better-than-average on the football field, first "lettering" on the Eagle's varsity team as a freshman. The coach first put me in during the waning moments of a game we were losing about fifty to nothing, and he was impressed when I broke through the defenders to tackle the opposing team's big star quarterback. As I recall it was a "late hit," but apparently the referees failed to notice, and I was credited with being an aggressive player! Never a star running back, I nevertheless started some games at fullback and alternated playing on the line. It was as a defensive middle linebacker that I really shone on the field, resulting in being named by Minnesota's WCCO radio as our conference's defensive player of the year my senior year.

My other athletic ability, in which I was perhaps even more adept than at football, was wrestling. In junior high physical education classes, I consistently ended up on top at the end of a match and was strongly encouraged by the coach to join the Eagle's traveling wrestling team. But my father said no to that one extracurricular activity since it involved a prolonged winter season, during which he needed me to help with the evening chores during the brutal cold weather. Coach Don Hauskins probably never forgave Bennie for that and would hound me every fall to make another effort at convincing Dad to let me wrestle.

In addition to concert and marching bands and football, my extracurricular activities included speech, debate, yearbook staff, student government, and one theatrical debut. I wrote and delivered an original oration every year in the regional speech competitions. Our senior year, my debate partner Jon Schroeder and I came away from most area competitions with more wins than losses. As in sports and music, once again Elbow Lake debaters were often up against the best talent from schools several times our size. Absent the kinds of student/administration tensions that would arise in the years after our 1968 graduation, I recall the Student Council meetings as being harmonious, marked by our school administrators' genuine interest in gaining student input. I was elected the council's president my senior year by my peers.

As student council president, I was asked to offer a brief address when a new addition to the high school was dedicated in the fall of 1967. With local and state dignitaries present, together with hundreds from the local community gathered in the large new gymnasium, I felt honored to offer words of gratitude. To my surprise, excerpts from my speech were not only published in the local paper but got picked up more broadly and gained attention as far away as Indiana where a newspaper reprinted the following editorial from *The Grant County Herald*:

> We can't let the opportunity pass without offering our thanks and congratulations to Mike Cooper, Elbow Lake high Student council president, for an exceptionally fine and inspiring speech at the new school dedication last week. For the benefit of those who might have missed the dedication, we'd like to reprint here a couple of paragraphs from Mike's speech that we thought particularly outstanding. Here they are:
>
> "Above and beyond improved educational offerings, the presence of this new building means something else to me. In this day of the hippies, teenage uprisings in our cities, teenage alcoholism and drug addiction, the cry of many misguided and miserable teens is 'Nobody cares! Nobody cares what I do or what happens to me!' I can never say this. I can never say that nobody cares about me. Nor can any other student in this high school."
>
> "Each morning when I get off the bus out front here, I see before my eyes a mighty big and unmistakable sign that somebody cares about me. I know that hundreds of you have been

willing to work and to dig a little deeper in your pockets to build this educational institution because you care enough to provide a place where we can learn and grow. We students want to say to all of you, 'Thank You!' Thank you for caring."

And all we can answer to Mike is a duplication of his own words: Thanks, Mike.

My one and only theatrical appearance was as Jeff the drunk in the musical *Brigadoon*. The favorite line, which peeved Coach Hauskins and the teetotalers in our somewhat pious community, was when after a night of drinking, my character said to the bartender: "Put it on my bill." To the barkeep's reply, "Your bill, sir, is getting mighty high," I replied with the appropriate slurred speech, "And sho am I. And sho am I!"

In both my junior and senior years, I received recognition for my academic performance and overall "leadership" abilities. Near the end of my junior year, the faculty named me as the one to represent Elbow Lake at Minnesota Boys' State, a coveted weeklong mock governmental leadership event in which I joined young men from high schools across the state. Some school official must have forgotten to notify my family and me of the nomination. We learned that I would be the 1967 Boys Stater when my picture appeared in the local *Grant County Herald* newspaper!

As the senior year drew toward graduation, at the annual National Honor Society banquet, I was informed that the faculty had selected me as the class "Most Representative Boy" to deliver one of two student addresses at commencement on the theme, "It's not where we stand; it's where we're going." When graduation came, I was valedictorian of the Elbow Lake High School class of 1968.

My high school senior photo, 1968

Beyond Church and School: Airplanes, Cars, and Girls!

The preceding paragraphs might well convince the reader that Michael's schedule of church and school activities, together with the daily hours of farm chores, left no time at all for a social life or recreational pursuits. Such was not the case. My senior year I was finally able to plunge into what would become my primary lifelong avocation. Having been fascinated with airplanes since my earliest memories, I persuaded Mom and Dad to let me join a handful of other school buddies and take flying lessons at the Elbow Lake Municipal Airport. After nine hours of challenging dual instruction with our local Certified Flight Instructor, John "Kip" Coleman, (during which I got upchuck airsick on a number of the first flights!), I soloed a 1950's vintage Piper Super Cub on March 10, 1968. I wrote the following in my journal that evening: "Important! Today Mike Cooper soloed in Piper 105, (call sign) N7276K. Yes, today was my first as solo pilot of an airplane." The summer after graduation I worked on the ground crew of a local crop duster, and after the spraying season was over, I flew his pristine Super Cub, gaining a total of just over 30 hours before I went off to college in the fall. While I had hoped to earn my Private Pilot license, I did not complete enough cross-country time. That milestone would have to be put off a few years until I had enough financial wherewithal to resume flying. But that early introduction to aviation further reinforced my desire to become a military and/or airline pilot.

My solo flight certificate: March 10, 1968

While not a fanatical car-lover like many young fellows, I enjoyed learning to drive, which came easy given my experiences with tractors and the pickup on the farm. In that era, Minnesota offered a "farm license" for fifteen-year-olds to drive during the daytime within thirty miles of home in the aid of a family's farming operations. I acquired that handily as soon as I was eligible through a driving test preceded by the usual written exam. Since there were significant auto insurance discounts for families whose young drivers had completed a Drivers' Education course, the following year I drove myself to town every day for two weeks of instruction in how to drive! About the time I got my license, my parents traded in their rather stodgy 1961 Rambler sedan and bought a sporty 1965 Ford Galaxy two-door hardtop—a really neat automobile for a teenager to borrow, and one they later sold me at a bargain when

I needed a car in college. I have always enjoyed driving and still do on occasions when I get behind the wheel for an extended road trip.

Gaining the driver's license granted new freedom and opened the way for another typical aspect of teenage life—dating. Unlike many people, I cannot point to a time in adolescence when I suddenly became interested in those of the opposite sex. I always liked girls! As a youngster, my primary playmate was our nearest neighbor, Margaret "Margy" Aseleson, three years my senior. While there was some segregation by gender in our structured or pick-up sports games in elementary school, much of our recess and P.E. time was also in coed configurations. Come junior high, however, like many of my peers, I began to pair off with a special friend for a time until moving on to someone else. With one exception, I recall the breakups of these brief romances as quite amicable and probably by mutual agreement. And then, my junior year in high school I fell head over heels in love!

Doris Weigand and I had started first grade together at Wendell Elementary. Always friends, as mentioned above, however, each of us had paired up with others in our early high school dating. She'd been dating my good friend Jon Schroeder, and I her friend Victoria Nordholm. Sensing it was time for me to move on from dating Vicky, I asked Doris out for a movie one evening, and we quickly proceeded to "going steady," ritualized in those days by wearing each other's high school rings and her wearing my football letter jacket. Naturally, our newfound love resulted in rather strained relationships with our friends Jon and Vicky! In my adult years, among all our high school classmates, I've had most frequent contact with Jon, so our friendship was not irreparably damaged. Doris' and my relationship continued to deepen, and we were married two weeks after our college graduation on May 15, 1971.

A Dashed Dream and Teenage Angst

Given my keen interest in aviation, I set my sights on the U.S. Air Force Academy when it came time to contemplate college choices. In that era, the only pathway to a military academy was by means of a congressional appointment. From Minnesota's seventh district congressman I received appointments to West Point, the Coast Guard Academy, and Air Force Academy. Of course, I chose to attend the latter. Midway through my senior year I went to the Twin Cities for the standard physical examination.

I was devastated when I was informed that I failed it due to the series of abdominal operations in my youth. A journal I kept during the later months of my high school senior year reveals the depth of disappointment I felt when the door to the academy was slammed shut. On March 4, 1968, I wrote: "Today I found out for sure that I have been disqualified for the Air Force Academy because of my bowel obstructions. Oh heck, what's the use? Everything I've worked and dreamed and hoped for is all gone."

During one period in my senior year, a sensitive English teacher noted my downcast demeanor when I was verging on the edge of depression. Shirley Lindbeck asked me to stay after class one day and handed me a note I have carried in my wallet ever since that day in 1968. On it appears this simple verse attributed to Theodore Tilton, which has given me comfort and courage at times I have faced daunting tasks or discouraging prospects:

> Once in Persia reigned a king, who upon his signet ring
> Graved a maxim true and wise, which, if held before the eyes,
> Gave him counsel at a glance, fit for every change and chance;
> Solemn words, and these are they: Even this shall pass away.

My teenage diary also confirms my highly competitive nature and almost frantic efforts to graduate top of my class. Many nights I studied until 1:00 or 2:00 a.m. and was almost desperate to maintain my grades even as I was involved with multiple extracurricular activities, farm work and an intense dating relationship with Doris. The diary reveals my wrestling with vocational options other than aviation when that door appeared shut. In mid-March I wrote one evening, "The ministry is starting to call me again." A few days later, another entry reads: "I am thinking a lot tonight about the ministry and serving the people of rural America. I am really concerned about rural problems and rural people." In addition to encouragement from Pastor Underdahl, the local Missouri Synod Lutheran minister, at the church where I attended release time sessions, suggested I should consider the ministry. He urged that I consider going through that denomination's rigorous preparation, which involved a seamless eight-year process of college and seminary. Little did I know it at the time, but ministry in that conservative church body would not have been a good match for me.

Knowing I could not count on academy appointment, I had submitted applications to two colleges—a Lutheran school, Gustavus Adolphus, where I had been impressed by the campus the previous summer when

Boys' State was held there, and the University of Minnesota. So, when a last-minute decision was required after the academy option evaporated, I felt I would be more comfortable at the small church-related college.

Out of the Nest: The College Years

On a warm late summer day in 1968 we unloaded our Ford Galaxy and carried my clothes, stereo, and a few boxes of personal items into a dormitory room of Sorenson Hall on the beautiful hill-top campus of Gustavus Adolphus College, in the Minnesota river town of St. Peter. I recall feeling a measure of both sadness and excitement as I bid farewell to my parents and took the plunge into the days of freshman orientation. Quickly settling into college life, I enjoyed my classes and made new friends in my dormitory. By the end of the first year, I had decided to major in philosophy while exploring a wide range of other courses.

During the summer after my freshman year at Gustavus, I was asked by the dean of students to join another student in forming a personal care team for a new student who had tragically become quadriplegic in a snow sledding accident. Rooming with "Pete" was an eye-opener for me as I witnessed the incredible courage required on his part to navigate every aspect of life totally dependent on me and others. Sadly, we could not sustain the level of care needed to keep him safe and healthy in a dormitory environment, and he had to withdraw from school after a few weeks. The experience left me with better understandings of the challenges faced by people with disabilities, and the burdens borne by so many among us in the human family.

Much as Gustavus was a fine school, I found myself with a growing sense it was not the best fit for the duration of my undergrad education. I felt somewhat out of my element with many peers from urban and suburban backgrounds in the Twin Cities. Added to that was the fact that by the end of my third semester, I had taken many of the courses offered by the two philosophy professors who constituted the department. I determined my major would be enhanced by exposure to a larger pool of teachers. I also experienced a growing loneliness, being across the state from where Doris was studying at Concordia College in Moorhead. I began to explore possible transfer to Concordia and made the move after Christmas 1979.

Because of the way Gustavus' courses transferred to Concordia, I discovered it was possible by attending one full summer to complete my B.A. in three years. Doris was also on an accelerated schedule including summers, so we graduated together in early May 1971 and were married two weeks later at her home church, Trinity Lutheran in Wendell.

Focused on excelling in academics at college (I graduated *summa cum laude*, second in a class of nearly 500), I limited my extracurricular involvement to singing in the concert choir at Gustavus and serving as a Resident Assistant (RA) at Concordia. The Gustavus choir experience included a 10-day tour that took us eastward from Minnesota to New York and Washington, D.C. Arriving in the nation's capital in mid-winter, I immediately fell in love with the place and recall hoping that I might live and work there at some point in my life. After a semester as RA at Concordia, I was invited to serve as Dormitory Manager overseeing all the RA's of Concordia's Brown Hall. Despite the fact the dormitory positions were remunerated, and I received substantial scholarships, I finished my bachelor's degree owing about $10,000 in student loans. Retiring them required payments for a decade after I finished seminary.

As the end of college was on the horizon, the big question was, "What comes next?" My interest in philosophy continued to deepen and I considered pursuing graduate work as a ticket to college teaching. The situation in the late 1960's and early 70's was such, however, that teaching positions were few and far between, and many with earned Ph.D.'s in the humanities found themselves making a living outside of academia. So, despite strong encouragement from my professors to go on for graduate study in philosophy, I decided against that option. Still yearning to fly professionally, I briefly considered going on for further education in one of the schools that offered pilot training combined with courses in airport administration and the like. There too, however, in that era it was virtually impossible to land an airline or other professional pilot position without a resume that included flying jets in the military.

Doris and I recognized we would need to earn a living, and although she planned to teach, we also wanted to start a family and could not depend on her salary alone. I sought to prepare myself for possible employment in business or government. Since I had fulfilled all the requirements for my philosophy major, my senior year curriculum consisted mostly of courses in economics, accounting, and administration, enabling me to graduate with a minor in business. Interested in government and excited at the prospect of a possible career in Washington, I also sent off applications to a number of federal agencies for civil service positions, including the CIA, FBI, and FAA. My score in the general civil service test was high enough to qualify for special management training and advanced placement with a federal agency, but when an offer came to be a technical writer in the U.S. Department of Agriculture, it just did not seem like my calling and I declined.

So, what was I going to do? In the fall or early winter of my senior year in college I saw the movie "Love Story," in which the main character is a law student. In the days following, I kept coming back to thoughts about what life as a small-town lawyer might be like, deciding "Well, that could be cool." Given my interest in scholarly pursuits, I saw the law as a profession requiring engagement with legal texts and documents as well as engagement with people. For many, it led to public service and politics, in which I had an abiding interest ever since President John F. Kennedy had been one of my childhood heroes. And one could make a good, even fairly substantial income as an attorney. Therefore, one Saturday morning in the winter of 1971, I headed up to Grand Forks, North Dakota, and, with no preparation whatsoever, sat for the Law School Admissions Test (LSAT). With a score well above average and my strong high school and college academic records, I was accepted by five fine law schools, the Universities of Arizona, Minnesota, and Michigan, as well as Georgetown and Valparaiso. Despite more generous scholarship offers from some of the others, given my fascination with Washington, it was an easy choice to enroll in the prestigious Georgetown University Law School.

Some Reflections on What It All Means

As we move further along in years, childhood, adolescence, and younger adult experiences recede more and more into the mists of memory. But high points and low moments stand out from all the ordinary times that constitute the various phases of life. Even in the best of circumstances there are bound to be some regrets over roads not taken, and perhaps even remorse over things said and done that were hurtful to other people or harmful to oneself. While even in my seventies, I am by no means free of self-centeredness, looking back on my youth from this vantage point I realize the degree to which in many ways I lived in my own insulated small world. Psychologically, I suppose the fact that I became de facto almost an "only child" by virtue of being so much younger than my siblings had its impact in my having a sense of being special and deserving of favorable treatment. I also suspect my place in the birth order contributed to my becoming frustrated when incapable of doing certain things since siblings a decade older were obviously more competent than little Mike in many areas. This family configuration probably also had its impact in my anxiety about being left out, since I usually was the one sent up to bed alone while the others remained downstairs playing cards and having grownup conversations.

To my parents and siblings, I owe profound gratitude for constituting what by any measure can only be regarded as a loving family. There were never prolonged seasons of estrangement or simmering anger as far as I can recall. While rare, my parents would on occasion have heated arguments, but quickly cleared the air and moved along. I'm sure my brother and sister had spats on occasion, but I cannot recall any, and am grateful we have enjoyed warm fraternal connections in our adult years. It was a hard blow to us all when Bernice died suddenly of a post-surgery pulmonary embolism at age fifty-eight. While I don't think any of us had "unfinished business" in our relationships with her, the lack of a chance to say goodbye weighed especially heavily on my parents, whose health concerns at the time precluded their traveling to Florida for her funeral.

I do recall a period in my pre-teens when my father suffered some significant depression. This may have coincided with his developing an ulcer that required a special diet, and perhaps also his watching many of our neighbors expand their farming operations, buying fancy new equipment and so on while Dad appeared content to remain a small dairy farmer. There was at least one frightening occasion when I interpreted Dad's words as suggesting he might contemplate taking his own life. For the most part, however, my parents were emotionally stable, and their relationship was strong. Mom also had some low moments, but even while in them could "name her feelings" and soon return to her generally optimistic and adventuresome spirit.

My generation was the first, especially in rural American communities, when completion of high school became the norm rather than exception. Accordingly, my academic "book learning" surpassed that of my parents by the time I reached junior high school. I was fortunate in being a fairly quick learner who did not need much help with homework, since particularly in subjects like algebra or trigonometry, my parents would have found themselves unable to assist. While I don't recall strong feelings of disconnect from them at the time, looking back now I realize that in some ways it was probably impossible for my parents to "get me" as my interests expanded into areas foreign to them. When I took flying lessons, for example, I don't recall either parent ever coming out to the airport to watch, even on the big day anticipated for my first solo. I carry no resentment but simply a small measure of sadness about those parts of my life that my parents seemed unable to share.

The insular and "small world" syndrome described above were manifest in what can only be named honestly as racist and sexist attitudes so common among WASPs (white, Anglo-Saxon protestants) of that time and place—and still sadly so in many ways today. A new organizing effort to help farmers band together and negotiate higher prices for their production was called the National Farmers Organization or NFO. I recall the acronym being refashioned by some in our area as a racial slur in describing African Americans from Nebraska as "n_ _ _ _ _ s from Omaha." When the Lutheran pastor of Trinity in Wendell and his wife adopted two African American children there were raised eyebrows and hushed whisperings about their bold decision.

My own early attitudes about gender relations were certainly shaped by the societal ethos of male domination. In my relations with girls, I expected to be "the leader," and I don't recall that being challenged back then, though on one occasion I was humbled when a girl named Diane beat me (and probably all my male classmates) at arm wrestling! Team sports were limited to boys, with a girl's only option to be a cheerleader. Boys and men drove cars; girls and women were passengers. When two couples went out for a Sunday drive, the guys usually sat in front, the women in the back. Few women worked outside the home or off the farm, and on that score, I remember being quite proud that my mother had a job in town.

To the degree that some of my peers and I began to question the attitudes that were in the air we breathed and the water we drank, we owe it in large measure to role models found in some courageous teachers, clergy, and others in our communities. A few of them spoke of the compelling need for racial equality and questioned the wisdom of escalating U.S. military action in Vietnam. Soon the latter would be on everyone's minds as the local draft board began calling many young men from our own community into military service.

Even before Vietnam and the struggle for civil rights became predominating societal issues, the ever-escalating Cold War cast a constant dreadful specter. I recall sitting in front of the television watching

President John F. Kennedy's address to the nation at the height of the Cuban missile crisis. At the age of twelve, I was terrified that nuclear war was imminent, and I might never grow up. While our rural schools did not have the "duck-and-cover" exercises common in some urban areas where it was expected Soviet missiles would fall in the event of nuclear attack, we were required to watch the movies about nuclear fallout, which would bring about miserable slow deaths if we did escape the fireballs. We were keenly aware that no one would be out of harm's way in a nuclear Armageddon. I recall looking up in the sky at jet contrails, wondering if they might be from Soviet bombers about to release the weapons of terror that would kill us all, and perhaps even bring about the end of the world.

So, as I left the farm and our rural community for college in mid-1968, in addition to wondering about my own pathway forward, all these bigger issues were swirling within me. I had a long way to go on a journey toward living out the values of equality and justice for all, espoused in the U.S. constitution and undergirded by the faith tradition in which I was raised. I still have a long way to go. To the degree I began and continue moving in the right direction, I owe it to patient but persistent mentors going all the way back to Rock Prairie and the Wendell-Elbow Lake schools and community. As I have pondered more deeply their lives, I have also come to recognize that, for all their traditional ways and socially conservative values, my parents demonstrated a spirit of openness to reconsider things and change some convictions. In their later years, Mom and Dad joined some others of their generation in wondering why so many of their peers seemed so afraid of gays and lesbians. They were cared for in their assisted living and nursing homes by hands of all colors, and I heard them say a genuine "thank you" to the many attendants who helped them, regardless of their race. While they never said as much in my hearing, I have the sense that as Bennie and Alice approached their final life chapters, they remembered those early days in Stony Brook when they felt themselves the "outsiders." Always suspicious of people who had a superior or arrogant air, my parents retained an intrinsic Midwestern sense of humility and lack of entitlement.

While my folks had attained a solid middle-class existence, by virtue of their longevity (to ninety-two for Mom and 100 for my Dad) they eventually outlived their retirement resources. My brother and I were so grateful that the Diakon (Lutheran) agency that owned the assisted living facility in which they spent their final years has a "benevolent care" fund, which supplemented their social security resources and provided for their continuing care after their bank accounts ran dry.

To sum up my reflections on the first two decades of my life, I end on a note of gratitude and humility. I was fortunate to be born into a loving family that instilled values of hard work and gave me a foundation of common sense and respectfulness that is not afraid to question or even challenge when I sense unfairness or injustice. I was coming of age in an era and context that afforded quality public education, albeit not without its limitations and socialization that reinforced certain prejudices already described. A few key individuals—especially teachers—gave me affirmations I may not have fully merited but that challenged me to grow beyond the limits initially fixed in my self-image. Representative of what I'm trying to describe here is an English teacher's comment on an essay I wrote as a high school junior (and still have among my files): "This is the finest statement I have ever read." When you get that kind of affirmation at a young age from elders you regard highly, it builds self-esteem and lifts your sights.

To a much greater degree than I recognized at the time, the very fact I survived at all is due, literally, to the luck of the draw that determined the fate of young men of my generation. Despite my failure to meet the rigorous Air Force Academy medical standards, I likely was still eligible to be drafted into the Army. In the fall of 1969, we sat around my college dormitory lounge as balls with birth date numbers were drawn in the first draft lottery. When mine was among the last to be selected at random (333), I knew I would avoid the jungles of Vietnam, from which many returned in coffins or severely wounded physically and/or psychologically. Decades later, when I first visited the Vietnam Memorial in Washington, I was shocked to find my name! Michael L. Cooper from West Virginia was killed in action in the late 1960's. I made an etching of his name that I have frequently displayed in my office as a reminder of his life and the sheer randomness of life and death for all of us in the human family.

As I reflect upon the course of my life, it is impossible to express adequately my gratitude for the opportunities and experiences I've been privileged to enjoy. I have lived and worked in some of the world's greatest cities with all the richness they have to offer. I have been offered positions of leadership that come with a modest measure of prestige and public recognition. But even now, in the final quarter of the game of life, I remain at a deep level the farm boy from western Minnesota. Rural roots and rhythms run deeply in my soul. Come five o'clock on a crisp fall afternoon, it still feels like it's time to head down to the barn, call the cows in from the pasture, and begin the milking!

— 3 —

Moving East and from Law to Gospel

FOLLOWING GRADUATION FROM CONCORDIA, and Doris's and my wedding on May 15, 1971, we moved to Minnesota's Twin Cities where we both worked in a powdered metal factory. My aunt and godmother Helen was the office administrator for the FMS Corporation in Bloomington, and I had worked there the previous summer as a laborer mixing various powered metals that then went into the giant presses and blast furnaces. Those two summers were eye-openers into the challenging world and demanding work of hourly laborers. As a farm kid, I was no stranger to manual labor. But working in a dust-filled factory, where the blast furnace heated conditions to 100 degrees, and moonlighting at a truck wash where I washed out rotting meat from refrigerator trailers with an acid-infused power washer, made me more sympathetic to those who labor their entire careers in back-breaking and life-threatening environments.

As summer ended, we packed up the 1965 Ford Galaxy and pulled a small U-Haul trailer with all our possessions on a trip from Minnesota to Washington, D.C. Doris had been offered a teaching position in the affluent suburban Montgomery County Maryland school system. After searching for apartments closer to the law school in the heart of D.C., we instead chose to reside in the "new town" of Columbia, Maryland, which provided an easier commute for Doris. It was an experimental planned community being developed by the Rouse Company, and we felt it would be an exciting place for us to live as newlyweds. In hindsight, living so far from the school and my classmates contributed to my never really feeling at home at Georgetown Law.

Where I found most enjoyment in those months of law school was in a part-time unpaid internship in the office of my Minnesota congressman, Bob Bergland, who would later serve as President Jimmy Carter's secretary of agriculture. I enjoyed doing some legal background work assigned by the congressional staff and responding to constituent letters from the many persons who write their representative seeking help with a wide range of issues and problems. By the time I decided to leave Georgetown and move in other vocational directions, I was informed that had I stayed the congressman's office might have been able to provide a small stipend for some continuing work. But it was time to move on and I needed to make more money than Bergland's office could provide.

After the first semester, in which I felt I was doing fairly well at keeping up with the hectic demands and new ethos of law school, I became increasingly clear that the law was not my calling. Beyond a growing dislike for the tediousness of legal research, writing briefs and the like, I began to realize that the glamorous lawyerly life I had seen on television shows and movies is far from the reality of what attorneys actually do most of the time. And I was troubled by the lack of ethics on the part of some of my classmates who were cutthroat and highly competitive in their drive to excel and land prestigious high-paying jobs after law school.

Notes in my mother's hand, which I discovered among her papers long after her death, appear to be a record of a phone conversation in which I explained to my parents my decision to leave law school. Mom quoted me as saying, "The law, like everything else, is not for everybody. Life is too short to plunge ahead into a career you can't put your heart and soul into." In that conversation, I apparently quoted one of the philosophers I had most appreciated in my undergraduate work, Ludwig Wittgenstein: "I wish you good, not necessarily clever thoughts and a decency that won't come out in the wash." I had discerned the law was not my calling. So, shortly after the second semester of law school began in early 1972, I made my decision to withdraw. When I went to inform the Georgetown Law dean of my plans, he was not happy. "Don't you realize you took a spot that someone else was eager to fill"? he asked, laying some guilt at my feet. "And besides," he said, "I don't think you'll find your life greatly different whether you're a minister or lawyer in some town somewhere." I was not persuaded. I followed through with my plans to withdraw from Georgetown, informed my congressman that I could no longer afford to work on a volunteer basis, and closed out that brief chapter of my life.

As I have said on many occasions, especially throughout my ministries in church executive positions, where I interacted regularly with attorneys, I hold good lawyers in high regard. I admire their professionalism and dedication to seeking the greatest possible justice in complex and challenging conditions. Like any vocational calling, the law is right for some and not for others. It wasn't my calling. At the same time, I have also often expressed gratitude for the one semester I spent at Georgetown which, I say, "taught me when I needed to call a lawyer." I gained enough insights to help me navigate the kinds of turbulent waters I encountered more and more as I moved into increasingly responsible administrative positions. The fact that in seventeen years as a seminary president our institution was never sued, apart from a minor personal injury matter that quickly went away, might be attributed in some measure to my ability to navigate complex legal and regulatory matters (or maybe we were just lucky on that score!)

Drawn toward Seminary

In my teaching on dynamics of personal, organizational, and institutional change, I have encouraged students to consider that major life changes typically come about as a combination of push- and pull-forces. When a significant change occurs, it's often initiated by a push to leave the place where one has been for a season. Graduation forces a student out of the nest. Job loss forces a worker to look for new employment. But just as change is frequently driven from behind, so it also often is accompanied by the draw toward something new. If the push- and pull-factors occur more or less simultaneously, and if one is successful in landing in the desired new place or position, that's probably the optimal transition. In my case, apart from feeling that the law was not for me, by the time I was convinced I needed to leave Georgetown, I had gained clarity that a "call" to full-time ministry seemed to be heard with greater and greater clarity.

As noted in the reflections on my youth, the church and religion had always been important to me. At various points along the way, I had been encouraged to consider "the ministry," and had felt drawn toward it. But I also went through a somewhat rebellious phase in my college years where I chafed at some aspects of the institutional church. I needed to work through those, which was aided greatly by a very positive parish experience during my short stint in law school. Living in Columbia, Doris and I quickly became involved in an avant-garde new mission, Living Word Lutheran Church. Living Word's pastor, Bob Grochau, was a far more "hip" clergyman than I had previously encountered in a congregation. Bob was involved in social issues. He had been a civil rights champion early in his ministry, became involved in groups protesting the Vietnam war, and spoke to current issues in his sermons. I also gravitated toward his more liberal personal habits that departed from the piety experienced in my youth. Bob and his wife Joan served cocktails in gatherings at their home! Living Word had innovative liturgies planned by the members. On occasion, I would play my alto sax in a small combo that accompanied "contemporary" worship services. "If the church can be like this," I began thinking to myself, "I can see myself as a minister in that kind of church."

As I considered the possibility of seminary, and shared my musings with Grochau, he was very encouraging, as were some of my fellow members of Living Word. While Bob had graduated from the Lutheran seminary in Philadelphia, he had served on the board of Gettysburg Seminary. He strongly encouraged me to check out Gettysburg. Since it was only about an hour's drive from Montgomery County Maryland where Doris was teaching, we determined she could keep her job and support us financially during seminary. I came away from a visit to Gettysburg with positive feelings and a sense the school would be a good place to prepare for ordained ministry and life as a parish pastor. I was particularly intrigued and excited upon learning that Gettysburg had a vibrant satellite in Washington, where it was a founding member of the Washington Theological Consortium. My plan was to commute to Gettysburg for all required courses and take as many electives as possible in schools of the consortium. Doris and I realized it would be an easier commute for me, both to Gettysburg and Washington, were we to move to the western side of Montgomery County. She requested and received a transfer from the elementary school in Olney, Maryland to one in Gaithersburg. Having enjoyed living in Columbia, we learned there was a similar "new town" community called Montgomery Village, where we found a new apartment complex just a mile or so from her school.

Temporary Jobs Further Expanded Horizons

With plans for entering seminary in the fall in place, after I was accepted in early 1972, I needed to find temporary employment for the spring and summer months. I spent a few weeks laboring in local construction. The most memorable part of that experience, aside from back-breaking labor as a hod carrier for a bricklaying outfit, was working with hardcore convicts on work release. Working shoulder to shoulder with convicted thieves and murderers taught me a great deal about the realities experienced by those who live on the underside of society. After a short stint doing some of the hardest physical work of my life, I was eager to find a more intellectually challenging job. I discovered that Maryland's Howard County where we lived was in desperate need of substitute teachers and required no education credentials other than a bachelor's degree in any field. As I recall, within a day or two of applying to the school district (there were no background checks back then!) I got a call from a principal and was off and running on my brief public school teaching career. For readers who may be unfamiliar with substitute teaching, it's a challenging and interesting lifestyle. Typically, a teacher calls in sick early in the morning and a principal must scramble to find a replacement for the day. So, it was not uncommon to get a call less than an hour before school began, and I would rush off to whichever school needed a "sub" that day. I apparently developed a reputation as a reliable sub in whom principals and teachers had confidence, so the work became quite steady. Another factor is that unlike most subs, this hungry young guy would take any assignment. Many of my counterparts were reluctant or outright refused assignments in some of the more challenging subject areas or with older high school or special education students. "I'll take anything," was my attitude. For the most part, I enjoyed the work and discovered I had some degree of aptitude for teaching.

As summer approached, when there would be no substitute teaching available, I applied for a summer intern program offered by federal agencies. A general civil service application was circulated among dozens of agencies, and I was hired for duty in the computer tape library of the U.S. Census Bureau in Suitland, Maryland. Throughout the summer of 1972, I commuted to that suburb on the east side of Washington and entered the huge complex where giant mainframe computers hummed away, processing data from the 1970 census. To say the least, the work was far less stimulating than substitute teaching or even the construction jobs. We interns were tasked with retrieving large reels of magnetic data tapes from the library and placing them in a staging area from which they would be loaded onto the computers that filled cavernous halls. Given the number of hands who touched any given tape box, our work often involved searching for missing tapes. "We're missing Las Vegas," a supervisor would say, "and you damn well better find it!" Back then, the bureau's data processing went on 24/7, and the interns were most often assigned the graveyard shift from midnight to 8 a.m. With little work required, since most of the tape-staging occurred in daytime hours, a couple of us would be directed by our supervisor to disappear into the bowels of the tape library and read or sleep. "If anybody asks what you're doing" (which they never did), the boss said, "tell them you're engaged in file maintenance."

During that time of transition, I learned most from interactions with my coworkers, the majority of whom were African American. Those pre-seminary extended conversations with construction workers and career federal employees broadened my horizons and gave me insights into the realities of racism, subsisting on low-income wages, and coping with urban problems in poorer neighborhoods. One vignette perhaps encapsulates the kind of learning that I experienced. A college student intern from a southern state was searching one night for a lost beige-colored magnetic tape box. Asked to describe it by our coworkers, he said, "Oh, you know it's that flesh-colored kind." Surrounded by a half dozen or so African American colleagues, one piped up and with a big grin asked, "Just whose flesh are you talking about?" I had begun my journey learning about white privilege and how permeated our society is with overt and subtle manifestations of racism.

Soon my summer working in the federal bureaucracy drew to a close. Doris and I made our move from Columbia to Montgomery Village. Since I would be making a daily round trip commute of 110 miles, we also decided it was time to buy a new car and purchased a flashy red 1972 "Rally Sport" Nova Chevrolet that would be our vehicle for the next dozen years or so. Especially after a few summers in the east and then years in California, we wished we had spent a few hundred bucks more and bought a car with air conditioning!

Seminary Student Years: Even Better Than Expected

In the early fall of 1972, I joined about sixty others for new student orientation on the campus of the Lutheran Theological Seminary at Gettysburg. With just a handful of exceptions, we were all recent college graduates aiming toward careers as parish ministers. While the Lutheran Church in America had decided two years previously to ordain women, all but a half-dozen of my classmates were men, and we were all white. A couple of Methodists made us nominally ecumenical, but by and large we mirrored the all-white and almost all-male cadre of students, as was then the case in all U.S. Lutheran seminaries.

To sum up my experience of seminary in a nutshell: "I loved it!" I found academic studies interesting in ways and to degrees I had not anticipated. With my philosophy major background, I took readily to topics like systematic theology that seemed forbidding to some of my peers whose undergraduate education was weak in the liberal arts. I enjoyed learning Greek in a month-long intensive January "boot camp" that provided foundations for New Testament studies. In tandem with the more purely academic areas of study, I enjoyed the practical studies in ministry, particularly homiletics or preaching and courses in human development and congregational leadership.

As noted above, after my first year when all courses were required on the Gettysburg campus, the bulk of my remaining seminary studies occurred in the half-dozen schools of the Washington Consortium. Two of my classmates and I had elected an option offered uniquely at Gettysburg. Called by the esoteric name of "Option B" (!), the program was patterned after European university models. Rather than completing required courses and electives, Option B students had to sit for five comprehensive written and/or oral examinations in Bible, Church History, Ethics, Theology, and Ministry. After the first year, we had no standard requirements, and were free to audit courses of interest throughout the Consortium as well as at Gettysburg. That flexibility enabled me to reengage in the political context of the nation's capital. A course called "The Minister and Public Affairs" found a handful of us in weekly conversations with some of the nation's highest governmental officials, like then-Associate Supreme Court Justice William Rehnquist. Another course, "The Bible and the *New York Times*" required daily reading of the *Times* and biblical texts. At our weekly seminars, students presented brief papers and led discussions on how scripture was speaking to the issues of the day and vice versa. I also completed a January-term internship at the Lutheran Council in the USA's (LCUSA) Office of Government and Public Affairs in Washington. It was at the zenith of the Watergate crisis, when it appeared that the impeachment of President Richard Nixon was imminent. Since the LCUSA office was beginning to receive inquiries about how the impeachment process would unfold, I was asked to compile a briefing paper on that hot topic.

As I successfully completed the Option B comprehensive exams one-by-one, my Gettysburg professors seemed quite impressed with my academic work, and several encouraged me to pursue graduate study and prepare for a teaching and scholarly career. In historical and theological studies, I proposed that instead of an exam, I write a thesis tracing Lutheran hermeneutics (Scripture interpretation) from the Reformation to the current era. The professors who read the thesis commented it was an excellent comprehensive piece of work.

Alongside seminary academic studies, we future ministers were required to participate in "field education," which involved immersion in a congregation. Given my residence in the greater Washington area, I petitioned to be assigned to a nearby parish where I could have frequent involvement without a lengthy commute. The Lutheran Church of the Redeemer in Damascus, Maryland was just a short drive north of Montgomery Village, and I liked Redeemer's pastor, the Rev. Irvin Staph, when we met to get acquainted. "Irv" was a second- career pastor, meaning he had worked in another vocation and attended seminary at an age older than most of his classmates. He was eager to mentor a young seminarian and spent considerable time sharing his insights with me in our supervisory sessions. He also offered me a wide range of parish involvement, including preaching, teaching youth and adult classes, accompanying him on pastoral visits, and observing meetings of church committees etc. In his final evaluation, Irv indicated he regarded me as a colleague in ministry, not merely a seminarian.

As I got to know Pastor Staph, I also learned that he was deeply involved in the charismatic movement that was sweeping through churches of all denominations in the late 1960's and early 1970's. With elements of Pentecostalism, those involved in the movement had high expectations for "charismatic" spiritual experiences like speaking in tongues, miraculous healings, and similar emotionally charged events. Increasingly, I grew uncomfortable with what I perceived as a somewhat elite attitude on the part of the pastor and some members, who seemed to see themselves as the super-Christians. In one of his sermons, Irv told Redeemer's members that were he to experience a major medical crisis like a heart attack or appendicitis, he would refuse medical treatment and just trust that God would heal him through prayer. At that point, I realized I did not share such theological convictions, which I regarded as rather naïve and overly prescriptive of how God might choose to act in the world. I recall asking Irv questions like, "Don't you think it limits God by decreeing he (few used inclusive language in that era) can't work through doctors and hospitals"? As time went on, I was saddened when Pastor Staph continued veering more and more away from mainstream Lutheranism. Ultimately, he led a faction of Redeemer members to leave the LCA and form an independent (and from their perspective I suspect "true and pure") Lutheran congregation in northern Montgomery County. Despite our growing apart theologically, I remain grateful for the way in which the Staphs and members of Redeemer welcomed Doris and me into their community and provided opportunity for me to begin testing my pastoral wings.

Another required component of field education was completion of a summer as student chaplain in a hospital or other institutional setting. Clinical Pastoral Education or "CPE" remains a requirement in many seminaries today. Beyond the practical learnings of working with people in times of crisis, navigating one's way around medical centers, interacting with doctors and nurses etc., CPE is for many an intense laboratory for personal growth. That surely proved the case for me. Initially assigned to a general hospital in Fargo, North Dakota, I was informed shortly before finishing up my "junior" year at seminary that I was being switched to the State Hospital in Fergus Falls, Minnesota. That change enabled Doris and me to spend the summer "back home," where we could live with her parents and save on living costs. I was not thrilled, however, when I was assigned to the Drug and Alcohol unit at the facility. "I can't imagine that's going to be all that useful in my ministry," was my naïve reaction at that point, little knowing precisely how helpful would be learning the basics of addiction, recovery, and pastoral care for people in life crises.

As I arrived at my CPE center, there was an additional shock. "Your first two weeks," our supervisor informed us, "You will live in the unit as patients." What?? Me?? Pretending to be an alcoholic or addict"? To be sure, the first few days for my peers and me were awkward as we would protest, "No, we're not alcoholics." Given the reality that denial is a key dynamic in addiction, our fellow residents were quick to respond, "Yah, that's what we all say!" Those two weeks "on the unit" were intense and valuable learning experiences, during which I had to confront aspects of myself and how I relate to others in ways I had not done previously.

CPE cohort groups in the 1960's and '70's were notorious for being intense cauldrons in which young seminarians were confronted harshly by peers and supervisors. Perhaps akin in some degree to military basic training, the underlying philosophy of many supervisors was to "break them down and then rebuild them the right way." Ours was no exception. While in the trenches some intense bonding with peers occurred, during group sessions the supervisor encouraged us to confront and sharply challenge one another. The CPE experience often causes strains in a marriage when one partner is in a high-pressure environment that may cause dramatic change and the other is a bystander. That was the case for us, to the extent that upon returning to the seminary, Doris and I engaged in a brief period of marriage counseling. Despite the challenges, I successfully completed my CPE and returned eager for my second year of seminary. It would be another year of interesting and challenging further development as a budding Lutheran minister.

Embracing an Atypical Internship

Since the 1960's, U.S. Lutheran seminarians have been required to complete a year of internship in a congregation as part of what's commonly referred to as "contextual education." At Gettysburg, early in the spring semester of one's second year, the internship placement process began. Both back in my student years, and to this day, Gettysburg (now part of United Lutheran Seminary) has a unique process of "matching" whereby students can interview with several parishes and then state a preference for where they wish to serve.

In a meeting preparatory for our matching process in the spring of 1974, our field education director, Daniel Sandstedt, mentioned that, in addition to the internship sites that would be represented on campus, there might be the possibility of an overseas experience. My interest was piqued regarding that option. I thought, "That's probably a once-in-a-lifetime opportunity to live and work in another country for a year." Doris also was game, so I expressed my interest to Sandstedt. I indicated that since Doris and I had both studied Spanish in high school and college, a Latin American setting would be ideal. After an initial inquiry, he said there was uncertainty over whether the Lutheran Church in America's (LCA) Division for World Mission would have any openings. But we agreed that I would remain open to the possibility, and he would continue pursuing it with national church officials.

Given the uncertainty of an overseas placement, I went through the matching workshop interviews along with my peers. While most of the possibilities presented didn't excite me, I was enthusiastic about a parish in New England and indicated to seminary officials that if offered I would accept it. Fortunately, as things would turn out, that setting was the most hotly desired one among my classmates, and one of them was assigned. Sandstedt assured me that if an overseas option did not emerge, he would find a U.S. placement. Within a few weeks I was called to his office and informed that if I were willing, I could go to South America and intern with a pastor in the Evangelical Lutheran Church in Chile (*Iglesia Evangelica Luterana en Chile*/IELCH). Sandstedt explained that while the LCA had not budgeted an internship in Chile, unexpected early repayment of a loan had freed up a few thousand dollars that could be made available.

To prepare for internship, I made a trip to New York City where I met with the World Mission staff person responsible for South America. He informed me that beyond just providing a good learning experience for a seminarian, church officials had an agenda for me. "We never see your supervisor do much more than sit and smoke his pipe," Milton Olson told me. "So, we hope you can light a fire under him and help get some things going in stewardship and evangelism." That was a surprise! I thought that supervisors were to be the teachers and motivators, and here I was being told that I was to mentor my boss.

Another shocking revelation came when, on that same trip, I visited David Kalke, a seminarian from Hamma Seminary in Ohio who had interned in Chile the prior year. Kalke was spirited into the U.S. Embassy in Santiago and rushed out of the country in the aftermath of the military coup that took place on September 11, 1973 (the first 9/11 to be forever ingrained in my consciousness). Kalke and his wife had become involved with efforts regarded by the brutal military junta as aiding and abetting the socialist regime of Salvador Allende. After the coup, the Kalkes had helped deliver fugitives to embassies and were otherwise involved in activities regarded as subversive. Following my visit with the Kalkes in New York's Hell's Kitchen, where they were living at the time, I was convinced that my internship would be anything but routine or boring.

Along with the uncertainties surrounding internship, there were complications related to my ecclesiastical process toward ordination. When I entered seminary, I was oblivious to denominational requirements beyond earning a degree. I had grown up in a congregation of the American Lutheran Church (ALC), but Gettysburg was an LCA seminary. "No big deal, it's Lutheran," was my uninformed attitude. While Pastor Grochau and Gettysburg Seminary officials were aware of my denominational status, they also signaled that it should not be an insurmountable problem to attend an LCA school and then be ordained as an ALC pastor. From what I could see, there were no major differences of theology or parish life between the two largest U.S. Lutheran church bodies. The fact the two merged to form the Evangelical Lutheran Church in America (ELCA) some years later is testimony to the accuracy of my assessment.

Midway through my first year of seminary, however, it became clear that it was in fact a big deal. I met with an official of the ALC responsible for working with seminaries and ministerial candidates. He explained that while Gettysburg was a fine seminary and he was confident it would make me a good Lutheran pastor, I needed to learn the ALC ethos and polity, and get to know seminarians who would be my colleagues in ministry. In short, he said that if I wanted to be an ALC pastor I'd have to transfer to an ALC seminary as soon as possible. Given Doris's teaching position, on which we depended for our living expenses, and that Gettysburg had awarded me one of two coveted full-tuition scholarships based on my academic promise, I was very reluctant to contemplate changing seminaries mid-stream in my formation.

A Gettysburg classmate, Wally Jenson, was in an identical situation. Wally had grown up in the ALC in North Dakota, but after a stint in the Army married an east coast woman and enrolled at Gettysburg. As we contemplated our futures together in several conversations, Wally and I decided we would make a joint visit to the nearest ALC seminary in Columbus, Ohio. (As a side note, during my years as president at Gettysburg, Wally was one of my vice presidents for a period when he worked in an ambitious endowment-building effort.) We were received warmly at Capital Seminary, including by its very gracious president, Fred Meuser, who would later become a good friend when he and his wife made frequent trips to Gettysburg during his retirement years. Despite our positive experience in Columbus, upon returning to Gettysburg, Wally and I both remained reluctant at the prospect of uprooting and transferring to Capital. What finally freed me to make a move in another direction was a conversation with the ALC's vice president, who was passing through Washington in early 1973. David Preus, who would later become the ALC's presiding bishop, confirmed what Wally and I had already heard from others. If we wanted to be ALC pastors, he stated, we'd need to attend one of their seminaries. But Preus then went on to ask, "Why don't you just think about becoming LCA pastors"? He confirmed my assessment that there really were no significant differences of theology or practice between the two church bodies. "Besides," Preus went on to say, "I think within about fifteen years or so we'll merge, and all be together anyway." (Exactly fifteen years later, on January 1, 1988, the ALC and LCA joined a small break-away group from the Lutheran Church-Missouri Synod and formed the ELCA).

In another manifestation of my youthful naivete, after making the decision to pursue ordination in the LCA, I thought that too would be no big deal. My views on that would change quickly upon presenting myself to the Maryland Synod of the LCA as a candidate for pastoral ministry. From my seminary peers at Gettysburg, I was soon to learn that the Maryland Synod's "examining panel" was notorious for the way its members grilled candidates and rejected some altogether. One of the panel's members, a well-known pastoral psychotherapist and CPE supervisor of the old school, was described like this: "You don't realize that Bob Lance has got you until you stand up and your ass stays on the chair!" My one encounter with Lance in the spring of 1976 was not to be my last. During the early years of my seminary presidency, Lance chaired Gettysburg's investment committee, but ultimately left angry when others marshalled efforts to break his stronghold on the committee and broaden the seminary's investment strategy.

I had come to the Maryland synod as an "outsider" with no prior connections to a congregation beyond my involvement with the Living Word mission in Columbia. In an era when there was growing talk of a "clergy oversupply," the synod had little incentive to take on additional candidates for ministry, but reluctantly did so when I applied during my second year of seminary. While I did not feel enthusiastically embraced after presenting myself to the Maryland Synod, I was determined to fulfill all their requirements and demonstrate that I was capable of being a good colleague and team player in the LCA's ministerium. At the same time, I balked at their standard expectation that all seminarians engage in personal therapy. I didn't feel the need to see a counselor but did engage in informal conversations with a highly regarded pastor in Washington and let that be known as a way of signaling my openness to continuing personal growth.

Where things came to a donnybrook between me and the "professional preparation committee" (the group that helped us get ready for our one-time encounter with the infamous examining panel) was in the matter of internship. When I presented my plans to intern in Chile, they strongly advised against it. "You won't really learn to be an American parish pastor by going off to Chile," was their stance. "And be aware if you do that, we'll probably require you to complete another internship stateside when you return." Faced with this dilemma, I sought the counsel of seminary professors, Pastor Grochau, and others. They helped me get back in touch with my feelings that a year abroad would be a unique opportunity to expand my horizons, develop fluency in Spanish, and in other ways gain experiences not afforded to my classmates. They also assured me they would go to bat for me and exert what influence they could with the Maryland synod upon my completion of a successful international internship.

Based upon that support from mentors I respected, I decided to forge ahead and proceed with the internship in Chile. In and of itself, that was a crossroads in my formation as a leader. While I may chafe on occasion at rules and authorities that I deem unwarranted or unreasonable, I don't believe I have huge "authority issues." At the same time, I am willing to push back, refuse to be bullied, and accept the consequences.

— 4 —

Chile:
A Life-Changing Pilgrimage

In every life, there are moments that loom large as one reflects back upon them. For some it is a stint in the military, particularly if one's service involves a combat tour. For others, the life-changing events may involve a medical crisis, divorce or other series of events. For me, the year spent in Chile was one of my life's most significant crossroads experiences.

As noted, from the conversation with the Kalkes, as well as reading newspapers, I had some hints of the political situation in Chile in the early 1970's. But nothing prepared me for the realities that I was about to experience as I was plunged into one of the most dangerous places in the world in that era. Living in a country under the brutal and repressive grip of a military junta headed by Agosto Pinochet would change forever my view of the world, as well as my theological convictions and political analyses.

The first glimpses of what we were about to experience in South America came with the hassles of securing a travel visa. With airline tickets purchased for us by the modest LCA grant, we expected to simply go to the airport and head for Santiago. It turned out that the visas required by Chile were not made available for our departure from Minnesota, where we had driven to leave our car in storage at my parents' farm for the duration of our year abroad. After repeated calls to the airline, LCA headquarters in New York, and the Chilean embassy in Washington, we were advised to get to Miami, from which our international flight would depart. Assurances were given that visas would be issued promptly by the Chilean consulate there. This was our first encounter with cultural differences when it comes to time. "Promptly" turned out to mean something quite different for Chilenos than for Americans!

Fortunately, my sister Bernice and her husband Ron lived in Homestead, Florida, about 30 miles south of Miami. So, we could stay at their home and enjoy a short visit before heading on down to South America. Again, "short visit" turned out to be nearly three weeks as we awaited a letter from Chile requesting the visas. Taking advantage of the chance, Doris and I made a day trip to the recently opened new Disney World and a few other tourist spots in south Florida. Mostly we studied Spanish and just enjoyed hanging out with Bernice and Ron until finally a visa was issued and we boarded an Aerolineas Argentinas flight to Santiago.

Arriving at the Pudahuel Airport, we were met by my supervising pastor Esteban Schaller and the Lutheran bishop Helmut Frenz. On the drive into Santiago city, we got briefly acquainted and were told there had been some changes in plans. We had been told that an apartment would be provided for us, as well as a vehicle. Instead, the two pastors informed us, we would be sharing a house with another intern and his wife. Bill Gorski was an intern from the Lutheran School of Theology at Chicago (LSTC) sponsored by the Lutheran World Federation. He and his wife Cindy had arrived a few days before us and were staying in temporary quarters. Esteban and Helmut also reported that the promised vehicle would not be available for some time until one of the missionaries left for home.

Weary from our long flight, we were taken to the two-story brick house in one of Santiago's nicer neighborhoods, Las Condes. The house, owned by a retired Chilean Air Force General, was unfurnished. Our local hosts delivered four cots, linens, and a few kitchen items. From their perspective, we were all set! There were some major limitations to the arrangement. The house was several miles from Bill's and my assigned parishes. Buses were crowded and the commutes took an hour or more, though Esteban or Helmut sometimes came by to pick us up on the way to various meetings. I soon bought a bicycle and could make the trip to La Trinidad (Trinity) parish by that means faster than via bus. But Doris and Cindy remained isolated in the suburban community, unable to communicate with neighbors—who kept their distance in any case given the climate of widespread fear and suspicion that existed everywhere in the country.

It also soon became apparent that, while we appreciated the presence of another young American seminary couple, our personalities and values were quite different from the Gorskis. The degree to which that was the case would become fully revealed decades later when Bill Gorski, who had returned to Chile as a missionary and became the IELCH bishop, was defrocked in 1996 when found guilty of financial embezzlement. We were relieved when a few weeks after moving into the house together the Gorskis announced they had persuaded Bishop Frenz to let them move into an apartment near Bill's assignment.

Experiencing Culture Shock in a Climate of Terror

Beyond the constraints of the initial living arrangement, the greater challenge was posed by what can only be described as a high degree of "culture shock." Common to many if not most persons who travel to places very different from their home turf, this syndrome is difficult to describe adequately. Components include a sense of being out of control in a place where the rules and norms differ greatly from those to which one is accustomed. If a language barrier is involved, as was our case despite having some rudimentary Spanish, the discomfort is exacerbated since one is often mostly unaware of what's being said by others. The typical challenge of navigating a strange territory is heightened when signs, maps, menus, and other things we take for granted are in an unfamiliar language.

A further element of the culture shock experienced by most North Americans making their first trips to a "third world" country is the extent and depth of poverty. While we had been exposed to poor inner-city neighborhoods, especially in our years in the Washington area, the degree of "living on the margins" was simply not the same as we first witnessed on the drive from the airport into Santiago. Peasant farmers still used oxcarts to transport their meager crops, and many people walked great distances carrying burdens in their arms or on their heads. Beggars in tattered rags were ubiquitous, and literally millions of people lived in dirt-floored shanty town huts constructed of cardboard and corrugated steel scrounged from dump grounds. Public buses overflowed with free riders hanging out the doors or clinging to roof racks. Bus and train passengers also frequently brought animals aboard, so it was an everyday thing to find oneself seated next to a live chicken or other creature on a bus.

Beyond these harsh realities that those of us from "first world" societies experience traveling many places in the world, Chile in 1974 was a country in the throes of a mostly underground and sinister civil war. Its illegitimate military government had declared war on large segments of the population. Widely documented elsewhere, a detailed history of the brutal takeover by Pinochet's armed forces need not be recounted here. By way of a short summation, on September 11, 1973, Chilean air force bombers attacked the Moneda palace where the democratically elected president, Salvador Allende, lived. Allende died in the attack, reportedly by suicide, but five decades later, the nature of his death remains in dispute. Storm troopers followed up with raids that rounded up Allende's affiliates and thousands of others around the nation regarded by the military as "communists." Without trials or even questioning, thousands of Allende supporters were summarily executed in the weeks following the coup. The military junta declared martial law, which disbanded the legislature and court system, shut down universities, and imposed a nighttime *toque de queda* or curfew. If people ventured out onto the streets after 10 p.m. they could expect to be hauled off to jail or perhaps shot on sight.

When we arrived in late August of 1974, nearly a year had passed since the coup. But rather than subsiding, the junta's repression had tightened its grip on the country. The dreaded DINA (internal intelligence forces) had expanded nighttime raids in which unsuspecting citizens heard a knock on the door and were never seen or heard from again. Bodies floated down the Mapocho River or were tossed beside roads and highways by way of signaling to the general populace, "You could be next." When my parents were visiting about midway through our year, my mother was awakened to gunshots one night, and she peeked out to see a body lying in the street in front of our house. The junta's informants were everywhere, so everyone held hushed conversations on the street, in restaurants, busses, and in other public places.

Throughout our year in Chile, I kept up correspondence with a couple of my seminary friends. In a letter sent to classmate Don Wilcox on April 3, 1975, I typed the first page and then shifted to longhand to finish the letter. My explanation offers a glimpse into the climate of terror in which we were living. "I decided to finish this by hand. It's after midnight and I always feel uncomfortable typing late at night. We live in a neighborhood where there are many military officers, and one never knows what sort of activities might raise suspicions."

Rather than enjoying a measure of protection in a culture that still regarded itself as a Christian nation, the church experienced some of the worst repressive measures. All public meetings were banned, so our Lutheran congregations could not hold annual meetings to elect officers, approve budgets or conduct other routine business matters. The same was true for all volunteer organizations, which were forced to keep the same leadership for several years and could not fill vacancies when board members resigned or died.

Our tiny national Lutheran church was under special scrutiny, resulting from the outspoken prophetic stance of Bishop Frenz and several other international pastors. In the immediate aftermath of the coup, Frenz worked with a Roman Catholic bishop to form the Committee for Peace that offered legal assistance to Chilenos being persecuted by the Pinochet regime. Helmut's courageous role in the years after the coup has been told in depth in his book *Mi Vida Chilena*, a portion of which I translated for the journal *Dialog* (September 2008), and also included in a lecture for DePaul University's 2017 World Catholicism Week.[1]

Frenz and several other German and American pastors were key players in running a kind of underground railroad that spirited persecuted Chilenos into the embassies of countries willing to grant diplomatic asylum. A surreptitious network was established to keep people in safe houses until "arrangements" could be made to deliver them at night to an embassy where, at a precise prearranged time, a side gate would suddenly open long enough for an individual or handful of people to sneak in from one of our Lutheran Church Volkswagen minibuses. While I never participated in those precarious runs, for over a week Doris and I sheltered in our home one of the top leaders in the Movimiento Izquertista Revolucionario (Leftist Revolutionary Movement). He was one known to be on the DINA's "most wanted list," and we were aware that had he been discovered the consequences for him and for us might have been dire.

As U.S. citizens, we did enjoy a measure of protection from harsh persecution by the Pinochet regime. Dependent upon continuing good will from the U.S. government, which had opposed Allende's administration and aided and abetted the military takeover, the military regime was reluctant that any harm should befall Americans. But at the same time, Pinochet and his minions were far from being in control of elements within

---

1. *Gathered in My Name: Ecumenism in the World Church*, William T. Cavanaugh ed., Wipf and Stock, 2020; pp. 70–83.

the shadowy DINA and other paramilitary entities that roamed the streets eager to eliminate anyone and everyone deemed in any way suspect.

Not only were we in the same state of constant fear of Pinochet's regime as the Chilenos, but we grew increasingly wary of U.S. officials supposedly stationed in the embassy and elsewhere for our protection. Our embassy was not among those willing to help persecuted Chilenos get out of the country. By contrast, official U.S. policy was to back Pinochet as a shining example of the kind of anti-communism it was hoped was spreading throughout Latin America. As mentioned above, David Kalke had already been expelled from the country when he was suspected of anti-Pinochet activities. Kalke was convinced that his ouster was a joint effort involving both U.S. and Chilean officials.

During the early months of our sojourn in Chile we had little contact with the embassy or U.S. officials. That changed when Doris began teaching at the international English language school called *Nido de Aguila* or "Eagle's Nest." Most U.S. embassy personnel sent their kids to *Nido*, which brought us into social contact with several high-level officials. For us, the best part of this arrangement was that some of our newfound friends had access to U.S. commissary privileges and could get us things like peanut butter and other commodities that were nowhere to be found in Chile's stores at the time. We suspected that some of those congenial folks who worked "at the embassy," and whose kids were Doris's pupils, were involved in surreptitious activity and doubled as CIA operatives. Those suspicions were confirmed years later in a revelatory book that chronicles the brutal assassination in Washington of a former Allende cabinet officer and his aide. *Assassination on Embassy Row* is a 400-page detailed history of the 1976 car-bombing that killed Orlando Letelier, former Chilean ambassador to the U.S., and his associate Ronni Moffitt. The book provides names and detailed information about U.S. embassy officials believed to have played a hand in the plot against Letelier. Among them was an embassy official, probably doubling as a CIA operative, whose wife was one of Doris's colleagues at *Nido*.

Those kinds of experiences prompted soul-searching and reassessment of my youthful naïveté and unquestioning patriotism. I was forced to revise my views about the role our nation plays throughout the world. This led me to more critical thinking and a growing realization of the interconnected nature of the global community. I became much more sympathetic to the plight of refugees, especially those fleeing political persecution in their native lands. Thus, when a few years later my parish in Los Angeles decided to sponsor a Chilean refugee family, I felt that was a "natural" and took the lead in resettling the Ibañez family of four. Leonardo Ibañez had been a university art professor and rising poet in Chile. Such intellectuals were universally suspect by the Pinochet regime. Tortured and exiled to another South American country for months, Leonardo was finally reunited with his family and allowed to emigrate. Our congregation helped the family start a new life in the U.S. After my retirement, I enjoyed a wonderful reunion with the Ibañezes after forty years had passed since seeing them. We continue to stay in touch occasionally through social media.

A Church in Turmoil Amidst a Country in Crisis

In addition to the crisis in Chilean society in the early 1970's, there was great turmoil in the country's Lutheran church as well. The Iglesia Evangelica Luterana en Chile or IELCH was a tiny church body with only fifteen parishes in the entire country. Founded in 1863 as a German Lutheran immigrant church, it was 100 years before the first worship services were held in the Spanish language. The parish I served, La Trinidad in Santiago, was the first congregation to be founded in which Spanish was the primary language.

A Chilean president in the early 20th century was eager to attract Europeans with skills and the capital to develop industries and agriculture. He was especially impressed by German industriousness and made large tracts of land available to immigrants. Another wave of German immigrants fled their native land during and in the aftermath of World War II. Among them were a significant number of outright Nazis and Nazi-sympathizers, many fleeing accountability for their war crimes and atrocities in the Hitler regime. The Germans brought with them personal wealth and high-level education in many cases, which enabled them to forge an elite and parallel society. In Chile's major cities and even many small communities, wherever significant numbers of German immigrants settled, there was a German school, fire company, German-speaking doctors and other professionals, since many of the transplants deemed native Chilenos to be racially inferior and unworthy of their patronage. They also formed German-speaking Lutheran churches to keep alive and pass on to their children the language and culture through a transplanted *Volkskirche*. In one of his sharpest prophetic critiques, Helmut Frenz was quoted in the newspaper as saying, "They are Lutherans because they are Germans, not because they are Christians." Needless to say, that remark did not endear the bishop to a large segment of his flock!

While Frenz's remark might be regarded as judgmental and overstated, in large measure it was the bald truth. Since they were among the elite who feared the loss of status and wealth during the years of the socialist (or from their perspective "*comunista*") Allende presidency, most of the German Lutherans were staunch supporters of Pinochet and the armed forces. When Frenz and most of the other pastors began speaking out against the brutal junta, their German-heritage parishioners rebelled and began to demand they be removed from their pastorates. Helmut and most of his colleagues stood firm, insisting that the gospel was on the side of the poor and persecuted. Not surprisingly, conflict was inflamed within several congregations and in the entire national church, as fierce political debates were waged between pro- and anti-Pinochet factions.

On Saturday, September 14, 1974, just days after our arrival in Chile, a full-page ad in the front section of Santiago's foremost newspaper, *El Mercurio*, carried a list of almost 500 "Members of Evangelical Lutheran Communities in Chile" calling for Frenz's resignation. Their demand was based upon what they alleged to be "the grave damage he has caused to our communities, his activities and distorted information regarding the developments of September 11, 1973, which he has been circulating overseas." Not only were these members calling for Helmut's being deposed as bishop, but "as Chileans we would be pleased to see his removal from the country." While church records were not all that accurate, Frenz and other pastors of the German-speaking congregations were confident the majority of the 500 signers were not, in fact, active Lutherans.

During the following weeks, a barrage of personal and public media attacks against Frenz continued. Helmut and members of his family received numerous death threats. At a worship service in one of his parishes in the southern city of Osorno, Frenz was accosted and told, "We do not speak with communists." He indicated that the synod, meeting in November, could take a vote of confidence on his leadership, but absent a majority asking for his departure he would continue his work in Chile. While contentious, the assembly did not issue a call for Frenz's resignation.

Even as he was being denounced by many within Chile, Frenz was being hailed in international circles as a heroic champion for refugees. In October 1974, he received the Fridtjof Nansen Medallion from the UN High Commission for Refugees at a grand ceremony in Geneva. First conferred upon Eleanor Roosevelt in 1954, the annual award is given to one who has "demonstrated perseverance and courage, and who has personally, directly and significantly helped forcibly displaced people." (Another champion for persecuted Chileans during the 1970's was U.S. Senator Edward "Ted" Kennedy, who received the Nansen award posthumously shortly after his death in 2009).

Upon his receipt of the Nansen award, Frenz made his most famous statement, which summarizes his life and witness. He said, "I try to identify myself with those who are suffering in our world, because I find that in giving myself to them, I encounter Christ the Lord." In his typical humility, Helmut said the award did not honor him alone, but all who serve the oppressed: "In the conferral of the Fridtjof Nansen Medallion, homage is paid to those committed to suffer with the suffering." Ever the prophet, Helmut also went on to say that the very existence of the award and the necessity for its conferral, "accuses many governments of the world."

Bishop Frenz's reaffirmation at the November 1974 church assembly notwithstanding, the attacks against Helmut and the majority of pastors serving Lutheran congregations persisted. In January 1975, I wrote a letter to be shared with my seminary classmates in a newsletter called "Round Robin" that was circulated among those of us on internship. In that letter I described the crisis in the IELCH:

> The large, wealthy German congregations have formed a coalition to oust Bishop Frenz and all pastors who refuse to become ineffective puppets. And so, the death now is by economic strangulation. These large wealthy congregations have each pledged synod support of one escudo (2000 escudos equal one dollar!) The synod is now, therefore, without a budget. We are all driving cars (worth double their U.S. value here) without insurance. Here in Santiago, the large German-speaking congregation fired one pastor last week and has banned the bishop and another pastor from the pulpit. We are quite concerned about the possibility that the bishop may not be able to return from the U.S. following his speaking tour this month.

In early May 1975 I wrote a letter to my bishop (still called "synod president"), Dr. Paul Orso of the LCA's Maryland Synod. Beyond providing a personal update, and sharing developments in my parish internships, I informed Paul about the larger scene in the IELCH, noting that "five of the German-speaking congregations have voted to withdraw and it is certain the remaining ones, with one possible exception, will go the same way. This will leave the IELCH with five tiny Spanish-speaking congregations."

While the international missionary pastors were at risk for their courageous words and actions, those most vulnerable were the Chilean members of the small and fragile Spanish-speaking congregations. By virtue of his being a Chilean citizen, my supervisor Esteban Schaller was in a particularly perilous situation. Despite the risks, he never wavered in his support for Frenz and the IELCH members who stood up to the German-heritage dominant group.

On Palm Sunday 1975, it was my turn to preach at La Trinidad. In my sermon on the Palm Sunday story from Luke's gospel, I imagined Jesus entering the city—but Santiago, not Jerusalem:

> Imagine with me on this Palm Sunday a contemporary version of the story. He comes down out of the high peaks of the Andean mountain range—not in a Mercedes as foreign dignitaries arrive, but in one of the humble horse carts that are still seen on occasion here in our city. He comes down into the city, goes downtown in the heat of midday, and is jostled here and there by the city's teeming multitudes. The people there have no time to pause and speak with him. He goes to where the common people live—in the wealthy and middle-class neighborhoods, yes, but in the shantytowns and humble homes most especially.
>
> During this Holy Week, it is not hard for us to imagine our Lord crying over this city—no longer Jerusalem, but now Santiago. Crying in the halls of government, in the prisons where there is no hope; crying over the embassies where foreign nations are concerned only to protect their own national interests. Jesus crying with those who cannot sleep tonight because they are too worried whether the money will reach tomorrow to buy bread for the family and milk for the baby.
>
> Hosanna! God in the midst of us. Jesus, weeping over this suffering city. Christ the Lord among us in our weakness and suffering. That is the message that will not be silenced in Chile and throughout Latin America today!

On May 31, 1975, things came to a head at the IELCH gathering in the southern city of Temuco. When Frenz and pastoral colleagues refused to resign and leave the country, there was a walk-out followed by an announcement that the larger and wealthier German-heritage congregations would be forming a new church body. They promptly did so, even though holding official meetings to elect officials, adopt a constitution etc. was supposedly not allowed. "If you're in bed with Pinochet, there are different rules," was the common conclusion among those who remained within the much smaller but unified and newly energized IELCH.

The LCA, together with German and other European churches that financially supported struggling congregations and refugee organizations, continued solidly in support of Frenz and the IELCH. Forceful statements of unwavering support for Frenz and the IELCH also came from the Lutheran World Federation and World Council of Churches. A handful of German missionary pastors, whose congregations had fired them, were reassigned to other posts and remained in Chile a while longer.

Not satisfied with their internal coup that took over the majority of Lutheran churches in Chile, the reactionaries continued their barrage of efforts to get Frenz and other foreign pastors deported. Articles ran in the major newspapers calling upon the Pinochet regime to investigate Frenz's and other pastors' alleged "systematic damage to Chile, their schismatic and divisive impact with the church community, and their external collaboration with forces outside the church that aid their corrosive efforts." On June 17, a nationwide television program aired in which nine so-called "evangelical" leaders lent their support to calls for Helmut's expulsion.

The efforts to oust Frenz did prevail within the next few months. While on a whirlwind tour of Europe, where he continued his advocacy for refugees and garnered support for Chile's most vulnerable, on October 3, 1975, Frenz was declared *persona non grata* by the Pinochet government and barred from returning to the country. An international outcry against the Junta's actions ensued, with many churches and other groups issuing statements supportive of Frenz. A Lutheran Council in the USA (LCUSA) press release on October 9, 1975, reported that "telegrams to Chile were sent from Europe and North America, and Protestant and Roman Catholic church leaders in Chile have requested a meeting with government authorities to discuss the matter." All U.S. and many European Lutheran and ecumenical church leaders issued telegrams, as did those of the Lutheran World Federation, and the National and World Councils of Churches. Despite the international protests in Frenz's favor, the Chilean Junta stood firm and his expulsion from his beloved Chile would persist for nearly thirty years. Esteban Schaller succeeded Frenz as bishop and provided the IELCH with steady leadership for several years.

Back in the States for my final year of seminary by that time, I organized a letter-writing campaign protesting the junta's actions. At a conference of Lutheran leaders from around the country in Washington,

I garnered signatures of several dozen prominent Lutherans on a letter to Pinochet, with copies to President Gerald Ford, the U.S. Ambassador in Santiago, and Latin America desk personnel at the U.S. State Department. I also warned and provided background information for national Lutheran leaders prior to their meeting with representatives from the newly formed schismatic "true Chilean Lutheran Church" who came to the U.S. seeking to garner support.

Within a few months of his rejection in Chile, I was privileged to help host Helmut when he made a visit to the U.S. to interpret the Chilean reality and advocate for continuing support to refugees and those being persecuted by the junta. I would not see him again for over three decades until we had a grand reunion when I visited Chile in 2007. Following his retirement from Amnesty International in Germany, Helmut returned to Chile and married a young woman with whom he had two additional children. Having been restored to a democratic government some years before, by the time of Helmut's return, Chile was once again a free society. In one of her most healing gestures of societal reconciliation, President Michelle Bachelet bestowed upon him honorary Chilean citizenship in honor of the work he had done in the 1970's.

Amid A Country in Crisis, Some Normal Parish Work

During the initial ride from the airport described above, I asked my new supervisor Esteban, "So how are things here in Chile"? "We are a church and a country in crisis," was his answer. As the above section of this chapter amply documents, that was an understatement. Nevertheless, despite the fact that these sweeping historical developments were playing out in Chile's national political scene and within the IELCH, my day-to-day work as an intern involved pastoral work similar to that in any parish anywhere in the world. I prepared sermons, with help cleaning up my dreadful early drafts in Spanish from a delightful high school student, Osvaldo Maldonado. On Sundays, I led worship together with Esteban and lay leaders of La Trinidad. I visited members in their homes and workplaces, helped with some administrative tasks, and taught Bible studies and other classes for adults and youth. I also participated in wider IELCH endeavors and programs, again particularly in the youth ministry arena, collaborating with Gorski and LCA missionary Susan Birkelo, whose primary role was Christian education. Birkelo later became an ELCA pastor serving in bilingual ministries in New York, Chicago, and California. Gorski, as noted above, went back to Chile after a few years pastoring in the U.S. After his criminal behavior as bishop came to light, he fled the country, ultimately returning to the U.S., where he died in 2015.

In my orientation at LCA headquarters in New York before leaving for Chile, as noted above, the South America director of World Mission had given me an assignment. Milton Olson was convinced that Schaller and lay leaders of Trinidad needed help in the areas of stewardship and evangelism. So, I was issued a "charge" to do what I could in stimulating outreach and more ownership of the ministry by the members of Trinity—a tall order for a seminarian under any circumstances, but particularly in a foreign country and a tiny church under siege! Some feeble efforts at "cold calling" by knocking on doors in the neighborhood yielded no discernible results, though developing relationships with a group of Mapuche native people did expand La Trinidad's outreach beyond its membership.

Esteban's gentle mentoring, together with that of Trinidad's wonderful lay members, taught me a great deal about cross-cultural ministry and the importance of "reading the culture" in every context. Soon after my arrival in the fall of 1974, Esteban mentioned that one of Trinidad's most active members, Don Julio, was in the hospital. "Can I go with you when you call upon him?" I asked my supervisor. "Oh no, senor!" Esteban blurted. "A pastor can't do that in Chile. If we show up in his hospital room, he'll be convinced he's dying, and you'll scare the hell out of him!" I learned many other nuances of Latin American and Chilean culture as I observed Esteban and the other pastors at work throughout the intense year of internship.

As the year progressed and I became more confident in Spanish and navigating Chilean culture and the delicate political realities, I was less dependent upon Esteban and began to spread my pastoral wings. We also gained a new freedom when one of the international pastors went back to Europe on furlough and I was finally assigned an automobile. At last, I could move about freely, and Doris and I took some longer trips to explore parts of Chile on our own. We spent the New Year's holiday of 1975 in a cabin owned by the Schallers at the seaside resort of El Tabo.

On one memorable occasion, we were touring a beauteous southern portion of Chile with my parents, who were visiting from Minnesota. Since it was virtually impossible in that era to make advance hotel reservations, we simply trusted that rooms could be found by cruising major streets in small cities and towns. That worked without a hitch, until one night it didn't! With what was obviously poor planning on my part, we arrived at our destination town late in the evening. After finding no available rooms in several inns or hotels, we were driving around in frantic search as the hour of the *toque* arrived. While we had tried to shield Mom and Dad from some of the more ominous realities with which we lived, they knew about the curfew and sensed my high anxiety as the clock ticked past 10 p.m. and we were still driving around in our bright orange VW bus. We finally lucked out and found a place with vacancies just minutes after the *toque* began for the night. While my personal theology isn't generally comfortable counting on divine intervention (especially when one's predicament is of his/her own making), in this case I'm willing to consider that maybe God really did save us from being snatched by the DINA!

As the year of internship neared its conclusion, I was given another opportunity to develop my pastoral skills. The IELCH's newest congregation was a mission established by Trinidad members in one of Santiago's shantytowns or *poblaciones*. By the time I arrived in Chile, the congregation Buen Samaritano (Good Samaritan) had been established for several years in the shantytown of La Faena. When its missionary pastor began a home furlough in the spring of 1975, I was asked to step in and provide pastoral coverage for the remainder of my time in Chile. That short-term assignment afforded opportunity for weekly preaching and a broad range of pastoral duties carried out largely on my own. It also plunged me into the harsh daily realities of those living on the margins of society to a greater degree than I had experienced earlier in the year. And it enabled Doris and me to move to a spacious home where we house-sat for the traveling missionary family. We felt much more in the center of things, living just down the street from Trinidad and the Schallers.

Soon the end of the intense year as *vicario* was on the near horizon and we made plans for our return trip to the U.S. Trading in our return airfare, we booked alternative travel by land that took us through several South American countries on our return voyage. Riding buses and trains through Chile, Bolivia and Peru, then flying to Ecuador, Colombia, and Venezuela further expanded our exposure to Latin American realities, including the diversity of cultures. In our homeward pilgrimage, we visited the breath-taking ancient city of Machu Picchu and many other historic sites, as well as the great cities of La Paz, Lima, Quito, Bogotá, and Caracas. A final stopover was in Puerto Rico where we were hosted by the Molinas, a pastoral family with whom we became familiar when Daisy

Molina visited Chile during the internship year. Pastor Rolando Molina was a famous Puerto Rican poet, who gave us an amazing overview of the island and Lutheran church's history, plus a delightful tour of the Bacardi rum distillery!

What Did and Does it Mean?

As I indicated at the outset of this chapter, the year in Chile was life-changing in so many ways. My horizons were broadened, and I became at least to some degree more of a world citizen. Navigating the turbulent waters of a country in terror, working through a major bout of culture shock, and learning to function in a multicultural environment was invaluable in preparing me for bilingual ministry in Los Angeles, as well short-term work in other parts of Latin America over the years. Beyond those external and surface changes, what happened inside of me is hard to describe. Mine was not the kind of dramatic conversion that others have experienced. I did not abandon a middle-class lifestyle and go off to live among the poor, as have some whom I admire. Nor did I become a radicalized anti-American revolutionary disillusioned with everything about my own country. Undoubtedly, I did become more critical of our government's policies and frequent foreign interventions, particularly in Latin America. But, following the year in Chile, I slipped back quite comfortably into mainstream U.S. society and the predominantly white, middle-class Lutheran church world.

Nevertheless, the internship year clearly made me more sensitive to the plight of the poor and to people living under conditions many Americans cannot begin to imagine. The cross-cultural plunge helped me become more comfortable with diversity, which served me well throughout the course of my career in ministry. What happened during the year from mid-1974 to mid-1975 is perhaps best summarized in my final internship report submitted to the Seminary:

> Personal growth has been greatest in flexibility, adaptability, and humility. Living and working in a foreign context with a distinct language and culture has been a challenge. Feelings of "at-homeness" developed gradually, as did independence from the initial leaning on colleagues for our most basic needs.
>
> Constant exposure to the manifold human problems caused by poverty, underdevelopment and unjust distribution of resources has caused a deep personal struggle. Being relatively

wealthy in an underdeveloped society posed constant struggles of conscience. I never buy now an item of clothing, a book or personal item without thinking what that money could mean in medicine, food or clothing for an unemployed Chilean worker or a starving child in another part of the world.

These feelings of "affluence-guilt" or "social estrangement" have not been resolved. I continue to feel bound to middle-class values and lifestyles, while feeling called in the gospel to a more radical identification with poor and suffering persons.

A Return Visit and the New La Trinidad

It would be thirty-two years before I once again set foot on the soil of Chile. When I returned in the fall of 2007, enroute to Argentina where I had a multi-year consulting relationship with the Lutheran Church, I was flooded with memories. Fortunately, I was able to enjoy a grand reunion with Esteban Schaller and Helmut Frenz. As noted above, the latter had returned to his beloved Chile, remarried and fathered two more children. I also visited La Trinidad and Buen Samaritano in the company of the Chilean Lutheran bishop, Gloria Cortez.

I have often spoken of the transformation in Chile when folks despair of the possibility for positive change amidst seemingly intractable situations. "If you had told me when I left Chile in 1975," I said on numerous occasions, "that within thirty years Chile would again be a free democratic society with a woman president, and the Lutheran Church would have a female native Chilena as bishop, I would have said, 'That's impossible.'"

One of the blessings of social media is reconnecting with friends and acquaintances out of the distant past. In a mid-2020 Facebook post, La Trinidad's pastor, Marcelo Huenulef-Ortega, described how the congregation had become a sanctuary for LGBTQ Chileans. That prospect, too, would never have occurred to me when I served there so long ago. The pastor's update, entitled "Christ on the Street in Santiago, Chile," also tells of a compassionate ministry among the homeless.

> Mrs. Elizabeth Grünholz, President of La Trinidad Congregation wrote this relevant and meaningful letter about "Christ on the Street":
>
> The Iglesia Evangélica Luterana Congregación "La Trinidad" from Ñuñoa, Santiago is a friendly open minded LGTBIQ (*sic*)congregation downtown Ñuñoa District, una "comuna",

a section of the Great Santiago City in Chile, South America. We have a great story of working with VIH-SIDA [HIV-AIDS] people back in the eighties and today we can proudly say that we are an open congregation to everyone. It is so because our desire is not being a ghetto but a living sign of the reign of God.

With that in mind, we started working with people who live in the streets, "gente en situación de calle," in Spanish. When this work started, we were few volunteers and we mostly made sandwiches and brought tea and coffee. The people we served were living around the Posta Central Hospital, the biggest ER Hospital in Santiago. Our desire has always been to establish relationships and deepen our understanding of the people in such a situation. We do not want to do just charity but get to know them as people, as human beings.

Now we continue to support our brothers and sisters during this pandemic. We cannot leave them alone. There are bonds that push us to serve God, who provides the good-hearted people. God provides the ones who donate, volunteer and makes this ministry of mercy, one of the biggest gifts God has given to our congregation. Thanks be to God!

In an email exchange with Pastor Huenulef-Ortega I wrote, "In 1974–75 I was Esteban Schaller's *vicario* at La Trinidad. It's so inspiring to get this update on the continuing courageous witness of the members. Saludos a todos!" Within hours, his kind reply came back on Facebook: "Great to know this información. Thanks! Pastor Schaller is very old right now and we don't see him much. The church you once knew does not exist, however, we are still La Trinidad and LGBTIQ people have finally found a home. Abrazos!" Abrazos means hugs. Nearly five decades after I served among the courageous Christians at La Trinidad and Buen Samaritano, I continue to feel their *abrazos*.

Bishops Helmut Frenz and Esteban Schaller in Chile, 2007]

— 5 —

Back to the U.S. and Final Year of Seminary

Following my return from internship in Chile, I was eager to complete my studies and receive a call to parish ministry. Before heading back to the east coast, Doris and I touched base with our families in Minnesota, retrieved our 1975 Chevy Nova from my folks' barn where it had been stored, and then drove back to begin my final year of seminary. We rented an apartment in Hyattsville, Maryland, just beyond the D.C. border, and retrieved our earthly possessions from where they had been in storage in an attic in the Staph home during the year abroad. I would take most of my remaining classes in the Washington area, while still commuting to Gettysburg one day a week for courses and contact with my peers and professors.

Before returning to the states, I had become aware of a Hispanic ministry in the nation's capital, and had contacted its director, the Rev. Charles "Chuck" Robertson, to explore possibilities of part-time work during my final year at seminary. I wanted to continue developing my Spanish, with an eye toward engaging in stateside bilingual ministry following graduation from seminary. His initial response was that while there would be value in my assisting, no money was available to employ me. After receiving Robertson's reply, I contacted the national LCA offices, inquiring whether a small grant might be available to further my preparation for future Hispanic ministry. We received $1,000, which provided a modest stipend for my part-time position. My work included one day a week at the ministry office in the Woodrow Wilson Center in northwest Washington, and Sundays at Augustana Lutheran Church, where a small group gathered for worship in Spanish. Chuck quickly became a good friend, mentor, and advocate as I approached the process of final approval for ordination.

Returning to the United States and seminary community was a time of mixed feelings for me. On the one hand, it felt good to be back on familiar turf with the comforts of home. Having newspapers, magazines, television programs and movies, and conducting conversations in English was such a relief after the year-long struggle to gain better command of Spanish. Rejoining the close-knit circle of seminary colleagues and other friendships was a joy. At the same time, I experienced the "reverse culture shock" of reentering middle-class American life. This was lessened somewhat by living in a large apartment complex where Doris and I appeared to be the only white residents in an otherwise all-Black community. My regular involvement in Washington's Latino community through the Hispanic ministry work was also a gift. Nevertheless, I found a deep disconnect between the internship experiences of my classmates and my own immersion in the daily life-and-death struggles of Chilean Christians. After my intense plunge into an impoverished "third world" context, I felt there was no way my peers could appreciate or understand all that I had experienced.

By virtue of my readings and experiences, I had become steeped in Latin American theology of liberation. While in vogue at many major universities and ecumenical divinity schools at the time, this radical new approach to theology was suspect at Gettysburg, and I found few with sympathetic ears. Despite my radicality, however, the seminary's two most renowned professors, Eric Gritsch and Robert Jenson, selected me as their teaching assistant. I read and graded all student papers and exams in two key courses, the Lutheran Confessions and Hermeneutics. Years later, I would sometimes quip that if there was an entire generation of heretical graduates from Gettysburg Seminary, it was all my fault! The affirmation from those key faculty members, combined with other expressions of encouragement by professors, led me to consider seriously the possibility of pursuing additional graduate study immediately following seminary. But I was eager to serve as a parish pastor.

Midway in my senior year, it was time for my final examination by the Maryland Synod's infamous examining panel. As the day to face the dozen or so examiners who held my fate in their hands approached, I was anxious, but also determined to help them see the growth I had experienced and how my Chile experience had prepared me for pastoral ministry. Early in the interview I spoke of how working among some of the world's poorest and most persecuted people had forced me to reexamine my own values and commitments. As had occurred prior to the internship, several appeared unconvinced and concerned that I was a radical rebel who would not serve well in typical Lutheran congregations. At one point in the interview, the bishop, who was also a psychotherapist, said he saw me as a pioneer setting out by myself in search of distant horizons. I responded, "Well, I do have a pioneering spirit alright, but I'd want to go in the company of others on such an exciting journey." Responding to my stated desire for urban ministry, one of the LCA's most well-known inner-city pastors offered his assessment that I didn't have what it takes for such tough work. Some years later, when I was a peer urban coalition director with a growing reputation as a national leader in Hispanic ministry, I reminded Hans Gobel of his discouraging words, which he insisted he had never uttered!

In the end, the panel approved my internship and granted final approval for my ordination. I am convinced that a key factor was strong support from Gettysburg Seminary in the person of the Rev. Dr. Leigh Jordahl, who was my faculty adviser. A few months after my approval interview, I was summoned to Dr. Jordahl's office. To my amazement, the conversation began by his posing the question, "Michael, what do you think would be the impact on the seminary of my departure"? How does a lowly student respond to an esteemed senior professor who raises such a question? As I recall, I stammered something along the lines of, "Well, Dr. Jordahl, that would be a great loss to this institution." He went on to explain that two offers had come to him; the first to become head librarian at a university in Iowa, and the second to serve as senior pastor at a large parish in Arizona. "If I decide on the latter," he explained, "I'd like you to consider being my associate." Taken aback, I stammered that I would be honored to consider such a possibility. But Jordahl ultimately accepted the librarian position, and I began exploring other possibilities for my first parish assignment.

Maryland Synod President Paul Orso indicated there would be no possibilities for bilingual ministry in my "home synod." Despite the Examining Panel's recommendation that I serve initially as an assistant pastor (given their reservations about the quality of my internship), Orso wanted me to consider a couple of inner-city "solo pastor" calls in East Baltimore. I declined, indicating I wanted to hold out for a bilingual context. Given the LCA's polity when it came to ministerial placement, I was then a "free agent" who could be in contact with any of the church's thirty-three synods regarding potential calls. I was invited to consider a call in Queens, New York at St. Paul's Lutheran Church. Upon my arrival to visit the congregation, I discovered the church still had an Assistant Pastor for its fledgling Latino ministry outreach. But he and the senior pastor had fallen into such deep conflict that they no longer spoke with each other. The senior pastor's strategy to move him out was to call a new assistant! As I met with Latino members of the parish, it was evident they loved their pastor, were confused by the attempt to replace him, and would only find acceptable a successor who was his clone and "preached with his hand on the Bible." During the interview with the search committee, which included no Latinos, I asked, "What role do you foresee your next assistant pastor fulfilling"? The church council president gazed across the table and said tersely, "If you come here, you'll just do exactly as the senior pastor says!" By the time the visit concluded, I knew I would not be welcomed by the Latino members and that I would chafe working as an underling with an authoritarian senior pastor. Within a few days, I declined further consideration and encouraged the New York synod office to sort things out before sending St. Paul's additional candidates.

Next came an invitation to consider serving as pastor (again, the sole/lead pastor) of a Spanish-speaking congregation in Weehauken, New Jersey. Virtually all the congregation's members were Cuban refugees who fled the Castro regime in the late 1960's and early 70's. As was common among Cuban immigrants in that era, they were fiercely anti-Communist and wary of anyone who would question any aspects of American foreign policy. Having just returned from Chile where, as noted in the previous chapter, the U.S. government had taken the side of the brutal Pinochet regime and supported the overthrow of the democratically elected government of socialist Salvador Allende, I simply could not in good faith promise to espouse the political values of the Cuban American community. I also sensed the members' continuing deep allegiance to their former founding pastor and felt that no "gringo" pastor would be readily accepted. So again, as with the New York parish, I declined further consideration by the New Jersey congregation.

During my years as seminary president, my faculty colleagues would chide me when I occasionally told students the story of my declining several potential calls during my final year of seminary. Bishops and veteran clergy tend to look askance at seminarians who appear too "choosy." I had my own concerns when a student seemed to exude an air of entitlement to a "plum call." But I shared my personal experience in order to underscore the seriousness with which one should take a potential call. While I feel a pastor should be open to serve a broad range of people, including those with whom we may disagree sharply at some points, accepting a call just to "get a job" usually proves disastrous for all concerned. As in other professional relationships, if one is convinced a pastor-parish "match" will prove unworkable, I believe it is unethical to enter into it.

After putting behind me the possibilities in New York and New Jersey, I went in search of other potential bilingual calls. I was encouraged by a response from the Rev. Lloyd Burke, president of the LCA's Pacific Southwest Synod (PSW) based in Los Angeles. He indicated the synod was eager to expand its outreach among burgeoning Latino populations in many areas, and that there could be a number of possibilities in the ensuing months. So, in August of 1976, I traveled from Washington to Boston for a meeting with Burke, who was there for the LCA's biennial national convention. He explained that a new Hispanic mission was being launched in Tucson, Arizona, and also that Angelica Lutheran Church in the heart of Los Angeles had received a funding commitment from the LCA to call a bilingual pastor. Either possibility sounded intriguing, and I enthusiastically asked that I be considered for them. Within a few weeks I was informed that an experienced bilingual pastor, the Rev. Richard Miller, had been interviewed for both positions and determined to accept the call in Tucson. I was then put in touch with the senior pastor at Angelica, the Rev. Jerald Ramsdell, with whom I felt instant rapport in telephone conversations.

In late August, I flew to Los Angeles for a round of interviews, all of which went extremely well. All signs indicated that I would be called as Associate Pastor for Hispanic Ministry at the historic LCA "mother church" of Southern California. The council recommended me and set the date for the congregational meeting to issue a call. When the day came, I waited anxiously for the phone call from Pastor Ramsdell, which came mid-afternoon. "Well, Mike," he said, "I have good news and some not-so-good news." The good news was that Angelica's vote to call me was unanimous. The bad news was that somehow amidst all the preparations, they had overlooked the fact that a congregational call vote would only be legal if a representative of the synod were present. Despite the fact the PSW Synod office was right upstairs in Angelica's educational wing, no one had informed the synod of the special meeting! Shortly, a new (and legally constituted) congregational meeting was held, and the call was issued for me to begin ministry at Angelica on October 1, 1976.

Arrangements were made for a service of ordination at Augustana Church in Washington, which had become so important in the final stages of my ministerial formation. Together with Chuck Robertson, I served Augustana in an interim role during the summer months when they were in pastoral transition. In addition to the small Latino contingent, I bonded with many of the other members in that richly diverse multicultural parish. President Orso's calendar allowed for him to ordain me on September ninth, and Augustana's members were very gracious in hosting a wonderful reception. Many of my friends, seminary classmates and members from Augustana, Living Word (Columbia), and Christ the Servant (Montgomery Village), which we had joined while living there, were present for the evening service. Members of Augustana's all-Black youth group, which I had led throughout the summer, sang gustily. My parents came from Minnesota and joined clergy in laying hands as the president/bishop pronounced me an ordained minister of the church.

Reflecting my growing love for urban ministry, I chose as the primary scripture for the service Revelation 21:1–7, which holds the promise of a "new heaven, new earth, and new city of Jerusalem." The preacher, a seminary friend, Randolph Barr, noted that the text is usually read at funerals rather than ordinations! Barr declared, "This text fits Mike Cooper to a T. On this night when he will be set apart for public ministry, Mike is declaring his intentions to be a freedom-fighter in Jesus' Name." He concluded by sharing his conviction that "neither Mike's work nor ours will ever be in vain as we strive for justice and mercy among all peoples."

In a letter to my "home pastor" in Minnesota, Harold Underdahl, I reported the mixed emotions of those days. I wrote to Harold that, while eager to begin ministry in a whole new and exciting arena in Los Angeles, the Washington area had become beloved, as had our many friends and especially the dear folks at Augustana. But it was time to move on. Within a few days, a moving van came to collect our belongings, and Doris and I began the long road trip westward to California. We enjoyed a week of vacation at a lake cabin in Minnesota, where we reconnected with our families. During that time, I preached at Rock Prairie, which hosted a lovely reception honoring my ordination and forthcoming ministry. By late September we arrived in Los Angeles. I was eager to plunge into ministry in a new and exciting environment.

Preaching at home church of Rock Prairie en route to CA in 1976

— 6 —

The Angelica Years: Farm Boy Becomes City Shepherd

ON OCTOBER 1, 1976, I began ministry as Associate Pastor (for Hispanic ministry) at Angelica Lutheran Church in the heart of South-Central Los Angeles' Pico-Union neighborhood. The congregation had a long and storied history. Founded in 1888, it was Southern California's oldest congregation of the former Augustana (Swedish heritage) Lutheran Church. At one point its membership exceeded 1000 members as congregants converged at Angelica from throughout the greater Los Angeles area. Angelica had been served throughout its history by outstanding pastors. Its two most recent senior pastors, Carl Segerhammar and Lloyd Burke, had both been elected presidents (bishops) of the five-state Pacific Southwest Synod of the Lutheran Church in America.

Angelica's impressive physical plant covered most of a city block and included a large and imposing worship sanctuary with a first-rate pipe organ and an altar carving of the Lord's Supper imported from Germany. Adjacent to the sanctuary was a large two-story administrative and educational center with a spacious auditorium, ample library, staff offices and space for a local Head Start program that served low-income children from the neighborhood.

During the 1960's, the congregation created a separate corporation, Angelica Homes Inc., and constructed a 38-unit apartment building for senior citizens; its residents included both members and persons not affiliated with Angelica. In brief, Angelica was known around the greater Los Angeles area, throughout the synod, and even nationwide as a so-called "tall steeple church." It was an honor to be called right out of seminary to such a highly respected parish doing important ministry.

As did many congregations with similar histories rooted in one ethnic tradition, Angelica found itself challenged as its neighborhood and the entire city of Los Angeles began to undergo sweeping demographic changes in the 1960's. Many churches founded in central city locations decided to "follow the people" who were fleeing inner cities for the suburbs. By contrast to these many congregations, most of whom were motivated by "white flight," Angelica made conscious decisions to stay in the city and seek to reach out to newcomers. The Pico-Union neighborhood went through a brief transition phase when significant numbers of African Americans moved into its relatively low-cost housing. Within a short time, however, the tide of immigrants from Mexico and Central America swelled and Pico-Union became one of the magnet neighborhoods for Latinos/as. The vast majority were undocumented refugees fleeing poverty and the violent wars erupting in places like El Salvador, Guatemala, and Nicaragua.

This rapid Latino in-migration to Los Angeles was mirrored by the swelling of other ethnic communities. It was reported that by the late 1970's, Los Angeles was the "second city" (in terms of population) of El Salvador, South Korea, Mexico, and some other nations as well. While there was, to be sure, some resistance from a segment of Angelica's longtime members, who wanted the focus to remain on "Anglo ministry," the parish leaders were committed to a vision of becoming a kind of "United Nations parish." At one point during my years there, the campus of Angelica hosted Sunday Lutheran services in Spanish, English, and Finnish, and rented space for two Korean independent congregations. Every Pentecost, all these groups converged for a festive combined worship using at least a half-dozen languages!

Angelica Lutheran Church, Los Angeles, California

A Challenging Start-Up

In accepting the call to Angelica, I knew the challenges would be formidable. While my Spanish had developed to a point of moderate fluency during the internship in Chile, it was still a challenge to preach, teach, counsel, and carry out all aspects of ministry in a second language. Unlike today, when Lutherans and most denominations have produced a wide range of resources in Spanish, we pioneers in Latino outreach during the 1970's had few tools at our disposal. Worship and educational materials had to be gleaned from disparate sources and many were created from scratch. The standard Lutheran worship book used widely from the 1950's in Latin America, *Culto Cristiano*, proved grossly insensitive to contemporary Latino cultural realities. So, we compiled our own little paper back liturgy booklet with songs appropriated from liturgies emerging at the grassroots throughout the Southern hemisphere.

To those coming from countries steeped in Roman Catholicism, the very concept of Lutheranism required interpretation. While the post-Vatican II ecumenical spirit had begun to pervade much of the U.S. Catholic world, some Catholic bishops and local priests still clung to anti-ecumenical resentment of other churches' outreach in Latino neighborhoods. Despite some good efforts at bridge-building, throughout my five years at Angelica we never developed close collaborative relations with the two large nearby Roman Catholic parishes.

By far the greatest challenges encountered in my early months at Angelica resulted from the continuing presence of a Lutheran former missionary who had been contracted to conduct Spanish-language worship prior to the arrival of a called bilingual pastor. The conditions under which he was brought to the congregation created a very difficult situation. He had consented to serve only if guaranteed total independence, with no accountability to the church council or the senior pastor and complete freedom to determine the Hispanic worship style.

The retired missionary's experience in Latin America had convinced him that Latinos seeking alternatives to the Roman Catholic Church would resonate best with a Pentecostal style of worship, and he intentionally eschewed anything recognizably Lutheran. He also insisted that the "Spanish congregation" would remain independent of Angelica, whose members desired one unified parish with worship and a full range of ministry in Spanish as well as English. While the expectation of Angelica's leadership was that the "interim Hispanic pastor" would cease to serve once the new regularly called minister arrived, that turned out not to be the case. Despite the fact Angelica ceased to compensate "Pastor Al" upon my arrival, he announced he would sacrificially continue serving anyway, since that was clearly the desire of the Latino "congregation" that he was pastoring. He also made it clear that, from his perspective, he would be the primary pastor of the Latino worshiping community and I would be in a subordinate role. The situation was untenable from my perspective. But unlike the situation in New York described in the last chapter, where I felt blind-sided upon showing up for an interview only to be told a bilingual pastor remained on the scene, Angelica's senior pastor and other leaders had been transparent in the call process that "Pastor Al" could be problematic. They were fully supportive as I assessed the situation and determined it would be nearly impossible for us to co-exist and work in a partnership.

After several weeks of deliberation among parish leaders, it was decided we needed to arrange a meeting with the bishop, Dr. Lloyd Burke, and LCA mission director, the Rev. Howell Foster, whose office was providing financial support for the Latino outreach. I approached that meeting with confidence that the bishop and Foster would support my position and that of the parish leaders. As the meeting unfolded, we presented the situation, and no one disputed the facts. Most of the information was already well understood by the bishop, since he was Angelica's most recent former pastor and had approved Pastor Al's leadership of the Latino group. After hearing all parties, the bishop mulled things over for a few moments and then rendered his counsel: "I think that Pastor Al should continue leading the Spanish worship, but he should do so in English and Michael can translate his sermon and so forth into Spanish."

I was dumbfounded! With only a moment's hesitation to collect my thoughts, I responded firmly and unequivocally, "No. That is not acceptable. I am the called pastor for Hispanic ministry and Pastor Al is welcome to stay but under the condition that he serve as my assistant." I went on to cite the Augsburg Confession[1] clause where the Lutheran reformers established the principle reflected in the LCA constitution: that no one should teach and preach in a congregation without a regular call. I held the call, and he did not. After my blunt response, there was silence in the room, and eyes got big as it dawned on everyone: This brash new pastor right out of seminary has just defied the bishop!

The next Sunday we began Spanish worship under my leadership, having issued what amounted to an eviction notice to Pastor Al upon his unwillingness to accept the conditions the senior pastor, church council leaders and I had established. Pastor Al's response was to circulate word that *his* worship service would continue at the usual hour and would take place in the park right across the street from Angelica church. The majority of the Spanish worshiping community—some fifty or so—went with him and only about two dozen attended the first services under my leadership. Soon, however, our group began to grow as we did intensive outreach in the local community, and a few of those who left with Pastor Al drifted back. After a few months, his "church" left the park and

---

1. The Augsburg Confession is a key 16th century document, in which the early Lutheran reformers set forth their most important theological convictions. To this day, we Lutheran clergy promise to preach and teach in accord with its tenets.

took up residence somewhere else unknown to us. While it was a sad and divisive situation, especially for the people who had been shepherded by Pastor Al and struggled to understand the dynamics between us, four decades later I continue to believe we made the right decision to carry out an authentic, culturally sensitive Lutheran witness rather than allow a Pentecostal ministry to masquerade under the banner of Lutheranism.

Since Angelica's vision for its ministry was to be one diverse congregation with multiple worship opportunities in both English and Spanish, it was also very important that both pastors and all the staff be seen as serving the entire membership. While somewhat inhibited by virtue of having little command of Spanish, my colleague Jerry Ramsdell made every effort to be available to the Latinos as well as Anglos. His stance at times brought sharp criticism from some of the longtime white members, who felt that the senior pastor should focus exclusively on their needs. But Jerry persisted in occasionally attending Spanish services, and he frequently greeted new immigrants eager to learn English in Angelica's popular ESL[2] classes. He and his family joined in fellowship meals and other events that appealed primarily to those who began referring to themselves as the *HispAngelica* contingent.

In turn, mine was a face seen regularly by the Anglo parish members. I preached once or twice a month at English services, conducted pastoral visitation with members of both language groups, especially hospital and shut-in calls with elderly members. And Doris and I were fully engaged with the young adults group made up almost entirely of Anglos. Not to the same extent as faced by Jerry, but I too heard complaints from time to time that Angelica's Latino members felt they were being neglected by *their* pastor (me!). I learned early on in my ministry that building and sustaining community in a diverse, multicultural church is very challenging. And I am eternally grateful for the opportunity to have served my first call in such a dynamic and exciting place.

Beginning a Family and Buying our First Home

After more than five years of marriage, Doris and I were eager to start a family. Our first son, Aaron Michael, came into the world on July 8, 1977, missing by one day being born 7/7/77. As so many young pastoral families have experienced, congregations love babies and young children. The

---

2. English as a Second Language

parish embraced our young son, and we loved being parents. Two days after his birth at California Lutheran Hospital on Hope Street in central Los Angeles, I was scheduled to preach at Angelica. My sermon title that day was, "Daddy, What's the World Like?" In the sermon I welcomed our firstborn to the world and shared my hopes for his life. Toward the end of the sermon, I said the following:

> So, when you ask me, "Daddy, what's the world like?" this is how I would answer. The world is big like you are (he was nearly ten pounds at birth). It's big and alive and beautiful. It also has a dirty bottom side, just like you. Sometimes it sleeps peacefully, and sometimes it screams with pain and cries out because it's hungry. It has a pretty face and delicate little fingers, and an uncontrolled underside. Sometimes it's nice and clean and pretty, and sometimes its insides get upset and it spits up and makes itself smell bad.

Preaching on the appointed epistle text for the day, in which Saint Paul reflects on the nature of Christian freedom, I assured the newborn and congregation, "It's a world called to be free!" I concluded:

> And that's what the world is really like. Our freedom, like your freedom, comes when we, like you, give ourselves into the arms of the waiting Father, who dries our tears. Our dirty bottom sides are made clean by the Christ, and the Spirit of love will teach us to walk free. So that's how I see the world, little one. I welcome you to it! It's time for us to get started together. It's time for us to put our hands to the plow and never look back.

Our first Los Angeles residence was a two-bedroom flat in Angelica Apartments, right next door to the church. Despite the proximity and being surrounded by elderly parishioners who were our fellow residents, our privacy was respected, and this was a good (and very affordable) first home. With Aaron's birth, however, we began to feel a bit cramped and started looking for a nearby house in which we might also capture some of the equity value increase for which Southern California was known in that era. With few properties for sale, I followed Jerry's suggestion, which worked for him in a prior locale, and began knocking on doors of houses we liked asking the owners if they might be thinking of selling. We came very close to closing the deal on a spacious home near the church, but at the last minute the owners decided to stay. After a few months of a house search, an older gentleman who taught English classes and befriended many of Angelica's Latino members proposed that we jointly purchase a three-unit property about two miles west of the church. He would occupy one of the two downstairs apartments, rent out the second, and we would have the entire spacious second floor unit, which offered large kitchen, living and dining rooms along with three bedrooms and a bookcase-lined study. In many ways, it was all we wanted in a house, apart from a large backyard for Aaron and any additional children that might come our way.

As things evolved, our relationship with our co-owner "Norm" proved challenging and taught some lessons about the importance of having clear understandings (in writing). We had not worked out detailed agreements about sharing costs and labor when major maintenance items affected the entire property. Badly in need of repainting, we decided to do the work ourselves. After a few months of observing that Norm appeared to be on a five-year schedule (painting a doorframe and then abandoning the project for several weeks, for example), I finally took about ten days of vacation and virtually painted the entire two-story house myself. When it came time for us to move on, we had no written agreement about how the sale of our portion of the home would transpire. An appraisal suggested that the value had nearly doubled in the three-plus years we owned the home, but we ended up selling our portion to Norm for a significantly lesser amount.

The greater challenge arising from our co-ownership, however, came to light as we learned to our dismay about his unethical lifestyle. It was common knowledge that the long-divorced bachelor enjoyed the company of women. What he successfully kept secret for several years was the way in which he manipulated innocent immigrant Latinas and took advantage of their undocumented status. When the full story came to light, we learned he first seduced one of the Angelica Latina members into living with him in his prior home in Watts. After that relationship ended, he established a pen pal correspondence with a woman in Central America and sent her photos of himself when he was in his twenties. When he proposed and somehow enabled her to cross the border, imagine her shock upon meeting this fellow in his early seventies! Pastor Ramsdell and I attempted to counsel the woman and assure her we would support her in leaving Norm. But probably out of fear of deportation, she declined our overtures and remained with him. Had we reported him to the police, the outcome indeed likely would have been her arrest and deportation. Co-owning property and living under the same roof with such a manipulative abuser was an extremely uncomfortable situation.

A Demanding and Exciting Crossroads Ministry

Throughout the years of ministry at Angelica, the pastors, interns, and our families gathered most Sunday evenings after a full day that included five worship services and other activities. Typically converging in the home of Jerry and Kris Ramsdell, we sat outdoors in summer and around the fireplace in colder months. Our typical fare was popcorn, cheese, beer, and wine. At the end of a long day and busy week, it was our time to let our hair down and rehash the week's events. More than forty years afterward, I still recall one of Jerry's favorite summations of the ministry at Angelica: "It's never dull or boring around here for long!" Indeed, it wasn't.

Beyond all the typical activities found in most Christian congregations—worship, Sunday School, Bible studies, choir rehearsals, committee and council meetings—because of its location and commitments, Angelica church served as a very public space and community center. Some years before our arrival, a wing had been added to the building to house the local Head Start classrooms as well as offices of the Lutheran Church in America's Pacific Southwest Synod. For many years, the California Lutheran Bible Institute (CLBI) was housed at Angelica. Lutheran Social Services of Southern California had a field office focused on providing immigration counseling and in other ways supporting the large population of undocumented immigrants in the neighborhood. A senior lunch program was offered daily in our auditorium, and four nights a week English Second Language classes were offered by parish members to as many as 100 recent immigrants from Latin America. Almost every evening one or more community groups assembled on our premises to conduct their business.

Since Jerry and I arrived at the parish within months of each other, and because of his very collegial style, ours was not a typical senior/associate pastor relationship in which he functioned as "the boss" and I his deputy. As time went on, I began to share more administrative duties in addition to the pastoral work. Without any formal change in roles or titles, ours evolved into what might be described as nearly a co-pastorate. Jerry was extremely gracious and supportive, to the point of recommending some years that I receive a larger percentage salary increase than him, to narrow the gap between our compensation. Our friendship deepened and continued after I left Angelica, albeit without the daily contact and close working relationship we experienced during our years together in Los Angeles. After a few more years there, the Ramsdells moved to the Bay area and Jerry served a congregation until his untimely death from a serious illness. During those years, our roles were reversed in some measure, in that I was the bishop's assistant providing "oversight" and support for all the pastors in my area of the synod. It was a privilege to accompany Jerry and Kris and the Ramsdell children on the difficult journey of his final days, and then to be the preacher at his funeral service. In her thank you note after the funeral, Kris wrote, "Jerry really did consider you the brother he never had, and your love and unwavering support over the last few years meant more to him than you can ever know."

From several perspectives, Angelica Lutheran Church lived at a crossroads. As noted above, its facility is right in the heart of the Pico-Union district of central Los Angeles. The maze of the downtown freeway interchange—where the Santa Monica, San Bernadino and Harbor freeways converge near the great University of Southern California (USC)—is less than a mile away. Because of its central location and the presence of the synod offices at that time, Angelica was also a crossroads for LCA Lutheranism. From throughout the five-state territory, pastors and lay leaders of the PSW synod were often on site. We also became increasingly recognized as a center of ecumenical work and shared some activities with other central Los Angeles Protestant congregations.

But the most rewarding dimension of working in this incredibly lively and diverse environment was my pastoral work, especially among the Latin Americans who began to come in increasing numbers. The Spanish language worship service attendance ebbed and flowed as the years went by, with the peak never exceeding about seventy-five or so. For people from countries and cultures steeped in Roman Catholicism, where one is a "member" of the parish simply by residing within its geographical boundaries, the whole concept of joining the church was foreign. Nevertheless, more than 100 Hispanic persons joined the church as official members during my years there, and dozens more in the community simply regarded us as their church. A decade after my departure from Angelica, testimony to the degree of its ownership by the neighborhood became apparent in the spring of 1992. After the devastating verdict exonerating Los Angeles police officers who brutally beat an innocent African American, Rodney King, widespread rage engulfed much of Los Angeles. As buildings citywide were set afire in the rebellion, it was reported neighbors surrounded the Angelica property, saying in essence, "Nobody's going to mess with our church."

As was the case broadly in the community, the vast majority of our Latino members and affiliates were undocumented persons who had either gained entrance to the U.S. without proper papers or overstayed their visas. After beginning my ministry at Angelica, I quickly learned it was important for me to wear a clerical collar when out and about. On the rare occasions when I donned a coat and tie, I would notice worried glances as I walked down the street or entered a local restaurant or other establishment. It soon dawned on me that the primary association folks in the community drew for a young Anglo guy was *"la migra"*—an agent of the Immigration & Naturalization Service. In that regard, it was also fun to see the looks on faces when Doris and I would walk down the street holding hands if I were clad in a collar. Again, for folks from a culture steeped in Roman Catholicism, where priests are expected to remain celibate, there was no small dose of "culture shock" to see a priest holding hands with a woman!

The immigration status of many Latinos embraced by our community outreach troubled some of Angelica's longtime Anglo members, who held varying degrees of law-and-order attitudes. So, finding ways to interpret the plight of folks fleeing poverty and political persecution was critical. We recognized that enabling personal relationships to develop would be more effective than criticizing racist and nationalistic impulses. A key bridge-building avenue in that regard was the ESL program. When a growing number of Anglo members—mostly retired folks, some well into their eighties—taught new immigrants recently arrived from Mexico and Central America, friendships quickly developed. When ESL teachers occasionally would hear fellow Anglo members speak disparagingly of "those people," they would quietly but firmly respond, "But you're talking about my friends Jose and Maria, Victor and Rosa."

There were times, of course, when a strong public stance had to be taken, even if it offended some of the long-time "pillars" of the parish. Early on in my tenure at Angelica, and fully supported by Jerry and key lay leaders, I signaled that if push came to shove, I would stand with the undocumented people we had begun to welcome. "I don't ask for green cards when they come to the altar and put out their hands for Holy Communion," I said on several occasions when asked how we dealt with people's immigration status.

In addition to Spanish worship services, bilingual Sunday and Vacation Bible Schools, ESL classes, a bilingual summer camp, sponsoring a soccer team, and other programs, our outreach in the Hispanic community included what is commonly referred to in church circles as "cold calling." Particularly on Saturdays, when we knew people were likely to be home, we simply began knocking on doors in the multiple apartment buildings that surrounded the church. "*Hola. Mi nombre es Miguel y yo soy un pastor en la Iglesia Angelica aquí en la vecindad. Le queremos invitar a nuestras misas, y a visitarnos, conocer los programas y nuestros miembros. Como iglesia, queremos servir a la comunidad y si Ustedes tienen necesidad cualquiera, nos gustaría ayudar.*" This was the essence of my message as I knocked on a door and was greeted in Spanish. ("Hello. My name is Michael, and I am a pastor at Angelica Church here in the neighborhood. We want to invite you to our worship services, to come and meet us, learn about our programs, and meet our members. As a church, we want to serve the community, so if you have any needs whatsoever, we would love to help."

Again, the fact that behind most of those doors were undocumented persons meant that a sensitive approach was critical. I was nearly always accompanied by a Latina who would be trusted by another woman in ways a gringo male never could be. I always wore my collar, took a step back from the door and tried to speak softly in my accented Spanish. We went with a simple Spanish-language brochure in hand that provided the church address, phone number, worship times and information about the ESL classes and other programs. Such outreach efforts were concentrated especially preceding holy days and seasons that are highly valued in Latino culture. In the Christmas season we celebrated Las Posadas, a wonderful tradition practiced especially in Central America, where wandering pilgrims go out in the evening in search of "posada" or a resting place for Mary and Joseph as they await Jesus' birth. Our processions through the neighborhood attracted keen interest from some who had enjoyed Posadas in their home countries. Similarly, the Lenten season offered a rich opportunity to invite folks for whom Good Friday processions were among the holiest occasions of the year. Each Pentecost we held one large joint service in which the several groups using Angelica's facilities worshipped together in English, Spanish, Finnish and Korean.

My pastoral sensitivity grew as I listened to people's stories and came to understand the dire circumstances from which our neighbors had fled to the U.S. As trust grew, some would tell me of the extreme poverty, political persecution and even torture they had experienced in their homelands. Some of these stories began to circulate also among the ESL teachers who became champions for our new friends and would confront any fellow Anglo members who spoke of "those people" as being lazy or a drain on society. The greatest champion of all was Esther Alm, a widow well into her 80's when I first arrived. A longtime teacher, Esther was the "community organizer" for the ESL classes. In addition to teaching several nights a week, "Señora Alm" offered personal one-to-one tutoring for many who worked evenings or for other reasons could not attend classes. I will never forget Esther's funeral when Latinos/as by the dozens came out (many probably missing work to do so) to pay her tribute. Mrs. Alm was chief among the saints who embodied the biblical mandate to welcome strangers.

But much as I tried to be a caring, sensitive pastor, I know there were many occasions when I failed. I recall one occasion in a Bible study group asking folks to take turns around the circle reading a few verses of scripture After a couple of folks "passed" when it came their turn, it finally sunk in that they had never had access to education in their homelands and were either totally or semi-illiterate. Another time, we were trying to resolve conflict with a group called *La Escuelita* (The Little School) that used our facilities for Spanish-language preschool. I could not sort out who the real leaders were and at one point in exasperation blurted out, "*No sabemos con quien debemos negociar.*" ("We don't know with whom we should negotiate.") A woman confronted me forcefully and said, "We are not a business with whom you 'negotiate.'"

Despite many such pastoral misfires on my part, the people were loving and forgiving, and embodied a graciousness in which I experienced God's love in the same ways I had in Chile, and among the poor I visited in Washington during my brief stint at Augustana and with the Hispanic Ministry there. When I last visited Angelica a few years ago, there were still a couple of members from that era, and we shared wonderful memories of our years of serving together. Sadly, Angelica's long-time pastor, Carlos Paiva, died suddenly in 2016 while on a visit to his homeland of Colombia. The congregation dwindled considerably after the loss of their beloved shepherd. Whether it can survive long-term remains in question now, as I write, though to some degree that can be said of a great many churches, particularly those in fragile, vulnerable inner-city communities like South Central Los Angeles.

Reigniting a Suspended Love Affair: With Airplanes!

After establishing myself in parish ministry with a work ethic that typically involved 60-hour weeks on the job, as the new year of 1979 began, I finally allowed myself to dedicate a few hours most weeks to reignite my passion for flying. After several hours of dual instruction in a Piper Cherokee at Hawthorne airport, I once again soloed following a ten-year hiatus. On August 2, 1979, I successfully completed the Private Pilot practical test (or "check ride" as it's commonly called). I was encouraged and supported by a member of Angelica, Ryden Richardson, an avid pilot and part-time flight instructor, who would later conduct portions of my advanced training for commercial and instrument ratings.

While the basic mechanics of flying a small aircraft are the same regardless of the locale, my second go at flight training in the greater Los Angeles area was a "different world" from my fledgling flights a decade earlier in rural Minnesota. Hawthorne airport is located less than five miles from Los Angeles International, amidst one of the world's most congested and complicated sectors of airspace. Training in this environment enabled me to become comfortable with and competent in communicating with air traffic controllers, precise navigation, and compliance with complex Federal Aviation Regulations (FARs). All of that served me well a decade later when I advanced in my training to become a Certified Flight Instructor (CFI) at Oakland International Airport in the equally congested San Francisco "Class B" (or back then, "Terminal Control Area") airspace.

After gaining my pilot's license, I joined the Civil Air Patrol (CAP)[3] as both chaplain and pilot in a squadron based at a small airport in the San Fernando Valley north of Los Angeles. On many Mondays, typically my weekly day off, I drove to that little field and enjoyed a few hours of flying either solo or with Ryden. Given his daytime demands as a chemist with a giant petroleum corporation, most of Ryden's and my airtime hours together were at night when the Los Angeles basin was an especially dramatic and impressive scene viewed from aloft. Access to the CAP-owned Piper Cherokee also provided a very inexpensive means of continuing to gain flight hours and experience.

---

3. The Civil Air Patrol is an auxiliary of the U.S. Air Force. In addition to providing educational opportunities for young people interested in aviation, CAP squadrons conduct search and rescue operations and support other humanitarian and public service activities.

While never realizing the dream of a true "flying ministry" that I sometimes envisioned, as the years went by, I was occasionally able to make work-related trips. While still at Angelica, I gave a handful of "greater Los Angeles orientation flights" to students from California Lutheran University involved in an urban studies program based at Angelica. In later years, both with the Northern California synod work and then during my Chicago years with the churchwide organization, some trips of medium distance were more convenient by small aircraft than by car or airlines. The same proved true when I became seminary president and occasionally flew to synod assemblies and other meetings throughout Pennsylvania. Though I do have an instrument rating and conducted a few flights "in the soup" of actual Instrument Flight Rules (IFR) conditions in California and the Chicago area, I realized that safely flying in less-than-visual weather requires doing so frequently. Given that I have not been able to keep at it regularly, and that the airplane I have owned for two decades is not IFR-equipped, I have confined myself to flying only in "visual flight rules" (VFR) conditions. A new chapter in my flying opened post-retirement when I trained for and received my commercial glider pilot rating and also became a busy tow pilot flying the former crop duster aircraft that tow the gliders aloft from our glider club's airstrip near the Pennsylvania-Maryland border.

An Expanding Sense of *Parish* and New Call Stirrings

After a few years at Angelica, word of its ministry began to spread. Interest in what we were doing was growing, especially among other congregations that were exploring the possibility of outreach in communities with burgeoning influx of Latinos. So, I was asked to speak about Angelica's ministry in parish and synodical gatherings. I authored a few articles about immigration issues for publication in synodical and Lutheran Social Service newsletters. One year, our Latino worship group was invited to sing at the synod's annual assembly. In short, while my primary day-to-day focus was at Angelica, I began assuming some wider church responsibilities. This expanded further when I was elected by my peers as leader of our regional grouping of LCA parishes, the Los Angeles Central Cluster.

Then, too, in the late 1970's and early 80's, the LCA's Division for Mission in North America (DMNA) consulted with urban pastors throughout the nation to determine key markers of effective ministry in metropolitan contexts. Out of a process led by the LCA's Director of Urban Ministry, the Rev. Harvey Peters, emerged a document entitled "Parish as Place." It reflected common convictions that ministry in any setting must be attuned to context and shaped to meet the needs and capture the excitement of the people who live in that place. "Neighborhood ministry within the shadow of the steeple" became our watchword, and Angelica had proven successful in serving many needs within the Pico Union community. While most of our Anglo members resided outside the neighborhood, including some who commuted long distances, many of our new members could walk to worship and other activities.

Another strong LCA emphasis in that era was the development of "area mission strategies," whereby a group of congregations in a geographic area would attempt to develop comprehensive strategic plans for future ministry in an entire region of a city or rural area. In the late 1970's, funding and staff support were made available by DMNA to develop a Los Angeles Area Strategy. Early in the process of laying groundwork, it was determined that developing such a mission plan for all of Los Angeles county would be nearly impossible given the metropolitan area included millions of people with more than 100 LCA congregations in dozens of cities. Accordingly, the strategy development would be limited to the territory of our Central Cluster. As cluster leader, I was asked to simultaneously serve as chair of the strategy development team. Over the course of about two years, we succeeded in charting a course for the fifteen or so urban-most congregations, as well as campus and other outreach ministries, in Central and South-Central L.A. and surrounding communities. Some years after I left Angelica, a smaller group of congregations formed the New City Parish that fostered an array of outreach and service ministries, as well as providing a support network for clergy and others engaged in the high-stress work of urban ministry. In post-retirement visits to Los Angeles, I have learned that some vestiges of that work continue more than four decades after our initial mission planning in the late 1970's.

In a number of cities across the country, the area strategy development process led to the creation of urban coalitions whereby a group of congregations forged deep partnerships that enhanced their outreach, service, and advocacy for justice in their communities. Most of the ministry coalitions hired a director, who provided oversight for programs and coordinated the work of the individual parish clergy and other church workers. At urban ministry conferences and training institutes, I began to rub shoulders with some of those coalition directors. Learning more about their work, I began to sense I could serve effectively and find fulfillment in such a calling should one come my way at some point in the future. I made known my interest in such a possibility to my bishop, and to Pastor Peters and other national staff who related to the coalitions and urban ministries around the country.

One day in 1980, I received a call in my office at Angelica from the bishop of the LCA's New Jersey Synod. He explained that the coalition director in Camden, New Jersey, had left for another call, and expressed the hope I might make a trip east to explore the possibility of serving in that challenging context. After mulling it over, praying and discussing with Doris, Jerry, and a few other trusted advisers, I decided I had really fallen in love with ministry in California. So, I called the bishop back and expressed my appreciation for his consideration but stated my sense of calling was to stay put in Los Angeles. Looking back, I now realize that the New Jersey invitation contributed to my becoming open to the possibility of a new call, especially one that might take me out of parish ministry for a few years. It had caused me to reconsider the prospect of settling in for a long-term pastorate at Angelica.

In the latter months of 1980, therefore, I began to pay attention to the process underway 300 miles to the north of Los Angeles where a newly organized San Francisco/East Bay Urban Coalition had been formed and was in search of its first director. Upon inquiring of Harvey Peters and my new bishop about the status of the director search, I learned that several candidates had been interviewed, and a finalist who was invited to move from a national staff position in the Midwest had just declined. Shortly after sending my resume to the search committee, I was invited to the Bay area for an interview early in 1981. Within days of my interview, I was informed the Coalition's executive committee had decided to call me, and we began planning for our move to northern California.

Our Big Christmas Present in 1980: Adam George!

We would be moving to the Bay area as a family of four since Adam was born in the waning days of 1980. Because Aaron had been delivered by Caesarian section, it was determined our second son would be also, as was standard practice at the time. Following Adam's birth on December

19, 1980, we took him home from California Hospital in a big Christmas stocking that the hospital auxiliary had made for all holiday newborns. Any worries we may have had about how three-year-old Aaron would react to his new sibling were dispelled the first afternoon. When we laid Adam in his bassinette for a nap, Aaron dragged his favorite blanket and laid underneath, as if to say, "Just in case he needs me!" While the boys would have the typical tussles among brothers over the years, they always had a strong bond. The two little guys who called themselves "ketchup and mustard" have become mature adult men who remain close.

We were eager to celebrate Adam's baptism in the Angelica community that had supported us during the second pregnancy and eagerly awaited his birth. So, I had the honor of baptizing him, as I had Aaron three years previously. Adam's took place on January 11, 1981, marked on the liturgical calendar as Baptism of our Lord. My sermon that day was crafted as a memo to "The New Adam" from "The Old Man." In my memorandum, shared with the entire congregation, I said:

> God makes the same promise to you today as that made to the first Adam, then to Abraham, on to Moses, to Isaiah the prophet: "I am the Lord; I have called you in righteousness; I have taken you by the hand and kept you."
>
> God takes your hand today, son, to lead you through the dark valleys and treacherous paths you may trod. We can't promise you that your generation will tread a path of luxury. You will become a man in the 21st century. Who knows what the world will be like then? We hope there will be a world as we know it. We hope that somehow yet, our generation can stop the rush to madness. Somehow, we search for the strength to stop the governments of the world from making bombs that will kill babies like you just as surely as they will kill us older folks who pay our taxes to build them.

I concluded the sermon reminding my newborn son of his heritage and our hopes for his life:

> ADAM—your very name comes from a Hebrew word that means "earth man." You come from a long line of farmers on both sides of your family. Stay close to the earth. Always keep a sense of your roots that are planted in the deep faith of your ancestors. So, son, congratulations today as you become a New Adam. Enjoy it. And please don't cry when I put water on your head, because there's a whole lot of people out there!

Saying Goodbye to A Beloved Congregation

The final weeks at Angelica were bittersweet. Many of the Latino members had tears in their eyes as I informed them of my imminent departure. Some of the Anglos to whom I had grown particularly close were sad as well. Since bilingual pastors were scarce in those days, there was anxiety about finding a successor who could carry on the work. Originally thinking it would be best to remain through the Lenten season, I later concluded that, both for me and the parish, leaving mid-Lent would be the better option. "That way," I interpreted my decision, "we can all celebrate Easter rather than have it be like a funeral!" I was primed to get on with the work in San Francisco, and the Coalition was eager for its new director to be on the scene.

A humorous moment occurred during my final Ash Wednesday at Angelica. Jerry Ramsdell and I were co-presiding at the somber service in which parishioners were invited to come forward and have a cross smudged on their foreheads. Issuing the usual invitation, I got tongue-tied and said, "And now it's time for those who wish to come forward for the imposition of asses!" Standing beside me at the altar, Jerry blurted out in a quite audible whisper, "I can't believe you just said that!" It was probably good I was about to take my departure.

A wonderful farewell send-off reception was held at Angelica on March 22, 1981. In my farewell sermon that day, I attempted to express my profound gratitude, and to encourage the congregation in its ongoing ministry.

> Thank you for sharing your lives with me and my family during these past four-and-a-half years. Thank you for your untold kindnesses, your up-lifting prayers that were spoken many times when I needed them and was not even aware you were praying for me.
>
> I shall always count it one of the great privileges of my life to have played one small part during one short act in the ongoing drama of this congregation. I consider Angelica to be one of a handful of truly great city congregations of the Lutheran Church in America.

The gospel text for the day was the story of Jesus putting mud on a blind man's eyes to restore his sight. I reflected that my years at Angelica had enhanced my sight and humbled me to recognize my own limitations. In my valedictory sermon, I tried to blend pastoral comfort with prophetic nudging people to overcome prejudices. I said that true Christians "are those who let themselves get dirty, who open their eyes to injustice and get themselves messed up in other people's problems." I continued:

> Clean and blind Christians wage campaigns against imagined enemies—the Russians, illegal aliens, homosexuals. Other Christians, those regarded by some as "dirty," sit down with people from these groups and try to see their pains, their wounds, their need for love and compassion.
>
> So, my last words of promise and challenge to you are these: Don't be afraid to get your eyes and faces dirty being God's people at Angelica. Let Jesus the great healer fill your eyes with the mud of humankind. Continue exposing your clay feet to one another. Continue to be, above all, a congregation that serves and gives, heals, and loves.

With the farewell behind us, and my start-date in the Bay Area April 1, it was time to prepare for the move. While we had purchased a modest ranch home in the Oakland foothills, it would not be available for a few weeks, so I went ahead, and Doris and the boys remained temporarily in Los Angeles. When moving time came, the two young fellows, named Randy and Jeff, who packed and unpacked our things obviously made a big impression on three-year-old Aaron. Some months after relocating to the Bay area, we were watching clouds blowing by in the sky overhead when he piped up, "I wonder if Randy and Jeff are moving them"!

Some Reflections

Four decades after I concluded my ministry at Angelica, I continue to cherish memories of those years in my first call. In the rich and diverse milieu of central Los Angeles, I was challenged to use all the abilities and knowledge I had acquired in seminary and in Chile. I enjoyed a wonderful collegial relationship with Jerry, and with Angelica's other staff members, including several seminary interns we hosted during my years there. In broader circles, I thrived in the work developing the area strategy and assuming some leadership as the synod sought to expand Hispanic outreach work.

As I announced my new call to head the Bay Area coalition, some wondered whether I was forever leaving parish ministry behind. I was quick to say that was by no means my intent, feeling that after a few years I would be eager to again serve as a congregational pastor. That was not to be. Apart from three congregations in the Bay Area, which I served for brief interim periods, Angelica was my only parish ministry. While I have no major regrets about that, I do reflect on how my life and ministry might have been quite different had I returned to serve a congregation at some point.

All in all, the years at Angelica and in Los Angeles were a time of amazing experiences, good and strong friendships, and growing more fully into my leadership. It was a heady time for the congregation as we celebrated Angelica's ninetieth anniversary in 1978, and the multi-faceted ministry was flourishing in many ways. Given Angelica's storied history and reputation first in the Augustana Synod and then the LCA, I was honored to serve in a widely recognized parish. For mainline churches, it was still a time of modest growth in many places, so our synod was an exciting place to be. I was also thrilled to get back into aviation, earning my private pilot certificate and instrument rating in the pressure cooker environment of Southern California airspace. We welcomed our wonderful two sons, Aaron and Adam, into the world and I presided at their baptisms in the font at Angelica. We bought our first home, though its co-ownership did bring complications and dimmed the experience to some degree. There were some early signs of a growing apartness in Doris's and my marriage, but I attributed that to the adjustments of being parents, and my failure to prioritize family life over parish demands. I hoped that a fresh start in a new setting would be renewing for us as a couple and family.

I described earlier that more than fifty years since I left the farm, there are still days when about five in the afternoon it feels like it's time to call the cows home and begin the milking. The rhythms that get embedded in us at an early age are probably never entirely left behind. And so, now, more than four decades after I said farewell to Angelica and parish ministry, some Sunday mornings I still feel a yearning to rise early and head for a long day pastoring a congregation.

— 7 —

Coalition and Synodical Ministry: A Dozen Years of *Syzygy*

AT MY SERVICE OF installation as Pastor/Director of the San Francisco/East Bay Urban Coalition on Palm Sunday 1981, our Pacific Southwest Synod bishop, Stanley Olson, preached on an obscure text from Ephesians 4:3. In that passage, Saint Paul offers greetings and entreats Syzygus (whose name means "yokefellow" or "loyal companion") to work in partnership with others. Stan's encouragement to me was to serve as a loyal companion dedicated to yoke together more strongly the diverse thirteen congregations of the Lutheran Church in America in the urban centers of San Francisco and the Oakland/Berkeley corridor across the bay. The image stuck, and for my birthday a few years later, Pamela secured a California "vanity plate" SYZYGUS for my car.

As noted in the last chapter, in several urban areas, coalitions were formed following area mission strategy development processes. In city after city throughout the country, urban Lutheran congregations had lost members, and in many contexts were teetering on the edge of survival. In most contexts, the decline resulted from demographic changes like those Angelica had experienced in the 1960's. Neighborhoods that were once all white, and typically of one predominant ethnic heritage group, changed rapidly with an influx of African American, Hispanic, or Asian citizens or immigrants. Lutherans among the newcomers were few and far between. Even more daunting was the sheer reality of racism whereby congregations were either disinterested in or outright hostile toward welcoming "people unlike us."

Some viewed the formation of coalitions as a last-ditch effort to save declining and faltering congregations by yoking them together in new alignments. Rather, the intent was to form laboratories for mutual learning in which pastors and other key leaders could teach one another ways to re-root congregations in their neighborhoods. Coalition directors were experienced urban pastors who were to motivate and coach, coax, and encourage colleagues engaged in tough inner-city contexts. When our San Francisco/East Bay Urban Coalition was founded in 1979, its bylaws described it as "a voluntary and intentional association of congregations, agencies and institutions working together to assist one another in common mission." Its purpose was to coordinate ministries, administer national church funding to parishes, consult in leadership selection, and help congregations better serve their neighborhoods. Not surprisingly, among those congregations, there was a range of commitment to a new way of relating to each other. A few seemed genuinely committed to a deeper level of shared ministry. While in some cases this was born of a sense of desperation and recognition they were declining, even dying congregations, in others there was a strong sense that "we can do better together than separately." A middle group of congregations and leaders appeared to have a moderate level of commitment, and a handful agreed to join reluctantly and somewhat resentfully, perceiving the Coalition as being forced upon them by high-handed synodical and national church officials.

As I began my work with the Coalition, I understood that my youthfulness and relatively limited experience in ministry would be a challenge. I could sense that some of the veterans who had been urban pastors for two or three decades were wary and doubted that a young pastor ordained less than five years could be of much help to them. Added to that were tensions between some of the local leaders and their "superiors" in the synod and LCA's Division for Ministry in North America (DMNA). While some of this resulted from personality clashes, and inevitable resistance to change, I sensed it was also generated by local resentment to expectations for a higher level of accountability. Inevitably, as the "yokefellow," I was often caught in the middle, with all parties in conflicted situations expecting me to be "their person" and take their side. I would quip to close confidants on occasion, "I feel like I'm riding thirteen headstrong horses simultaneously and they're all going in different directions—a situation sure to cause multiple hernias!"

The Coalition was in such a fledgling state when I arrived that we had to build everything from the ground up. There was no office or equipment, no support staff, no letterhead, and no logo or materials for interpreting the new entity to internal and broader constituencies. While a bank account had been established and a treasurer elected, no one had arranged how I was to be paid! So, the early weeks were devoted to those mundane tasks. Initially residing at Salem Lutheran Home for the elderly, while I awaited the family's move when we could occupy our Oakland home, I also worked from a temporary office there. Coalition officers and I decided to establish an office at First Lutheran Church in East Oakland, which had space and was eager to host me. That decision caused some controversy, as First Lutheran, in the relatively upscale Oakland hills, was among the least "urban" of the member congregations. Within a year, we moved the office to Bethlehem church near downtown Oakland, where more ample space was available. By being housed in a predominantly African American parish, the Coalition's identity and mission were more clearly signaled. Bethlehem's pastor was Rev. Will Herzfeld, widely known national bishop of the Association of Evangelical Lutheran Churches (AELC), the denomination formed by progressives who were exiled from the conservative Lutheran Church-Missouri Synod. As he became more familiar with our work, through our frequent chats in his or my office, Herzfeld began to spread good reports about the Coalition in his extensive travels.

Being the first coalition director, not only in the Bay area, but entire western U.S., I was questioned frequently, "Who are you and what are you about"? The very notion of a "coalition" was disturbing to some who equated it with radical initiatives to erode congregational autonomy and impose high-handed external authority over clergy and congregations. Some suspected there was a hidden "political" agenda at work. Still others saw the Coalition as too anemic and without real teeth to effect needed changes. Both out of my personal sense of calling, and to mitigate perceptions that my role was to be an authoritarian bureaucrat exercising unwanted control, I ascribed to myself the title of *Pastor-Director* (rather than the original simple Director in the job description). Perhaps more than any other symbolic gesture, that self-identification seemed to serve us all well throughout the Coalition's decade of existence. We adopted as our logo a bridge, so representative of an everyday iconic structure for all Bay area citizens, but also symbolizing our work of bridging together the diverse ministries comprising the Coalition.

I attempted to signal the "pastoral" image by preaching frequently in Coalition parishes. Additionally, I served—at no cost to the parish—as transitional or interim pastor when a congregation went through clergy transition. Those short-term intensive engagements in congregations conveyed my commitment to walk with people (to be a loyal companion!). They also eased my personal sense of loss in no longer being a congregation's minister. While excited to be in a new and multifaceted call, I missed the regular rhythms of parish life. I found it especially hard to sit in the pew as worshiper on high festival days like Christmas and Easter when I was accustomed to being up front at the altar and preaching.

Growing the Coalition, Embracing Expanded Responsibilities

By the time the Coalition was launched in the early 1980's, decisions already had been made by the three national churches—American Lutheran Church (ALC), Association of Evangelical Lutheran Churches (AELC), and Lutheran Church in America (LCA)—to explore merger. At all three national church conventions in the summer of 1982, strong majority "go" votes were taken to proceed in forming what would become known as the Evangelical Lutheran Church in America (ELCA). For congregations of the three denominations everywhere, but especially for us in greater San Francisco, it was a new day, and time for the Coalition to undergo significant change. Given that we would all be under one ecclesial umbrella within a few years, it seemed natural for the Coalition to expand beyond the LCA and become a forerunner for merger by opening full membership to parishes and affiliated ministries of the ALC and AELC. We proposed changing the bylaws to enable expansion, and the move was readily endorsed by the synod, which had to approve Coalition governing document revisions. From its original thirteen LCA member parishes, the Coalition grew year after year to a total of thirty-three congregations, and also included affiliated agencies—Salem Lutheran Home, Lutheran Social Services, and area campus ministries.

In my initial years with the Coalition, I worked very closely with Pastor Bob Herhold, who was the Pacific Southwest Synod's (PSW) assistant to the bishop for the coastal areas of northern California. Bob and I became close friends, often rooming together when in Los Angeles for synod staff meetings and otherwise frequently interacting in our shared work. In 1983, Bob, who always described himself as a "reluctant bureaucrat," determined the time had come for him to return to parish ministry. As Bob's departure neared, Bishop Olson and I entered into conversations about the possibility of combining my role as Coalition Director with the Assistant to the Bishop role. I was concerned about the increased workload, which would expand my portfolio with forty more congregations in northwest coastal California—from the Monterey Peninsula all the way to the Oregon border. But I was also excited at the prospect of an expanded role with broader influence and pleased at the prospect of a hike in salary as well.

As conversations continued about this possible reconfiguration in Coalition and synodical leadership, many in the Coalition were understandably reluctant. One of the more intense Coalition pastors, who initially resisted my leadership, John Frykman, declared at a meeting of Coalition pastors, "You're *our* staff person and we don't want to share you more broadly." There was also resistance from a couple of veteran pastors who saw themselves as the next Assistant to the Bishop. In the end, what sold the Coalition on the idea was the fact it would allow major budget reallocation since the bulk of my salary and benefits would be shifted to the synod payroll. This enabled us to fund a variety of parish outreach programs and provide other seed grants to parishes for experimental ministries.

Expanding Multicultural Outreach

As noted, one of the key motivators for the development of our Coalition and those elsewhere was the fact the Lutheran church remained overwhelmingly white in membership even as the U.S. population was becoming more and more multicultural, particularly in urban centers. Still today, despite forty years of efforts to better reflect the diversity of America's polyglot and ethnically mixed society, the ELCA remains overwhelmingly white in official membership. While not quite as bleak as elsewhere, the situation in the Bay area when I went to the Coalition mirrored this larger trend of Lutheran inability to reach out to persons of color. A high priority, therefore, in terms of funding decisions and placement of clergy, was making efforts to turn the tide and become a more diverse church.

During my years with the Coalition, new mission development efforts were begun in Chinese by providing salary support to place Asian pastors in three existing congregations, as well as developing a new congregation, Chinese Lutheran Church, in San Francisco's Sunset district. Latino outreach was supported at St. John's in the Mission District and efforts made in Oakland as well where a Latino pastor served a traditional English-speaking congregation. With added influence by virtue of my synodical role and growing national reputation as an effective change-agent, I garnered grants that enabled outreach in the Bay area Filipino community. The Bay Area Native American Ministry was another cutting-edge ministry developed by the Coalition. A strong outreach to the Hmong population in Richmond was launched when that East Bay community experienced a sizeable influx of Southeast Asian refugees. Significant financial support was provided for at least three congregations in predominantly African American communities as well.

Under the Coalition's auspices, anti-racism workshops were conducted, and other efforts made to equip pastors and laity for more inclusive outreach in their local neighborhoods. Children and youth involved in Coalition-supported summer programs included a high percentage of young persons of color. We seemed to be making some headway, though a number of those ministries faltered and were eventually discontinued as funding eroded, pastors moved on or retired, and church priorities moved in other directions. Sadly, today several of the congregations that made up the Coalition have closed or merged, and many of the toeholds in multicultural ministry established during its existence have evaporated.

The Coalition's, Synod's, and My Transition into the ELCA

As noted above, the go/no go decision about merging three national Lutheran church bodies was made in 1982. But it would be six years before the formal launch of the Evangelical Lutheran Church on January 1, 1988. All of us in "wider church" staff positions therefore endured a prolonged season of uncertainty about our futures. Many colleagues in synodical and national church positions sought and accepted calls to parishes or church or secular agencies which promised greater employment security. During those transitional years, I received a couple of intriguing invitations to consider parish calls. First Lutheran of Palo Alto, California, was a medium-sized congregation in an affluent area near Stanford University. When its long-time pastor retired, I received a feeler about my willingness to be interviewed for the call. Later, as the transition year of 1988 approached, I was invited for an interview at Christ Lutheran Church in New York City. In both cases, while I saw many exciting possibilities in these dynamic ministries with wonderful congregants and strong lay leaders, I determined my calling was to remain with the Coalition and PSW Synod until its end. I hoped thereby to sustain momentum and undergird the future of some of the still-fragile new outreach ministries we had established. In addition, I discovered I had come to love the work as an urban yokefellow and synodical shepherd.

During the mid-1980's, as the basic framework of the ELCA had begun to emerge, a host of task forces and work groups were established. Along with other synodical and district staffers of all three merging churches, I was asked to serve as a consultant to an appointed Transition Team. More than in many areas where synods and districts were smaller and tended to be mostly homogeneous with a preponderance of congregations from either ALC or LCA (the AELC being a tiny denomination with only about 250 parishes spread throughout the nation), ours was a huge task that embraced nearly a quarter of the territory of the continental United States. Our Pacific Southwest Synod included all LCA congregations in California, Arizona, Nevada, Hawaii and Utah. The ALC's South Pacific District was even larger and reached eastward to include some congregations in western Texas. In the ELCA, this vast territory would be carved up into a half-dozen new synods, each of which would have its own bishop and staff, would have to establish offices and become integrated into new relational patterns with national church structures and staff.

The questions facing those of us charged with creating an on-ramp to the ELCA even as we sustained all our regular ongoing work were legion, and the tasks needing attention rather daunting. How would each of the new synods be funded initially? What processes would be put in place to ensure openness and fairness in the selection of ELCA bishops and synodical and regional staff (since ELCA framers determined multi-synodical "regions" would play a major role in the new church)? Who would make decisions whether ministries financially supported from three national offices would continue to be funded? What steps were needed for the orderly wind-down of the existing structures, dissolution of synod corporate entities etc.? What measures might be taken to build stronger inter-church relationships prior to the merger, to avoid the typical post-merger sense that "they won, and we lost"? How would we overcome some of the disparities that existed between the churches' recommended salary parameters and the differing approaches to providing pensions for retired church workers? What reassurances could be given to clergy and parishes reluctant to remain in the ELCA that their local identities would be honored by yet-to-be elected leaders?

Given the fact that the ALC had no deployed staff in Northern California, and the AELC had eliminated a position similar to mine some years before, I was the one experienced church executive available to assist the many work groups tasked with establishing a framework for what would become the Northern California/Northern Nevada Synod (later renamed Sierra Pacific). At a series of meetings over two to three years, I provided needed background information and made suggestions based upon my observation of best practices in all three merging churches. Based upon the good spirit experienced as colleagues of the ALC, AELC and LCA met together, I was optimistic for our future in the "new church." I also was realistic enough to know there would be rough spots, personality clashes, and jockeying for position as long-established organizational patterns began to be dismantled and new ways of working emerged even prior to the official beginning of the ELCA.

The need and opportunity to work together existed in our area more than almost anywhere else in the emerging ELCA by virtue of the balanced mix of congregations from the prior church bodies. Since California and Arizona were primary "mission fields" for all mainline denominations in the 1950's and 1960's, dozens of congregations had been established by all three merging churches. Thus, at the time of the merger, the Sierra Pacific Synod was constituted by 110 ALC, ninety LCA and nineteen AELC congregations. Few of the new ELCA synods had such a balance of congregations from the three predecessor bodies. Especially in the metropolitan Bay Area, in good measure due to the Coalition's existence, relationships had been developed and there was a reservoir of good will and eagerness to cooperate, all of which served us well in the transition to the ELCA and new synod. We took steps to pave the way for the emerging ELCA in the west. Beginning at least two years prior to 1988, in several call processes we recommended ALC or AELC candidates along with those of the LCA to our LCA congregations, and forged understandings with our counterparts that such arrangements would bypass the normal need for transfer to the other church's roster. In other ways we creatively cut through bureaucratic impediments and began living and leaning into the new church even as we maintained the integrity of governance and ministry oversight until December 31, 1987.

My ability and that of my colleagues on the PSW staff to "hang in there" throughout the merger process was aided by the foresight of its synod council to guarantee conclusion-of-service (severance) compensation for a period of up to six months into 1988. In other words, any of us who did not land jobs immediately in new ELCA staff positions or parish calls would continue receiving our full salaries and benefits for a period of up to six months. I think that decision, together with continuing strong signals from our bishop and the council that we were valued, and our continuing work was important for the church, enabled the synod to retain its entire staff and sustain momentum to our last day in office. Looking back on that challenging transitional era, I continue to be grateful for that synod's foresight and commitment to and care for its staff.

As the final months in the "old churches" unfolded, a question batted around in every gathering of clergy and elsewhere was, of course, "Who are going to be the new bishops in our synods, the region and throughout the new church"? Speculations abounded, suggestions were wide-ranging as to who would emerge as viable candidates, and rumors began circulating about campaigns and efforts to promote one or another likely nominee. In a few conversations, it was suggested that given my experience and proven track record in leadership, I should and likely would be among those considered as the first bishop in Northern California/Northern Nevada. As I contemplated that possibility, I could see myself serving effectively in the lead position. Based on my love for synodical ministry, I knew that I would find being either the bishop or continuing as an assistant/associate a fulfilling calling. By early 1988, however, I sensed it would be highly unlikely the bishop's election would come my way. At that juncture, unlike most sitting ALC, LCA and AELC bishops not of retirement age, who were open wherever a call as bishop might emerge, my boss, Stan Olson, declared himself restricted to the new NC/NN (Sierra Pacific Synod). In the sequence of summer synod assemblies, accordingly, Stan withdrew from elections in some of the synods that met ahead of NC/NN, where he undoubtedly would have been chosen as the first ELCA bishop.

With my seasoned, widely known and highly respected boss in the running, it was clear any chances that I would become bishop were all but eliminated. I was rather confident Stan would be elected and, given his desire for the Coalition's continuation and my effective leadership of it, thought it highly likely I would be offered a position on the new synod staff. To my surprise, and that of many other people in the synod, an ALC pastor of a large parish in Fresno, the Rev. Lyle Miller, was elected. Suddenly, my own future became uncertain to a degree I had not expected.

Personal Upheaval and Embracing God's Grace

While work with the Coalition and expanded ministry opportunities as I became regular synod staff were rewarding and fulfilling, on the home front there was major upheaval beginning in the fall of 1984 as Doris and I realized our marriage was beginning to unravel. Unlike many couples who separate and divorce, ours was never a conflict-ridden relationship; nor was either unfaithful or involved with someone outside the marriage. It was simply a case of two people who had known each other since the first grade, been high school sweethearts and married young right out of college, growing apart over the years and losing the spark that keeps a marriage mutually enlivening.

We both dearly loved our two young sons and reeled at the prospect of breaking up a family that provided them with daily interaction with both parents. Nevertheless, following several months of counseling, and an intense discernment experience at the ecumenical Center for Ministry in Oakland, we sadly decided to separate. I moved out of our Oakland home into an apartment. Since Doris had been a stay-at-home parent, and following our separation began work at a day care center where little Adam could be enrolled, she became the primary custodial parent. All of a sudden, my days waking up to young boys tugging at my sleeve or tucking them in with a story at bedtime were reduced to weekends and longer periods in summer when the boys were in my care.

In a life that now spans seven decades, this was undoubtedly the most painful and disruptive period. Others who have been through separation and divorce can identify with the sense of loss and upheaval, and with the guilt experienced especially by the non-custodial parent who often feels like s/he has abandoned one's children. Such guilt tends to be ratcheted up acutely for those of us who are clergy. While I was fortunate to serve at a time and in a denomination where clergy divorce did not mean unquestioned and automatic defrocking or dismissal, attitudes persisted that pastoral couples should model marital perfection and promises "'til death us do part" should under no circumstances be broken. I recall the pain of sharing the news with our parents and siblings, in immediate families where divorce was still a rarity at the time. Convinced that transparency in such matters is far superior to entrusting news to the rumor mill, after informing my bishop, our families and a few trusted close friends and associates, I sent a letter to all my clergy colleagues with forthright acknowledgement that my marriage was ending.

A gift of immense proportions, for which I am eternally grateful, was the support received from my boss and bishop, Stan, colleagues on the synod staff, and several close friends and clergy colleagues. Rather than judging or adding to the sense of failure, guilt, and shame I felt already, they listened, offered comfort and assurances that this disruption in my personal life would in no way impede or undermine my ministry. In the months and years after our separation, I discovered that the clergy and others entrusted into my shepherding as bishop's assistant seemed freer to confide their own struggles and personal challenges. When other pastors, friends and associates were going through divorces, I made special efforts to be available to both spouses as well as congregants and others affected. As in few other seasons of my life, those months dominated by the dissolution of my fourteen-year marriage to Doris surrounded me with the love and care of the "great cloud of witnesses," bearers of and vehicles for the enormity of the grace of God.

As time went on, Doris and I developed a workable rhythm for shared parenting and meeting our responsibilities to our wonderful boys. Within months of our separation, we were each in relationships that led rather quickly to remarriage. Doris's reconnection with and remarriage to a former junior high school boyfriend, who was a career Air Force officer in Omaha, Nebraska, faced me with the further challenge of maintaining a close relationship with Adam and Aaron at great geographical distance. I made periodic weekend trips to the Midwest, and we enjoyed portions of the summer together in the Bay area. The fact that both our sons developed into the outstanding men they are today bespeaks the success of our efforts to be the best parents possible under challenging circumstances. Both their stepparents also deserve credit for the ways they welcomed the boys into their new family arrangements and extended their love and care. Today, our shared granddaughters are each blessed with three sets of grandparents who adore them.

A Surprise New Love and a "Life Squad" Pilgrimage

One of the amazing ministries that evolved out of the turbulent 1960's was the San Francisco Night Ministry. Each night, either the full-time night minister or a volunteer clergy person is on the streets of the city offering pastoral care and counseling. The ministers roam among bars and nightclubs, especially in some of the seedier neighborhoods of the city's underside. In the fall of 1984, I served on a planning committee to celebrate the Night Ministry's 20th anniversary. When a gala banquet was held in November that year, I was to be seated with members of Oakland's Bethlehem Lutheran Church. But when it came time to be seated, there was an extra person at our table. So, I volunteered to be seated at another table with some folks from a group called the San Francisco Partnership Ministry—an urban coalition of six United Church of Christ congregations, who were deeply engaged in youth and refugee ministries. As the meal progressed, I enjoyed a lively conversation with Partnership's executive director, comparing notes on our common challenges leading multi-parish coalitions. I also was aware that Rev. Pamela White is a very attractive and enticing woman! As the evening concluded, we exchanged business cards and agreed we might meet at some point to continue conversation about our respective ministries.

A few days later I followed up and arranged lunch with Rev. White. When I showed up at her office in San Francisco's Tenderloin, she was wearing knee-high cowboy boots and jeans, a striking image for an urban pastor! During our lunch conversation, Pam mentioned she was planning a trip to El Salvador to accompany church leaders who were receiving death threats because of their prophetic ministries. I recounted my experiences under similar circumstances in Chile, and Pam perked up when she discovered I speak Spanish. Issuing an invitation to join the delegation, she definitely captured my attention. In a follow-up meeting a few days later, I confessed my attraction for her and said I thought it could get in the way on a trip to a war zone. In the following weeks I continued to ponder the invitation and my feelings for this winsome bright young woman. On Christmas Day I called her at home to report I had decided to join the delegation. She expressed delight to have me onboard with my prior experiences in South America and ability to help translate. As we both have said in recounting our love story on many occasions, "You learn a lot about a person in a war zone." Although we kept things professional during the trip, by the end of our month-long pilgrimage with three others, we had each concluded that things might progress to a serious relationship. While in El Salvador, we had to remain focused on our mission. Those who were being threatened lived in terror that they might become the next victims of that country's infamous "death squads." As it had been in Chile a decade earlier, there were bands of soldiers and civilians who roamed the streets by night snatching people out of their homes and murdering or "disappearing" them. The Lutheran Bishop, Medardo Gomez, had received such death threats and left the country for a time. A few years later we would return to El Salvador on a second visit and accompany Medardo and other Lutheran leaders for several days.

Our charges on the January 1986 trip were Baptist pastors, and our shields to protect them were simply our U.S. passports. As it had in Chile, the U.S. government was supporting the Salvadoran military. To avoid jeopardizing support among the American people for continuing aid, the Salvadoran government wanted to avoid harm to U.S. citizens. So, our constant accompaniment of those being threatened, serving as their human shields, was their best and only real protection. We accompanied our hosts on visits to many churches, non-governmental advocacy organizations, and communities that were under threat by the military and death squads. Everywhere we went, the people asked that we understand their harsh realities and tell their stories back in the U.S., to generate more support for their heroic efforts. This was during a time when media attention to the war in El Salvador was scarce and sporadic.

There were many occasions during that month-long sojourn when we found ourselves in precarious situations. Sitting in a restaurant or at an outdoor café, a vehicle with darkened windows would drive up and we feared it could be a death squad. We were told that a trip to the countryside could be deadly, if caught in the crossfire between soldiers and guerillas or swooped down on by a helicopter with its guns blazing. On one occasion I was driving in a remote area with a Salvadoran church worker who said she thought an encampment of guerillas might be just up ahead on the rocky cow-path roadway. "What will happen if they stop us"? I asked. "Well, they might just ask us questions," she replied, "or they might kill us!" To fortify protection for our hosts and ourselves, we made visits to the U.S. Embassy in San Salvador. On one of those occasions, Pam and I were granted a personal audience with the ambassador, Thomas Pickering, who would later serve as the U.S. Ambassador to the United Nations. In all those meetings with U.S. and Salvadoran high officials, we stressed that our hosts were simply carrying out their faithful Christian ministries of caring for God's people regardless of political persuasion. As our month-long sojourn progressed, we began referring to ourselves as *"el escuadron de vida"* (The Life Squad) in contrast to the Salvadoran death squads.

It was in the cauldron of those intense dynamics that Pam and I got to know each other well and found common values and commitments, despite our quite diverse backgrounds. On many occasions, this Minnesota farm boy and Boston-bred suburbanite have described ours as a cross-cultural marriage! Following a year of courtship and engagement, Pam and I were married at St. John's United Church of Christ in San Francisco on April 26, 1986. Pam's maid of honor was her close friend, the actress Carol Potter, from California, and my brother Dave served as my best man. Our other attendants were Valorie Villela, a dear friend who had been the other translator for our El Salvador delegation, and one my closest synod staff colleagues, Rev. Ev Nielsen. Aaron and Adam were present under my parents' close supervision. By the end of the evening, little Adam had turned beet red, as unbeknownst to us, he was coming down with scarlet fever. For our wedding, I wrote the following poem that sought to capture the history of our relationship and cast a vision for our shared future. We had chosen as the gospel reading the story of the Road to Emmaus, in which the resurrected Jesus appears as a stranger to two travelers who are despondent in the aftermath of his crucifixion.

THE GIFT

The gift was given, out there on the road,
Somewhere between Jerusalem and Jericho,
And somewhere between La Libertad and San Salvador.

The gift was given, in the midst of pain and sorrow,
After the death, of Calvary and Good Friday,
And the crucifixion of the displaced and disappeared.

The gift was given, not first love nor infatuation;

Love born of friendship, born of common commitments,
Love unknown, unrecognized as first we walked along.

The gift was given, at the table,
As conversations entwined themselves with sunsets,
And bread was broken by gentle, trusting hands.

The gift was given as we walked the freedom trail,
Setting each other at liberty to live and believe our own way,
Free to lift our voices in chorus and sing songs of solitude.

The gift was given on an island vineyard,
As we made promises to make promises,
Binding ourselves together in a faithful trust.

The gift is given, here in this waystation,
Wherein we bid the unseen giver God and Goddess,
Surround us with an unseen, unbounded love.

Suffice it to say that the love I have experienced with Pamela in our three-and-a-half decades of marriage thus far has been among the greatest gifts of my life. And our joy in being together took on new depth with the birth of our daughter, Macrina Amanda. More about her to follow.

Our wedding photo: April 26, 1986

— 8 —

Serving a New Church and Unity-Challenged Synod

THE SUMMER OF 1987 proved pivotal in many ways as constituting conventions of the "new ELCA synods" were held across the country. As noted in the previous chapter, I played a significant role as foundations for a new synod in Northern California and Nevada were established. At various points along the way I had the opportunity to weigh in on aspects of the constitution and bylaws, budget, governance structures, and attention to many details that would facilitate as seamless transition as possible from the "old" to "new church." And, as also mentioned, my imagined future continuing with a synod staff team headed by Stan Olson evaporated within a matter of hours as the bishop's election proceeded at the NC/NN's constituting convention in San Jose.

In hindsight, it should not have been such a surprise that an ALC pastor would be elected the new synod's first bishop, since that church body had the largest number of congregations and voting members of the assembly. But I had thought that Stan's experience and reputation as a strong leader would put him over the top and yield a ready election as the synod's first bishop. I later came to realize that it was Stan's very strength, willingness to hold clergy and congregations accountable, and outspokenness on issues of social justice that probably made him a scary candidate to those who did not also know from personal experience his generosity of spirit, compassion, and deep commitment to pastoral care for all in his "flock."

Both in the immediate aftermath of the election, and in the years since, I have felt a measure of responsibility and even guilt for having perhaps contributed to Stan's defeat. Some months prior to the constituting convention I wrote an op ed piece for our national magazine, *The Lutheran*, that was regarded by many as coming from the "radical fringe." In that brief opinion piece, I shared a vision of a fully inclusive new church that would embrace gays and lesbians, commit itself to more widespread use of inclusive language, and in other ways help our church serve a much broader portion of God's beloved people in our society. The degree to which my op ed may have contributed to Stan's loss in the election will never be known. What I am confident about is that, were he still living, Stan would smile lovingly and say, "Mike, you did the right thing; it needed to be said and you said it." It was a gift to visit Stan in the memory care unit where he lived the last months before his death, and to thank him for all he meant in my life. Probably more than any other mentor, Stan's support and encouragement were the key to opening doors that led to the rest of my career opportunities.

With the surprise (to me and many others) election of Lyle Miller as the first NC/NN bishop, my own future was suddenly much more uncertain. My new bishop did not know me, so within days of his election I sent a letter with my resume and expression of eagerness to continue serving in synodical ministry. As I look back on that letter, I am somewhat amazed at my youthful brazenness. I felt if there were any possibility of my serving as one of his assistants, ours needed to be an open and honest relationship. So, I started off the letter confirming that I had not voted for Lyle! He told me years later that the letter got his attention and gave him pause as he considered his initial staff appointments. He also revealed that many who knew me—clergy and laity from all three predecessor churches with whom I had worked in the Coalition and Transition Team—encouraged him to include me among his associates.

After sending my letter, several weeks went by with no response from Bishop-elect Miller. I understood that he too was surprised at his election and needed to wrap up his ministry at a large parish, even while being overwhelmed by all the demands of establishing a new synod. Given the uncertainty, I redoubled efforts to explore and be open to other options. At one point during those transition weeks, I was interviewed for a position as Director of Urban Ministry with the new churchwide offices that were being established in Chicago. As with Miller, the person chosen as executive director of the Division for Outreach wherein that position was lodged, James Berquist, did not know me personally. He did, however, know that I was among a small group of coalition directors around the country who formed a kind of kitchen cabinet for the LCA's urban ministry leaders. Prominent among the latter was Harvey Peters, who had been Berquist's rival for the prestigious executive position. Following my interview with Berquist, I was told by one of his associates that I was doomed from the start because in demeanor and my verbal responses I reminded Berquist too much of Peters!

Toward the end of the summer, I was finally invited to meet with Lyle Miller to discuss the possibility of my serving on his staff. Imagining a lengthy formal interview in an office setting, I was surprised when after chatting for a few moments on a bench outside a church somewhere (I can no longer recall the exact location) Lyle offered me the position. It was evident he had consulted with others and probably had his mind made up before our "interview." Since his election, I too had been checking out my new bishop with a number of folks who knew him well. Despite my continuing disappointment at Stan's defeat, I liked what I was hearing about Lyle's collegial leadership style, humility, sense of fairness, and experience as a volunteer leader in the ALC District, of which he had been vice president. So, without hesitation, when Lyle offered the position, I accepted on the spot. For the remaining months of 1987, I felt like I was riding two horses at the same time—and they weren't always moving in the same direction! There was still work to be completed in wrapping up many aspects of my work with the Pacific Southwest Synod. At the same time, the tasks of organizing the new NC/NN synod placed additional demands upon my time and energy.

As Lyle began assembling his staff team, I was the only one chosen with prior full-time synodical field staff experience. Coupled together with that was the fact the others selected were all serving congregations and had to finish out those ministries before they could transition to their new roles. As a result, it fell to me to work closely with Lyle and the new synod's other officers in developing policies for pastoral call processes, setting up an office, staffing various committees and commissions. And as always occurs in a time of transition, attention to and requests from constituents increasingly shifted from former leaders of ALC, AELC and LCA to those of us who would constitute the NC/NN staff. Once again, I was the available person with experience in dealing with congregational conflict, clergy personal crises and the like, so my plate was very full during that time of transition.

Those early years in the new NC/NN (later renamed Sierra Pacific) Synod were exciting and fulfilling. I quickly developed a warm collegial relationship with Lyle and other colleagues, especially Pastor Noreen Meginness, whom I had known for several years in the former synod. Moving into a modern building at the Oakland airport office complex found me surrounded daily by good colleagues, as opposed to the rather spartan and lonely quarters occupied by the Coalition at Bethlehem Church in West Oakland. Day to day, the work was similar to what I had been doing for several years with the Coalition and Pacific Southwest Synod. I worked closely with parishes in pastoral transition, call processes, and conflict mediation; visited active and retired clergy; staffed committees, particularly in areas related to urban and social ministry. In virtually all those circles, I found that my experience was valued, and the work was fulfilling.

A surprise development about midway in my years with Lyle and the new synod was being asked to move into increasing areas of administration. Discovering that I was adept at and enjoyed planning, coordinating various work groups, responding to correspondence and supervising others, Lyle moved me into a role that might best be described as chief of staff. I prepared staff agenda meetings, coordinated the work of the whole staff, led a synod-wide strategic planning process, consulted with synod council leaders and conference deans, and in other ways played an ever-growing role in overall synod leadership. Among my staff colleagues I was known affectionately as "Memo Mikey" for the volume of memoranda I circulated to keep administrative process and synodical programs flowing smoothly. (Those were, of course, the days before email and other electronic means of broadcasting paperless messages!)

A Third Job for a Season

Another surprise development a couple of years into the new synod came when I was asked to serve as Interim Director of the large Northern California Ecumenical Council (NCEC). This decades-old organization, made up of most of the Protestant denominations in Northern California, found itself in a time of financial crisis following the resignation of its long-time executive director. I had served on the NCEC board for several years and became its chair shortly before the crisis came to light. When the executive resigned, some of the other board members asked if I would step in temporarily to manage the organization. Along with other denominational executives, Lyle Miller had his misgivings about NCEC's future. In addition to its management issues, NCEC's focus on social justice made it controversial in some circles, so those leaders felt a fresh start might be wise. Nevertheless, Lyle did not resist my taking on the interim directorship. So, at least one day a week I worked in the San Francisco office and helped carve a pathway forward for the agency, which sadly required staff layoffs and other drastic measures.

In one of those surprising synchronicities, it so happened that a few years before I assumed the helm of NCEC, it had taken under its umbrella some of the programs formerly housed with San Francisco Partnership Ministry, the organization Pam headed when we met. My understanding of the crucial nature of those programs fortified my efforts to help save NCEC. After a period of several months, things had stabilized and NCEC was able to call a part-time executive leader. It lived on for several years, and the efforts to replace it with a new entity never gained traction. During those months when I was serving simultaneously with the synod, Coalition and NCEC, I would quip on occasion, "Since I have three offices, I never actually do any work at all; they just think I'm at one of the other offices!" My service with NCEC expanded my skill set and deepened my commitment to ecumenical partnerships.

Closing Out the Coalition

As the new synod gained momentum and its subunits (called conferences) became effective in supporting parishes and other ministries, some began questioning the need for the Coalition's continuing existence. It became increasingly difficult to bridge the parishes of the East Bay with San Francisco. Frustratingly, the new ELCA Division for Outreach headed by Berquist and his team not only questioned, but overtly worked to dismantle coalitions by withdrawing funding, eliminating national cohort gatherings, and other measures. Thus, following a year-long process of internal discernment, the decision was made to dissolve the Coalition a dozen years after its official founding. Once again point person for a major transition, I oversaw an orderly closure, preserving key historical documents in archives, and handing off Coalition functions to other synodical entities. And we held a final benedictory celebration and entrusted to history the Coalition I had led throughout its existence. My final report reflecting on all that had been accomplished stated:

> As we gather, I find myself flooded with memories, hopes and concerns. When I came to the Bay Area over a decade ago as the Coalition's first director, I accepted a two-year term call. I fully expected to stay no more than four or five years and then return to parish ministry. As way has led on to way, to paraphrase Robert Frost, the years have come and gone, and the Coalition has gone through many changes and transitions.
>
> There is a certain sense of satisfaction that while the Coalition has not revolutionized Lutheran urban ministry in the Bay Area, we have made some significant contributions. Countless are the joys I have personally experienced throughout the past decade: the hundreds of conversations and consultations where we have struggled together to be faithful in our mission; dozens of call processes where I have sought to assist urban congregations in finding appropriate leadership; the great privilege of preaching and leading worship in virtually every congregation.

In early 1992 I received a letter from the Rev. Thomas Anderson, who had been the Coalition's board chair early in its existence. Anderson wrote of the Coalition that "its passing deserves more than a mere footnote." He went on to reflect on the organization's legacy and my leadership:

> Under your leadership that coalition did so many favorable actions to foster communication and healing between the Bays [San Francisco and the East Bay, which had little to do with each other before the Coalition was formed] and give solidarity and purpose to the Lutheran witness.
>
> You more than anyone remember the difficult task it was to bring order, much less cooperation, to the disparate parishes, some of whom had never spoken to each other. I hope you find a moment to congratulate yourself for that work and to recall with some acceptable pride what a Himalayan effort it was.
>
> Maybe the crowning glory, though, is to simply say—it was done! It happened! Then to pause a moment in celebration that there was for a long moment in the late 70's and 80's, a time when Lutheran congregations stood together as one. Since you were the key ingredient to its success, I am passing along these words with gratitude.

An Ongoing Crisis and Struggle of Conscience

The ELCA and new NC/NN synod were barely out of the starting gate before we were thrust into a whirlwind that would claim so much of my time and energy over the following two decades. Early in 1988, three seminarians at Pacific Lutheran Theological Seminary (PLTS) in Berkeley came out as gay and announced that they would refuse to remain in compliance with expectations that they refrain from sexual intimacy. While the fledgling ELCA had not developed a definitive stance regarding clergy sexual behavior, the firestorm that spread throughout the church caused a hasty adoption of policies that precluded ordaining the Berkeley Three and other gay and lesbian persons who would not commit to sexual abstinence. All throughout the ELCA congregations and clergy were up in arms, with many threatening to leave the church or withdraw financial support if the new policy were not strictly enforced.

Since PLTS was in our synod's territory, just a few miles from the synod office, and the most well-known of the three seminarians, Jeff Johnson, was a candidate of our synod, we were at the epicenter of the crisis from the outset. Shortly after the public coming out of the three seminarians, Lyle Miller summoned Jeff to our office, and the bishop asked that I join him as he informed Jeff he could not be ordained given his current status. That was one of the most anguished times of my ministry, since I felt the policy was wrong and Jeff was being treated unjustly. At the same time, I understood Lyle was doing what he felt was a bishop's responsibility to enforce the church's policy. Given his understanding of scripture and the church's historic perspectives on homosexuality, Lyle did not disagree with the policy. As happened with many open-minded people willing to listen to the compelling stories of members of the LGBTQI community, Lyle's personal views changed in later years.

As word spread of the decision regarding Jeff Johnson and his two fellow seminarians, a tsunami of anger was directed at church officials, especially the bishop and me. Given my very public declarations and leadership within the Coalition, which had strongly affirmed ministries among gays and lesbians, many were especially upset with and felt betrayed by me. I was accused of being a weak-kneed hypocrite unable to stand up to my boss. Some called for my resignation. Internally I was deeply torn. I loved my work with the synod and felt I was making strong contributions in many arenas. At the same time, I worried that the angry response over the sexuality issues would weaken my ability to provide leadership.

More importantly, I simply felt the church had made the wrong decision through a rushed process to placate homophobic and hostile elements. Over the course of several weeks, I wavered back and forth. I had a letter of resignation composed in my mind and discussed with Pam whether to put it on paper and submit it. I also discussed my anguished internal debate with the ELCA Presiding Bishop Herbert Chilstrom when he made a pastoral visit to the PSW Synod in the throes of the conflict. Little could I imagine at that time that a few years later I would join Herb's staff as his assistant for synodical relations. While Herb's personal views favored lifting the church's ban, as would come to light more clearly in his later years in office,[1] like Lyle he felt he had to uphold the church's policy. He counseled me that if I could not support my bishop, I should resign. In the end, I decided not to resign but to remain in my position, from which I believed I could exert influence and contribute to a growing movement that would eventually result in change. Regrettably, it would take twenty years for that change to happen, and thousands of LGBTQ persons continued to be harmed by the ELCA's discriminatory stance.

In the PSW Synod, the crisis deepened when two San Francisco congregations declared their intent to call Johnson and two lesbian pastoral candidates, Ruth Frost and Phyllis Zillhart, who also refused to declare their commitment to celibacy. In a series of meetings with leaders of both parishes, Lyle and I tried to avert what we knew would generate new waves of anger throughout the church and provoke a constitutional crisis. ELCA congregations can call as pastors only those already on or approved for the clergy roster. Since the candidates were not so approved, the calls would be invalid from the wider church's perspective, and the congregations would place themselves in open defiance of a central criterion for recognition as an ELCA congregation. In one of the meetings, Lyle and I encouraged pursuing another pathway that would enable the two churches to achieve their objective of outreach into San Francisco's large LGBTQ community. "Why don't you form a separate corporate

---

1. During his last year in office, Chilstrom circulated a memorandum to the three of us who were his assistants in which he sought our counsel as to whether he should issue a bold public call for changing the church's stance regarding ordination of partnered or married gays and lesbians. While he concluded such a "parting shot" might be counterproductive, in his retirement years he seized many occasions to publicly say he felt he had been wrong in upholding the policy while in office. After the church's policy finally changed in 2009, at a service welcoming to the ELCA clergy roster pastors who had been excluded by the unjust policy, Herb read a "litany of confession" lamenting the harm caused by the unjust policy.

entity to employ and call these three"? I suggested. "As long as it's not an ELCA congregation, no one would be defying church policy," I explained. Lyle chimed in to say that if that pathway were followed the synod would help fund the ministry. While a separate ministry, the Lutheran Lesbian and Gay Ministry (LLGM), was formed, the congregations insisted on issuing the calls by way of challenging the unjust policy. In a grand ordination service with more than 1,000 in attendance at St. Paulus Lutheran Church in San Francisco, Jeff, Ruth, and Phyllis were ordained on January 20, 1990. Sympathetic to what was occurring, I fervently wanted to be in attendance on that historic occasion. But I felt that in so doing I would undermine the legitimacy of the bishop's and synod's authority. So, instead, I joined a friend in his sailboat on San Francisco Bay on that balmy afternoon, from which I could see the spire of St. Paulus and be in prayerful communion with those inside. It was one of the most anguished days of my ministerial career.

Despite my strong counsel that he take a hands-off stance, Lyle felt he had to bring charges for the congregations' disregard of the church's governing documents. As the disciplinary trial unfolded, I quietly offered my counsel to the discipline committee's chair. On a sunny afternoon she came to our home in Oakland, and we sat on the deck discussing options. I affirmed the discipline panel's inclination to censure but not expel the congregations, giving them a five-year period to come into conformity with the church's policies. Many on the discipline panel shared my hope that within that period the ELCA would change its stance and thereby avoid losing the two urban parishes. While that did not occur, in 2009 the ELCA changed policy to allow openly LGBTQ persons to serve as clergy. The congregations were reinstated, as were the three whose ordinations were originally deemed "irregular." In mid-2023, Jeff Johnson was elected bishop of the Sierra Pacific Synod, which 35 years before had refused to ordain him.

Amidst those high tensions that marked the entirety of my ministry with the new ELCA synod, I strove to maintain positive relationships with those who at some points were sharply critical of me. While a few found it difficult to continue working together, most remained gracious and collegial despite their disappointment in my not publicly disavowing Lyle's responses. In 1992, I worked closely with First United Lutheran in San Francisco as the congregation was experiencing some internal conflict and financial challenges. Rev. James DeLange, lead pastor at St.

Francis, which had joined First United in the unauthorized ordinations, later wrote:

> Having been part of the sometimes-painful process at First United these past two years, I want to commend you and Lyle for the patience, understanding, and care you gave to this congregation during this time—especially you, Mike, as you were in the forefront.
>
> Given the history of conflict with the synod, it would have been expected by some that you would have taken the opportunity to strike back at First United for their action. Instead, you recognized this situation for its reality, offered a process for healing and financial assistance when they needed it.

My Wonderful Fortieth Birthday Gift: Macrina Amanda!

While all these events were unfolding for me professionally, Pam was also engaged in challenging work. After her years singing opera, she was executive director of a large domestic violence and battered women's service agency in Mountain View, across the Bay from Oakland. By 1990, she was serving as Director of the Center for Women and Religion at the Graduate Theological Union (GTU) in Berkeley. In addition, she was affiliated part-time with St. Paul's Episcopal Church in Oakland as an associate priest. We were ecstatic when she became pregnant, and eagerly awaited the birth of our daughter. With a due date around my August 30 birthday, Pam had accepted a regular preaching assignment for Sunday, August 5. We were surprised late afternoon on Saturday when she went into labor. After arriving at Alta Bates Hospital in Berkeley, I called St. Paul's rector, Rev. Donald Seaton, and alerted him "Don," I said, "Pam won't be showing up at church in the morning." Ironically, her sermon title, printed in the bulletin, was "God's Time is Not Our Time." That was so true for us that day!

Mid-morning on that delightful Sunday morning (easy for me to describe it that way; things were more challenging for Pam!), Macrina came into the world. We had become intrigued with the unusual name when Pam met an Episcopal priest so named. Discovering Saint Macrina was a fourth century Christian held in high esteem, including by her more famous brothers (in that era, due recognition for women's leadership was even less forthcoming than now), we decided to give it to our daughter.

We also liked Amanda, and before the birth, had been undecided on the order of names, whether Macrina would be the first or middle name. The moment we saw her face we both agreed, "She's Macrina." Like her brothers, she has been an absolute joy throughout the years. Given that my birthday falls later in August, I've always thought of her as the best fortieth birthday gift a dad could ever receive.

A few months later, when Macrina was to be baptized at St. Paul's on November 25, Pam and I were both invited to write some reflections about the meaning of baptism for the parish newsletter. I concluded my brief article, "Baptism: Her Daddy's View":

> As you are baptized, Macrina Amanda Cooper-White, welcome to the community of those who have been washed with the waters of eternal comfort. To you whose very name means "blessed," may the Spirit which brooded over the waters at creation bless you at the moment of your baptism and each day of your life!

Time for a Big Move

Despite the enduring tensions around the issues related to sexuality, I continued to love my work with the synod. Serving in the incredibly diverse and magnificent territory of Northern California was a rare privilege afforded to only a few. At national gatherings of peers, I would say, "Yes, I'm the guy who is forced to go to places like the Monterey Bay, Napa Valley, the Mendocino coastline, and other dismal spots!" I never wearied of consulting with congregations and felt my skills in that area continued to grow over the years. Likewise, I enjoyed offering support to clergy and other church workers, encouraging seminarians, and handling an ever-expanding portfolio of administrative work that stretched my leadership abilities. We had a good team in the synod office and hit our stride after the first couple of years in the start-up phase. Those of us based in Oakland would often break away on a midweek afternoon for an Oakland A's game at the Coliseum right across the freeway from our office. Occasional fellowship gatherings in one of our homes knit us together as a cohesive group for the most part.

In the ELCA's early years, bishops were elected to four-year terms. Discovering how quickly time goes, after studying the experiences in other churches with frequent leadership turnover, by the mid-1990's the constitution was changed to afford bishops terms of six-years. But in 1991, Lyle had to stand for reelection at the spring synod assembly. Since ELCA synods elect by means of an "ecclesiastical ballot" where voting members can nominate any pastor, there was not absolute certainty he would be reelected, especially given the ongoing tensions over the sexuality issues. Indeed, a number of other pastors, including me, received votes on the nominating ballot. But after a few more ballots, Lyle was reelected, after which he assured all of us on the staff that we could count on continuing in our positions.

By the early 1990's, there was also a growing trend in the ELCA and other churches to encourage sabbaticals for church leaders. This came in recognition that the stresses of ministry take their toll, and "burn-out" is widespread among clergy in all denominations. As the synod staff in what I sometimes described as the ELCA's most "unity-challenged synod," our stress levels ran particularly high those early years after the new synod's formation. We felt sabbaticals would help us sustain healthy long-term service, and also would model their value for parish clergy and others in high-stress vocations. A plan was developed whereby the bishop would be the first to have a three-month sabbatical. As the longest-serving associate, mine would follow in short order.

During Lyle's sabbatical, my role expanded as the person coordinating the staff's work. I convened staff meetings and in other ways functioned as point person during the bishop's absence. The three months went quickly, and we were eager to hear Lyle's report on his sabbatical as he rejoined us after his time away. After sharing a bit about the travels and experiences he had enjoyed, Lyle looked around the table and said that he had one key revelation during his time away. "I'm really called to be a parish pastor," he declared. Taken aback, all of us on the staff realized that the job security we felt following his reelection had just gone out the window. Within a few months, Lyle received a parish call in the state of Washington and the synod prepared to elect a new bishop. Given there were no guarantees a new bishop would retain us, each of us associates began to consider our own futures. While I felt as I had in the late 1980's that my experience likely would be recognized and valued by a new bishop, leading to reappointment, there were no guarantees to that effect. Also, as had occurred in the late 1980's, I began to receive signals that some in the synod saw me as one who should be considered a candidate for bishop. But I assessed the chances of being elected bishop very small. In short, Lyle's announcement pried me loose to be open to other possibilities.

Soon an intriguing possibility presented itself. A little-known but significant role at the churchwide office in Chicago was the position as Director of Synodical Relations. The director is an assistant to the presiding bishop and chief staff person for the ELCA Conference of Bishops. In the fall of 1993, that position had become vacant suddenly when the incumbent, a former bishop, resigned after being accused of past sexual misconduct. After reviewing the position posting and being strongly encouraged by Lyle to be open to it, I submitted my application, and was invited for an interview just before Thanksgiving. I flew to Chicago where I was interviewed at "headquarters" by Presiding Bishop Herb Chilstrom together with the chair and vice chair of the Conference of Bishops, Kenneth Sauer and Charles Maahs.

Midway through my interview I was asked, "Is there anything that would prevent you from accepting this position should it be offered"? Given what had occurred with the last incumbent, I sensed there was more to the question than just inquiring how serious candidates were about the job. Trying to lighten the mood, I at first responded, "Well, I've been living for years in California and don't have a winter coat!" But then I went on to assure the bishops that I had no skeletons in my closet and there was nothing in my background that would cause another embarrassing situation for the church. To my first response, Herb Chilstrom quipped in return, "Well, I still have my old college coat in the closet and could hand it over." I thought to myself, "The presiding bishop just offered me his coat, so I think this interview may be going rather well!" Two days later, Bishop Chilstrom called me at home and offered the position, to begin in early January 1994.

Following the public announcement of my appointment, I was surprised to receive dozens of letters of congratulations from bishops all around the ELCA. The gracious notes from many I had not even met foretold of a Conference of Bishops community I would experience as among the most supportive collegial groups of my entire career. Also much appreciated were notes of thanks from a number of pastors and other leaders with whom I had long-standing relationships in the synod. Most significant of those was the hand-written note from Stan Olson, in which he said, "I rejoice in this move—good for you and good for the life of the ELCA bishops! Blessings as you go into a transition that is long overdue and made to order. You have guided our old PSW and the new Sierra Pacific Synod. You have the experience and the gifts that will be taxed and put to full use. Way to go!"

My last few weeks with the Sierra Pacific synod were bittersweet. It was hard saying goodbye to a place and people among whom I had lived and worked for thirteen years. At the same time, I was excited about the new challenges in Chicago. Pam and I decided she would remain in Oakland until summer when she could wrap up her work as Director of the Center for Women and Religion of the Graduate Theological Union. We knew it would be a challenge for her to have our very active three-year-old daughter on her own for those months but felt it would also enable an orderly sale of our house and reasonable notice on Pam's part to support a strong transition in her organization. We were grateful when our closest neighbors, a lesbian couple who lived next door in a rented home, expressed interest in buying ours, and we arranged a mutually beneficial transition that did not require a realtor and enabled Pam and Macrina to stay in the home until July.

On January 16, 1994, I boarded a flight to Chicago. The temperature in Oakland was in the mid-60's; upon landing at O'Hare in Chicago, the pilot announced that with the wind chill factor it was 60 below zero. I asked myself, "Mike, are you sure this was a good decision?!" It would prove to be so indeed. A new and challenging chapter, that would unfold in surprising ways, was about to begin.

— 9 —

The Chicago Years: Living in the Whole Church

DURING THE FINAL MONTHS of Herbert Chilstrom's time in office as presiding bishop, we held an appreciation lunch for several dozen people from the greater Chicago area who volunteered at the ELCA churchwide offices. Going around the table for self-introductions, one of the volunteers said he lived in a Chicago suburb. Herb got a puzzled look on his face and said, "I'm sorry but I don't know where that is; in my years in this job, you see, I've lived mostly in the whole world rather than the Chicago area." The bishop was saying that his responsibilities involved a great deal of international travel in addition to constantly roaming throughout the U.S. and Caribbean, which comprised the territory of the Evangelical Lutheran Church in America.

By the time I concluded my seven years in churchwide ministry, it occurred to me that I had experienced the privilege of living in the whole church in ways experienced by only a small circle of people. While my travels did not take me overseas, as was the case for the presiding bishop and executives of the Global Mission division, I was frequently taking the short shuttle ride from the churchwide offices to O'Hare airport for travel throughout the country. As the ELCA's director of the Department for Synodical Relations and an assistant to the presiding bishop, I was responsible for tending the relationships between synods and the churchwide "expression."[1] A major part of the job involved serving as chief staff person for the Conference of Bishops, made up of the sixty-five synodical bishops, the presiding bishop, and the ELCA corporate secretary. In my role, I worked closely with the church's officers and Conference chair in planning semi-annual week-long bishops' meetings, as well as an annual Bishops' Academy continuing education event. I served as staff to a half-dozen committees through which the Conference did much of its work, generated reports to the Church Council (ELCA Board of Directors), and was the bishops' chief liaison to churchwide executives and a host of committees, task forces, and other groups.

My office also included the Bishop's Assistant for Federal Chaplaincies, who related to hundreds of military and other federal chaplains throughout the world, and the nine regional coordinators deployed throughout the ELCA to strengthen partnerships among and deliver various services to the sixty-five synods. As the years went by, I also had the privilege of working closely with an expanding circle of ecumenical counterparts in other churches as the ELCA forged agreements of "full communion"[2] with the Episcopal, Presbyterian, United Church of Christ and Reformed Churches. We were also expanding our relationship with the Evangelical Lutheran Church in Canada. I found this demanding role to require all the experience and skills I had acquired during my first two decades of ministry, and then some! I also absolutely loved the work with all its diversity and never-ending set of new opportunities to expand my influence and impact in multiple arenas.

I had accepted the position in 1994 knowing it was closely tied to the incumbent presiding bishop, and that Herb Chilstrom would be retiring in late 1995. While there were assurances of likely continuation under a new bishop, there were no absolute guarantees, so I experienced a measure of concern as the ELCA prepared to elect Chilstrom's successor in August of 1995. To my delight, George Anderson (who had on several previous occasions refused to stand for election) allowed his name to move forward and was elected as the second presiding bishop. I had first met Anderson during my senior year in seminary when he was

---

1. In the ELCA's polity, as set forth in the constitution, there are three "expressions" of the one church—congregations, synods, and the churchwide organization. Among other reasons for the nomenclature is to avoid the commonly used description of "levels," which implies hierarchy. ELCA principles of organization insist the three expressions are "inter-dependent."

2. The meaning of "full communion" is explained later in this chapter.

the speaker at a stewardship seminar where I represented Gettysburg. And he had spoken at a gathering of bishop's assistants we held early in my tenure in Chicago, where I got to know him a bit better. Shortly after Anderson's election, he interviewed each of us who were serving in the bishop's office. While I don't recall many details, I was impressed that George seemed genuinely interested in my advice about how he should relate to the Conference of Bishops. He said something along the lines of, "In your position you know the whole church better than anyone else, and I'll rely heavily upon your wisdom." And he did not waste time in assuring me of continuation into his administration.

A happy surprise that became evident as soon as Bishop Anderson took office was that he would include me in the inner circle of leadership to a degree I had not enjoyed with Chilstrom. I began regularly attending what we called the "OB Five" meetings, which included the bishop, executive for administration, director of communication, bishop's executive assistant, and me. That was the group that coordinated the work of all 600-plus churchwide staff, set agendas for the Church Council and Conference of Bishops, Churchwide Assemblies, and in all other ways fulfilled the leadership responsibilities entrusted to the Office of the Presiding Bishop. I also served with two others on the Crisis Team responsible for generating communications and managing all aspects of crisis situations, which in a church of five million people and 10,000 congregations, happened with some regularity.

During the first six months of his tenure, Anderson searched for a second executive assistant whose responsibilities included responding to the heavy load of correspondence arriving daily and relating to several of the churchwide divisions. While most of the candidates considered for the position had many of the gifts George was seeking, none seemed to meet all his expectations, and the position remained vacant. Walking back to my office one day after a meeting down the hall, George stopped me and said simply, "Mike, I'd like you to become my other executive assistant and also keep your job as director of the Department for Synodical Relations (DSR)." I was stunned, both at his confidence in me and the staggering workload that saying yes would thrust upon me. In subsequent conversations, the bishop promised that I could expand the DSR staff to help with its work, and if the combined job proved too burdensome, we would reevaluate after a few months.

As executive assistant, I responded to probably about ninety percent of the correspondence received by the presiding bishop, both letters and email traffic that was rapidly increasing in that era. I dictated responses that were transcribed and reviewed by the bishop, who rarely made any changes in my drafts. After a few months in that aspect of the work, George said to me one day, "Mike, you think my thoughts before I think them myself!" As time went on, I also drafted the bulk of the bishop's reports to the Conference of Bishops, Church Council, and major portions of his written reports to the Churchwide Assembly. Serving in that capacity as George's primary "ghost writer" developed a unique partnership between us that we have both acknowledged at every reunion in the years since we concluded our work in Chicago. I was also ghost writer for the Conference of Bishops chair's reports to the Church Council and other groups. Given what was often only a twenty-four-hour deadline after a meeting concluded to feed that report into the council's agenda, I would typically write the report ahead of a meeting! After a few years, I could anticipate the bishops' actions on a broad variety of issues with about a 95% accuracy. So, within hours of a meeting's conclusions, I could make any final adjustments and submit the report well ahead of the deadline.

As the years went by and I gained experience and credibility, leaders of the Conference of Bishops increasingly turned to me to carry out a variety of assignments. When, for example, the Conference decided it should issue a pastoral letter to the church as we approached the turn of the new millennium, I was the initial drafter of that document. On a growing number of occasions, when committees or the full conference would decide "Let's do it" and then ask, "Who will do it"? I found eyes shift in my direction.

Full Inclusion Kept Calling Our Names

As noted in the previous chapter, a big surprise during my years of synodical ministry was the degree to which they would be dominated by matters related to human sexuality. If I had any illusions those struggles would be left behind in California, they evaporated immediately upon moving into my Chicago office. When I became the DSR director in 1994, every meeting of the Conference of Bishops included extended discussions of matters related to homosexuality and ministry. By that time, a handful of bishops were beginning to go public with the fact they felt it was time to loosen the church's restrictive stance that precluded from ordained service gay and lesbian candidates who would not commit to lifelong celibacy. But by and large, the Conference adhered to the stance articulated in a document called "Visions and Expectations," which created great anxiety among many seminarians and closeted ministers of our denomination. As I got to know them, and grew close to a growing number of bishops, I learned that quite a few felt our policy was unjust, inhibiting the church's outreach to gays and lesbians, and depriving us of the gifts brought to ministry by many faithful and committed persons. In quiet one-on-one conversations, I encouraged bishops to become more vocal in urging change.

As the Bay Area had been the flashpoint for these issues previously, so it became again when Bob Matthias had succeeded Lyle Miller as bishop. St. Paul's church in Oakland, where I had been a member before moving to Chicago, was served by my friend Ross Merkel. I recall vividly how Ross, whom I had recommended for the call to St. Paul's, had responded during a meet-and-greet evening with the congregation. When a member blurted out the inappropriate question of why he wasn't married, Ross responded, "I just haven't found the right person yet." At that point, he did not reveal that for him the right person would have to be male. After serving St. Paul's for several years, Ross felt that his personal integrity required him to publicly come out to the congregation, which he did in a sermon. In the aftermath of that revelation, there simply was no question that St. Paul's would keep their beloved pastor and thereby follow suit with congregations that had been disciplined for their noncompliance with ELCA policy.

In a conversation with Bishop Matthias, I encouraged him to consider options other than bringing down the hammer of church discipline. I advised, "Bob, while the constitution says you should bring charges against St. Paul's, it doesn't say when you have to do so. I think the synod and perhaps most of the church can just live with this for an extended period. You could also just say the synod regards St. Paul's as without a duly called pastor but not bring any discipline charges." Matthias followed the course I advised and decided to let things rest and avoid another high-profile disciplinary case.

Another watershed moment in the church's journey on the road to full inclusion came during a Conference of Bishops meeting. Preparing for that meeting, I drafted a one-page document, which offered five positions that I thought reflected where the various bishops stood on the matter of ordaining openly gay and lesbian persons. They ranged from viewing homosexual orientation as a sinful abomination, to expecting gays and lesbians to remain celibate, to fully embracing homosexuality as but one more dimension of God's good creation of humankind. During the meeting, bishops were asked to get out of their chairs and stand at one of the five places along the spectrum. As I recall the moment, there were visceral reactions when the bishops and staff present saw the degree of openness expressed by a majority. That simple exercise opened the floodgates, as more and more bishops felt free to join the growing ranks of pastors and laity calling for change in the church's position. My own position of openness and advocacy for inclusion was increasingly known widely, and I was regarded by many as heretical or at least misguided and menacing to the gospel. By the time I left Chicago in 2000, there were many hopeful signs that the church would change and allow partnered gay and lesbian clergy. An increasing number of synods were adopting resolutions calling for such change, and the vote margins were growing in many places. It would take another nine years until that step would finally occur, but when the 2009 ELCA Churchwide Assembly made its historic decision, I felt a measure of satisfaction in having made at least some small contributions in the movement for full inclusion.

Ecumenical Unions Challenged ELCA Unity

While not carrying the same emotional freight that sexuality did for so many, issues related to our emerging ecumenical partnerships also demanded far more of my time and energy than I could have imagined upon moving to Chicago. In the early 1990's, following decades of ecumenical dialogues in multiple directions, the ELCA found ourselves at the forefront of church-to-church relations. There was not much energy for inter-denominational mergers, but growing numbers in several church bodies desired something more than episodic warm occasions of good fellowship. The paradigm of full communion emerged as a goal for churches that aspired to encourage a boundary-less free flow of members and even clergy who would be regarded as at least in-laws if not full members of more than one denominational family. Full communion means that members are fully welcomed, including at the Lord's table, in each other's churches, and that under special arrangements clergy of one denomination can serve in congregations and other ministries of a partner body.

Beyond my theological conviction that God's Church is ultimately one body, and my growing frustrations at continuing divisions within the Body of Christ, full communion is a deeply personal matter. Pamela is an Episcopal priest, so the prospect of the ELCA and Episcopal Church in the USA (ECUSA) taking this step was especially important to us "Lutherpalians," as we sometimes referred to the Cooper-White family. Of all the full communion agreements, however, the Episcopal/ELCA one proved the most troublesome for many in the ELCA. Their objections hinged primarily on the role and status of bishops. By virtue of my being the ELCA bishops' chief staff person and executive assistant to the presiding bishop, I was right in the heart of another heated controversy. My office in Chicago shared a wall with the director of Ecumenical Affairs, symbolic of how close I was to the center of action in these matters.

From 1996 when I became George Anderson's executive assistant until I left Chicago, I responded to hundreds of letters from ELCA members opposed to full communion with Episcopalians. For most, the stumbling block was the Episcopal understanding that bishops belong to a line of succession known as "the historic episcopate." To sum up a somewhat complex theological and ecclesiastical stance, Episcopalians, like Roman Catholics and Orthodox Christians (as well as some other Lutheran churches around the world), believe that ministerial authority and legitimacy is transmitted to the ordained by virtue of the laying on of hands by bishops who have in turn been ordained by other bishops who can trace their roots all the way back to the first apostles. As a matter essential to the Episcopal Church, therefore, the ELCA had to commit to involving ECUSA bishops in ELCA bishops' installations. And the ELCA had to pledge that all future pastoral ordinations would be conducted by bishops, discontinuing occasional cases where a bishop was not present. (In my synod staff days, for example, I conducted two ordinations when candidates wished the service to be held at a time when the bishop was unavailable.)

Particularly in the upper Midwest, many Lutherans were not about to accede to these stipulations. Since I grew up among "low church" Lutherans of Scandinavian descent, I fully understood the reluctance and even visceral opposition. Neither the LCA nor ALC had "bishops" until the late 1970's when we decided to call district or synod presidents by that title. The notion that bishops would wear special garb not used by all clergy—purple shirts, special copes, pectoral crosses, and even mitres or pointy hats like those worn by Roman Catholic bishops—was alien to a broad sweep of Lutheranism in the USA.

Personally, given my understanding of the arc of Lutheran theology since the time of the Reformation, I continue to believe that how the church organizes itself and determines to deploy its public ministers is a matter of *adiaphora*—i.e., non-essentials that can be debated and settled differently in diverse contexts. That this is the case is testified to by the fact the ELCA considers itself to be in full communion with all member churches of the Lutheran World Federation, some of which do not even have bishops but continue to be led by persons bearing the title of president.

In my responses to those who objected strenuously to ELCA/ECUSA full communion, I emphasized that in the mid-1990's we were striving simultaneously for full communion with three churches of the Reformed tradition—the Presbyterian Church in the USA, United Church of Christ, and the Reformed Church in America. I pointed out that those churches, like some other Lutheran bodies around the world, do not have bishops at all. Therefore, I argued, while we were willing to accede to Episcopal demands on the one hand, we were clearly signaling simultaneously that ELCA Lutherans do not regard bishops as essential. The degree to which that argument was convincing is impossible for me to gauge, but I can only hope that I played some small role in a historic movement. While their implementation and impact have been slower and lesser than I imagined, I believe our full communion agreements have been beneficial and an inspiration to many.

As is the case with most prolonged and complex processes, I conclude this brief description of my involvement in forging the full communion agreements saying, "There's more to the story." Included in the following chapter will be the story of how a meeting in Milwaukee amidst a January blizzard complicated my life at a critical juncture.

North Carolina: A Case Study in Ministry Amidst Crisis

In my seminary teaching in the areas of church administration, communication, and conflict management, I have used a wide range of case studies. One can wax eloquent with theoretical constructs and ideological convictions, but if you can't apply them to real life situations, what's the point? Given that conviction, I'll describe my role in one major crisis as another window into the scope and nature of my churchwide ministry chapter.

In the spring of 1996, my colleague in the Office of the Presiding Bishop, Lita Brusick Johnson, called me into her office one day and said, "Mike, we have a crisis with a bishop in one of our synods." She wanted me to have a heads-up and think with her and Bishop Anderson about how we might offer support to this synod that we expected to be in crisis in short order. It had come to light that the bishop of the North Carolina Synod had acknowledged past sexual misconduct with an adult woman. His victim was willing to go public, if necessary, to challenge the bishop's continuing in office. The bishop confessed to his misdeeds and agreed to resign, which he did just a couple of days before the synod's annual assembly. As the crisis was about to unfold, it was decided that I would be the churchwide official to make a hasty trip to North Carolina and assume the role of crisis manager in what inevitably would be a high profile and very public scandalous news story.

Arriving in Salisbury on a late afternoon, I hurriedly huddled with the synod's lay vice president and members of the bishop's staff to offer support and make plans for communication and conduct of the synod assembly. We had planned that Bishop Anderson would fly in for the assembly and preside. Since ordinations were scheduled, and only a synodical bishop can ordain, the presiding bishop would be designated as the synod's interim bishop for the period of the assembly only. We also identified a retired bishop from South Dakota who agreed to step in for an indefinite period of transitional leadership.

A letter was prepared to go out to all the ministers and congregations, and we anticipated having about twenty-four hours before public media would pick up the news. Within hours of its being dropped at the post office, reports began appearing on radio and television news! There had been a leak, so I hurriedly drafted some notes I would use in making the church's official response to the flurry of media inquiries coming into the synod office. I also met with the resigning bishop to offer some pastoral presence to a person in crisis, albeit of his own making. And I verified with synod officials that pastoral care was being provided for the victim. As all this was breaking hour by hour, we had to make plans for hosting an assembly of almost 1000 people who would be in shock at the news about their much-loved bishop. The staff and synod officers contacted a network of counselors who would be present during much of the assembly to lead small group conversations and be available to distraught individuals.

Throughout the two days before the assembly, I was in frequent touch with Bishop Anderson and my friend, Eric Shafer, the ELCA's Director of Communication, to coordinate our response. I had also been briefed by ELCA General Counsel Phil Harris, who was always a wise "counselor" in the best sense of the word. Our primary focus was pastoral care for all concerned, most of all the one who had been deeply harmed by the North Carolina bishop's failure to maintain appropriate professional boundaries.

This situation was among the most demanding I faced while in the presiding bishop's office and my role at DSR. Many referred to our work with the synod as a "textbook case" in crisis intervention and communication best practices. A few weeks after the North Carolina Synod assembly, a letter came from its vice president, Faith A. Ashton. She wrote:

> On behalf of the entire synod, I want to say a gigantic THANK YOU!!!! Your unassuming manner, your knowledge and your sensitivity were invaluable. On a more personal note, a special thanks from me! I don't think I would have been able to preside this weekend if I had not had the time with you to process this entire situation. Coming to North Carolina as early as you did helped all of us who had to keep the assembly rolling.

Notes of appreciation also came from several bishops who had themselves dealt with instances of clergy sexual misconduct. The bishop of the Central States Synod, Charles Maahs, who chaired the Conference of Bishops during my final years in Chicago, wrote, "I wanted you to know the bishops are extremely grateful for the ministry you do on our behalf." There were also some sharp critics, who felt the bishop should simply have been forgiven and allowed to remain in office. I had learned from previous instances of responding to instances of clergy abuse that some people are unable to be angry with the guilty pastor and instead blame those who simply tell the truth.

Hitting Our Stride: Some of the ELCA's Best Years

Reflecting upon the first thirty-five years of the Evangelical Lutheran Church in America, I have said on occasion that I was blessed to be there in some of the best years. The first half-dozen years were marked by some unexpected start-up challenges as leaders from the previous church bodies jockeyed for position, income fell far below initial projections, and painful staff and program cuts had to be made. By the time I arrived in Chicago in 1994, the "new church" was settling in and beginning to hit its stride. My first week in office I was told I would have to make budget cuts, to which I responded, "I don't even know where to find my budget yet!" In fact, since we were relatively lean on staffing, I did not have to make personnel cuts or enact other dire measures as did most of my colleagues. The remaining years I served in Chicago saw modest growth in income and rebuilding depleted reserve funds.

Particularly after George Anderson's election and a change in leadership of the Conference of Bishops, there was a growing harmony within the Conference, as well as between bishops and the churchwide staff. Strongly supported by my colleagues in the Office of the Bishop, I was given broad latitude to strengthen the churchwide organization's support for the sixty-five synods. I regularly convened a Synodical Services and Resources inter-unit staff team that strove to focus energies from all parts of the churchwide organization in increasing support for synods. Some felt those efforts were a key to increased financial support for churchwide work from a number of synods. Despite the tensions that arose among them over the "hot button" issues of sexuality and the ecumenical proposals, bishops developed a higher level of collegiality. In addition to Anderson and his other two assistants, Bob Bacher and Lita Johnson (and later Myrna Sheie who took Lita's position when she became director of the ELCA World Hunger effort), Director of Communication Eric Shafer was a key partner. Eric and his staff worked hard to build and support a network of communication specialists in the synods, to get synod leaders networked through the newly emerging technology of email and online chat meetings. With staff additions in Synodical Relations, we could offer more on-site training events for leaders throughout the ELCA.

In that era, the national Lutheran church bodies were recipients of substantial financial support from two fraternal benefit organizations, Lutheran Brotherhood (LB) and Aid Association to Lutherans (AAL). Annually, we received upwards of $3 million or more in support of various programs, major events, and hospitality support to enhance meetings of the bishops. Midway through my Chicago years, we proposed and were granted Synodical Initiative Grant (SIG) funds to support innovative efforts in synods. At about that same point, I replaced Lita Johnson as the ELCA's primary liaison to the two financial services organizations. That meant regular visits to their headquarters in Minneapolis and Appleton, Wisconsin, to tend relationships and interact with their CEO's and other senior executives. While there were occasional tensions as we sought to ensure continuing funding for important projects without allowing AAL and LB undue influence, by and large that aspect of my work was rewarding and interesting. As I was concluding my tenure with the churchwide organization, Lutheran Brotherhood's Vice President Louise Thoreson wrote the following:

> Thank you for your creative leadership as the ELCA liaison with Lutheran Brotherhood. I have greatly appreciated your listening ear, your candor, and your ability to navigate through land mines. A strange combination, but truly gifts from God. You were the perfect person to represent the Bishop's office. I value the insights you bring to the church and to our common mission. Most of all, I have valued your friendship.

A Personal Loss: Sister Bernice Died Too Young

In the summer of 1997, after the annual round of synod assemblies and other early summer events, Pamela, Macrina and I headed to Massachusetts for two weeks of vacation. After visiting her parents in Swampscott, we had planned a week on Martha's Vineyard, where Pam and I had become engaged and spent our delayed honeymoon. On our last afternoon in Swampscott, we were enjoying some time at the beach down the hill from the Whites' home when my father-in-law Tom appeared with obvious concern on his face. He informed us that my brother Dave had called to report that our sister Bernice had suffered a medical crisis and died suddenly in Homestead, Florida. As the hours went by, it appeared that there had been miscommunication, and she was still barely clinging to life. We debated whether to proceed to the Vineyard, and finally decided to go ahead with our plans. But shortly after we arrived there, word came that Bernice had died. I hurriedly arranged a flight to Florida for her funeral and to offer support to my brother-in-law Ron. Dave arrived in Homestead about the same time, and for several days we grieved together and helped Ron, as well as our nephew Steve and his family, absorb the shock of Bernice's sudden death from a pulmonary embolism. Only 58, Bernice had struggled her entire adult life with obesity. In the months before her death, she had lost upwards of 150 pounds in order to undergo a long-overdue hernia surgery. It appears that the combination of weight loss and the stress of surgery made her vulnerable to the fatal episode.

Her death was a blow to us all, but especially hard for our Mom and Dad, who were not able to travel for the funeral because of their own increasingly fragile health conditions. Ron and all of us received an outpouring of condolences from Bernice's many friends and especially her current and former pre-school kids and their families. Bernice's classroom was described as "Mrs. Anderson's Apple Gang," and over the years she had received a number of glass and ceramic apples as gifts. As I was leaving to return home after the funeral, Ron insisted I take one of those apples, which has graced a shelf in my offices ever since as a reminder of my beloved only sister. Sometime after Bernice's death, Ron remarried, but sadly, within a couple years thereafter, he also died. And on another sad note, for unknown reasons, Bernice and Ron's daughter Patti, who had married a Dutch man and lived in Holland her entire adult life, has broken all ties with the family.

Final Years and Leave-Taking from Chicago

As had been the case in my previous ministries, the Chicago position presented unending challenges year after year. As Jerry Ramsdell had said about Angelica, "It was never dull for long!" Every day was filled with a multiplicity of tasks, issues, and people in need of information, support or just a "listening ear." The longer I worked in my position, the more I was convinced of the wisdom of my predecessor, who phoned shortly after I arrived in Chicago and described it as "the best job in the church." My position placed me once again at a unique crossroads where almost every dimension of the ELCA's life intersected. My last couple of years brought an increasing sense of appreciation for my work and collegiality and friendship with literally hundreds of people around the whole church. As occurs in most jobs, a growing familiarity with the rhythms and institutional ethos of the churchwide organization relieved some of the stress experienced my first couple of years in Chicago.

As in my previous calls, I felt like my whole life had been preparing me for the challenges and complexities that were a given in my position. When the unrelenting flow of correspondence required daily hours spent dictating responses, I remembered the dailiness required by the herd of cows on the farm. When preparation for meetings of the conference of bishop and ELCA council called upon us to coordinate and oversee the work of all the churchwide departments, synods and many church agencies and institutions, I fell back upon my flight training to keep "situational awareness," see the big picture, and not get overly fixated on minor details. "Keep flying the airplane no matter what else is happening," was my mantra.

On occasion, my work brought unexpected and delightful opportunities. Arriving at the synod office in Detroit one day, where I was to conduct some staff training, the bishop said, "We're going to see Bill Clinton!" A last-minute invitation to a large rally, where the vast majority were African American church leaders, afforded me the opportunity to accompany the bishop and see the U.S. president in person.

My last year in Chicago, when Pamela and Macrina had moved to Philadelphia for Pam's new professorship at the Lutheran seminary, Aaron accepted a position in the World Hunger office of the ELCA and joined me in our home. It was a delight having that time together, especially since we had been apart the majority of his growing years when he and Adam were with their mother and stepfather in Nebraska. We enjoyed many evenings doing things together or just hanging out as father and son. Then, in December of 1999, I received notice I had been nominated for the presidency of my alma mater, Gettysburg Seminary. While I thought the possibility of being chosen was minimal, I responded by sending a resume and other materials requested by the search committee. The job intrigued me, but even more inviting was the prospect of being just 120 miles from Philadelphia, which would enable our family to be together more readily. To my great surprise, following the typical round of interviews in early 2000, I was chosen to be the twelfth president of that historic institution. More about that in the following chapters.

Following the announcement of my resignation, as had occurred when I accepted the Chicago position, I received an outpouring of appreciative notes from most of the bishops for my work with them over the years. In his response to my resignation letter, George Anderson was extremely gracious:

> Your letter of resignation brings a flood of responses to mind, beginning with "Oh, no. What will we do without him"? You have been more than just another member of the team. You have created a climate of cooperative work that has benefited us all and made us all mindful of the many people who depend on what we do. Your work ethic has kept things flowing smoothly even when the tasks threatened to overwhelm us. Your good

sense has helped us to avoid blunders. In short, you have helped to shape us into an efficient and caring staff.

My personal response, of course, is "Who can ever match his ability to catch my thoughts and present them so winsomely"? You have been able to deal with the varied correspondence, with its varied levels of passion, with detachment and grace. In fact, you often brought knowledge to the responses that I did not have, to say nothing of your general courtesy and compassion. In the reports to the Conference of Bishops, I particularly appreciated the way you could take my ideas and enfold them in a thought-structure that enhanced them.

But the feeling I need to fall back on is, "What a good gift for Gettysburg!" You know how institutions work, and you have had plenty of experience in planning. Above all, I believe you know how to "take it to the Lord in prayer," and you will be fed by the worship life of the seminary community. So, all will be well.

On May 30, 2000, a wonderful farewell event took place on the top floor of the Lutheran Center, just down the hall from the office in which I had worked for six and one-half years. Tables joined together were decorated as a long runway, and little balsam airplanes hand-decorated by dozens of staff colleagues adorned them. There was a cake with aviation themes as well. A number of colleagues offered verbal tributes, and written greetings from many bishops and others around the country were read as well. In his remarks, George Anderson did a take-off from my last name initials, C-W, describing my having been on a Closer Walk with synods and churchwide units, preaching in Chapel Worship, engaging in Collegial Work while never Crying Wolf but busting through Concrete Walls when necessary. The bishop described me as a Creative Writer, a Communication Wizard, a bit of a Computer Wonk (I was once described as the ELCA's first blogger for my posts on meetings of the bishops and other events), thought by some to be Captain Wonder. Finally, he wished me Clear Weather as I went off to head a seminary steeped in the history of the Civil War! A lovely "Ritual of Leave-taking" included this litany of blessing:

> You, Michael Cooper-White, have been very special to us.
> > Knowing you has changed us.
> > We are different people for having loved you.
> > We claim the gifts you have evoked in us and bless you.
> > We bless you to send you on your way and to let go as we have known you.
> > We proclaim with our words the blessings you are for us.

And the blessings we bring to each other and our world because of you.

Michael, you have been a faithful servant of our God and God's people in many ways, in the churchwide offices, in synods, in many units, in the congregations where you have worshiped, and in the lives of those near and far. You now step out with courage to the next phase of your journey in faith and vocation.

On June 6, 2000, I preached for a final time at the Lutheran Center's daily chapel service. In that homily, I offered thanks and a word of encouragement to my colleagues:

Dear friends and coworkers, this is my week of goodbye-saying to this place and all of you. Until a few months ago, I planned to be here for a much longer time. Then came an unexpected intrusion into my life. The seminary from which I graduated twenty-four years ago has called me back for some remedial education. It will probably take me several years to complete this second round of study at Gettysburg. So, I must say goodbye. My years here at the Lutheran Center have been some of the best ones of my life.

I ask that you pray for our whole church, especially a certain small Pennsylvania seminary in a historic little town where Abraham Lincoln once gave a short address. Know that this former colleague will pray often for you in gratitude. Know that before God and all who will listen, I shall say of you: They are a good and Godly people, given by God for the sake of the church and the world!

Nearly two decades after I left my position in Chicago, one with whom I worked closely sent a letter reflecting on my service at the churchwide office and with the Conference of Bishops. After he retired as bishop of the Central States Synod (Kansas and Missouri), I invited Charlie Maahs to teach New Testament for a semester while one of our regular faculty members was on sabbatical. In the same letter, he also said how much his time at Gettysburg meant to him.

Somehow when Pauline and I were having lunch together with you in Gettysburg, I neglected to mention how much I appreciated your friendship and the leadership you provided our synods during your service at 8765 W. Higgins Road. Working together with you was always knowing that everything would be done in a pastoral, caring, and right way.

I also appreciated your friendship and assistance and the professional and top-notch leadership you provided the Seminary community. Your service as Dean of the seminary presidents for so many years was a true benefit and blessing for our Church.

Ruminations on the Chicago Years

Before leaving this description of my Chicago years, I offer some concluding reflections. Just as I had loved my synodical staff work, I treasured the rare opportunity for *syzygy* in a much larger and far more complex arena. I don't recall many days when I woke up dreading a day in the office or on the road. As I had during my California years, I would sometimes say to myself, "You're just a farm kid from Wendell. What in the world are you doing in this place?" During those years I rubbed shoulders with hundreds of key leaders in every arena of the church. Having an office two doors down from the Presiding Bishop provided a vantage point that only a handful have been given in the life of the ELCA. Working with the church's top officers, more than 100 bishops who held office during my seven years in Chicago, as well as the senior leaders of several other denominations afforded me opportunities I could not have imagined when I began my ministry.

As I have described, in no other chapter of my life and ministry did I receive so many expressions of appreciation. I still maintain a bulging file of dozens of thank you notes from bishops, their assistants, churchwide colleagues and folks I encountered in synod assemblies or when preaching or speaking on various occasions. While I experienced a few challenging relationships during those years, the vast majority of the ELCA bishops and other leaders were among the most charitable, kind, and appreciative persons I have served alongside in four decades of active ministry. As so often is the case, a child may be able to see things with greater clarity than adults. In the fall of 1998, we worked with the ELCA's Washington office to organize a bishops' visit in the nation's capital. Meetings and briefings were arranged with leaders at the highest levels, including key aides to President Bill Clinton at the White House. While I was in D.C., Macrina had a conversation with her Mom. "So, Daddy's in Washington with all the bishops, right? And Daddy's not a bishop, right?" After Pam confirmed her assumptions, the eight-year-old concluded, "Oh, I get it.

It's like when there's a 911 call and all the firemen show up; there's always one policeman too!"

As I conclude this chapter, I also want to acknowledge with gratitude that Pam made the Chicago years possible for me by bearing the major load of tending the home fires. In making the move from the Bay Area, she sacrificed some enticing career opportunities that had begun to present themselves. With my constant travel, she spent many days and nights alone with our energetic young daughter. While she loved her ministry in a local Episcopal parish, the full range of her gifts and talents could not be exercised as an associate priest in a mid-sized congregation. Her coastal roots never really took hold in midwestern Chicagoland, especially a suburb where many held conservative views that did not align with ours. But, as she always does, she seized new opportunities, establishing herself as a highly respected therapist and gaining a second Ph.D. to prepare for the next chapters of her life and amazing career.

— 10 —

Gettysburg Seminary: My Early Years on the Ridge

DURING NEW STUDENT ORIENTATION throughout my years as president of Gettysburg Seminary a standard piece of advice I offered to incoming seminarians was, "Be open to surprises." I usually included a brief personal testimony, sharing that every place I was called to serve by God and the church came as a surprise. I went on to say that I also felt unqualified for each position, but once chosen took my best shot at fulfilling the demands of that call. "If you're standing at the plate and they hand you a bat," I would encourage, "take your best swing and see what happens."

A Surprising Invitation

At no time in my professional career did I feel more surprised and more challenged than when I received the invitation to serve as the twelfth president of the Evangelical Lutheran Church in America's oldest and most historic seminary. The possibility was first presented in the fall of 1999 when I was leading a staff retreat for the Allegheny Synod in central Pennsylvania. The synod's bishop, Gregory Pile, was an old friend from seminary days who had graduated a year ahead of me. On a break from the team building and planning retreat, Greg and I took a walk through the fields surrounding a Roman Catholic retreat center along the Pennsylvania Turnpike. Midway through our hike, Greg suddenly turned to me and asked, "Mike, have you ever thought of becoming the next president of our seminary?" Taken aback, I recall dismissing the suggestion out of hand, saying something like, "Greg, you know I don't have the qualifications for that job." His query reminded me that a few weeks earlier I had been going through my mail at home in Chicago and found a postcard announcing the seminary's launch of a presidential search. As I pondered it for a moment, I thought to myself, "Had I done some things differently—earned a Ph.D. and gained some experience in academia—this might have been a possibility for me." But without giving it further thought I tossed the "invitation" in our paper recycling bin. Despite my dismissal of the bishop's suggestion, however, when a formal letter from the search committee chair indicating I had been nominated for the presidency arrived in January of 2000, I could no longer avoid the possibility of seeing where things might lead. At that point, I also recalled a conversation with Pam the previous summer while we were in Gettysburg for an event at which I had been invited to speak. On a walk through the seminary campus one evening, she suddenly blurted out, "I have a feeling we're going to be spending a lot more time here!"

So, I sent a copy of my professional resume and written responses to questions posed by the search committee. A few weeks later, I was informed that the committee wished to include me among those being interviewed for the presidency. Because I valued his pastoral and personal support, and inasmuch as informing my boss was proper protocol, I sought George Anderson's counsel. I was also aware that he had served as a seminary president earlier in his career and could offer some "insider" perspectives on the nature of the job. In his very gentle and direct manner, George indicated he felt I had many qualities that lent themselves to a presidency, particularly my administrative experience, knowledge of the church, and confidence of many of its key leaders. At the same time, he pointed out, "There are some holes in your resume," noting the absence of a terminal degree and experience in the academic world. Concluding the conversation, George said he felt I had little to lose in allowing the process to unfold, and he would support the ultimate outcome.

On a frigid, stormy winter night in February 2000, a drive from Philadelphia to Gettysburg normally requiring two and one-half hours lasted over five. When we finally fell into bed at Gettysburg's finest hotel on Lincoln Square around 1:00 a.m. I felt exhausted and ill-suited for a critical interview the next morning. Despite a short and poor night's sleep, however, when morning dawned and I met a small group for breakfast in the hotel's dining room, I felt ready and eager for a good conversation. I had done careful preparation by reading all the background materials sent to me, as well as seeking counsel from several of the sitting seminary presidents. In my mind I had rehearsed responses to the typical kinds of questions asked in such interviews. It helped put me at ease when I looked around the room and saw several familiar faces, including the seminary's dean, Norma Wood, who had begun teaching part-time while I was a seminarian a quarter century before. As I have always done in such contexts, I was determined to be transparent and straightforward, letting the seminary's leaders know who I am and how I might approach working collegially with them.

At the conclusion of a morning-long interview, it was explained that I was one of five finalists for the presidency. The chair indicated the committee's plan was to narrow the field to three and engage each in an exhaustive round of on-campus conversations with all key constituent groups—students, faculty, staff, board members, and alumni—after which one would be recommended to the board for election. In the days after the interview, I had positive feelings and the sense I could offer some leadership the seminary needed at that point in its history. Due to a prolonged enrollment decline over several years, the departure of several faculty for positions elsewhere, and the absence of clear overarching future directions, the faculty and staff seemed somewhat demoralized. While the true state of the school's finances was not fully disclosed, I knew enough from reviewing the financials that suggested some "belt-tightening" would be required. Pam was encouraging, offering her perspective that, "They don't need an 'academic' leader right now; they need a strong administrator who has your experience with organizations and the wider church." Nevertheless, as I further pondered the process outlined, I had misgivings about proceeding should I be among the three selected as finalists. Continuing to believe I was a longshot on the basis of my inexperience in academia, I was reluctant to "go public" and be perceived in broad circles throughout the church as seeking to leave my position in the Office of the Presiding Bishop. Beyond anxiety about undermining my own position, I was reluctant to send signals that could be interpreted by some that Bishop Anderson's staff members were beginning to bail. And probably on a deeper level, I feared experiencing a measure of embarrassment at widespread knowledge that I had been passed over for an important and prestigious position.

Things changed dramatically a few days after the interview when I received a phone call from the search committee chairman, Rev. Kirk Bish. "Michael," he said in his straightforward and no-nonsense manner, "if you're willing, we have decided we want to proceed with you as our only candidate in meeting the broader seminary community." I was later told by search committee members that the quality of my interview stood apart from the rest and convinced them nearly unanimously that I was best qualified to serve as the next president of my alma mater. Given the strength of the search committee's endorsement of my candidacy, I had no hesitation in continuing in the process.

A Hiccup: The Milwaukee Meeting

As described earlier in the previous chapter, one of the joys of my years in Chicago was playing a small role as the ELCA forged its full communion relationships with several other churches. Given our family "Lutherpalian" identity, I was especially proud of the *Called to Common Mission* agreement with the Episcopal Church. Hotly contested, as described previously, the ELCA internal battles were not over when the agreement was adopted at the 1999 churchwide assembly. A vocal minority continued to protest the ELCA's acceptance of the Episcopalian understanding of bishops and the condition that all future ELCA pastors would have to be ordained by a bishop. Among the dissidents were several of the ELCA bishops and a number of prominent theologians, especially faculty members at our largest seminary, Luther, in St. Paul.

Tensions continued to build following the 1999 assembly, particularly in the upper Midwest, with a growing number of clergy and congregations threatening to leave the ELCA unless exceptions to the "bishop ordination rule" could be allowed. Following several months of protests, and with the encouragement of a significant number of synodical bishops, an attempt was led by Bishop Mark Hanson of the St. Paul Synod to reach a compromise. Shortly before my interview at Gettysburg, a small number of leaders were invited to gather in Milwaukee, Wisconsin in January 2000, to seek a pathway out of the impasse. In addition to bishops, invitees included a handful of seminary professors and other key leaders representing both sides of the controversy. In our discussions in Chicago, it was deemed unwise for the presiding bishop or other officers to represent the churchwide organization. George Anderson decided that

Joseph Wagner and I should be his two representatives in Milwaukee. Joe was head of the ELCA's Division for Ministry, the churchwide unit responsible for all matters related to rostered ministry, including recommending policies for ordination, the appropriate role of bishops and such.

In what I regard as one of the most significant meetings in a time of crisis for our church, about twenty of us hunkered down for forty-eight hours amidst serious blizzard conditions! Mirroring the frigid conditions outside our hotel were the frosty greetings and handshakes exchanged by some of the participants. The two days proved to be among the most intense occasions of my professional career. As the discussions proceeded, it became clear that objection to what the church had adopted just a few months before was indeed fierce and probably growing. The rumblings of massive withdrawals of congregations were not idle threats according to those best positioned to assess reality on the ground, the synodical bishops. Equally clear were statements by Episcopal representatives that the ELCA's reneging on the ordination-by-bishops commitment could jeopardize the entire agreement and prove a disastrous setback in broad ecumenical circles. At one critical juncture, when an Episcopal bishop serving as that church's representative was digging in his heels, I reminded him and the group that the ELCA had other full communion agreements whereby Presbyterian, Reformed and United Church of Christ ordained ministers would be welcomed onto the ELCA's clergy roster without re-ordination at the hands of a bishop. "Please remember," I said, "that from your perspective the ELCA will never have a totally 'pure' clergy roster." After pointing out that some wiggle room was baked into the agreement, I sensed that the tenor of the meeting changed, and the majority of those present were in a mood to seek a compromise. Except for Joe Wagner, all present agreed to recommend that under rare circumstances, and only with the approval of an individual ministerial candidate's synodical bishop and the presiding bishop, an ordination could take place by a pastor, without a bishop's participation.

When I returned to Chicago after the Milwaukee meeting (the snowstorm did finally subside), I had become *persona non grata* with some of the church's highest officials who felt I had sold out on our commitments to the Episcopalians. Fortunately, the presiding bishop was not among them. An old hand in ecumenical endeavors and church politics, George Anderson seemed to accept that the proposed exception rule would offer a way forward that hopefully enabled most of those opposed to the agreement to remain in the ELCA. At no time did he express displeasure with my going along with the stance that all except Wagner were able to embrace. He worked hard to interpret our proposal, both to the Episcopalians and broadly within the ELCA, and supported the exception when it came time for the Church Council to adopt it.

For me, however, the timing could not have been worse in terms of the presidential search process at Gettysburg. As word spread of the compromise proposal and my support of it, some of the faculty who were strong supporters of *Called to Common Mission* raised questions about my stance. I learned that some felt so strongly they were questioning the wisdom of the search committee's recommendation. As I got wind of the building uneasiness over this issue, I phoned the dean and assured her I would be eager to respond to any questions and concerns about the matter during my upcoming campus visit. I also found some comfort in the fact that another supporter of the compromise, Bishop Donald McCoid of the Southwestern Pennsylvania Synod, was Pastor Bish's boss and was likely to reassure the search committee chair of my integrity.

A Strong Vote of Confidence and Some Startling Surprises

During two mid-March days on campus in Gettysburg, I moved through a whirlwind round of meetings and conversations with the search committee and board leaders, faculty and staff members, and students. At every turn, I found myself excited at the prospect of becoming the Seminary's twelfth president who would lead my alma mater in the early years of the twenty-first century. My earlier misgivings about my lack of experience in academia began to evaporate as I felt myself embraced by the Seminary community, which seemed eager to open a new chapter under new leadership. The areas of the institution's greatest needs—to develop a long-term strategic plan, undergird its financial base, enhance constituent relationships and communication, and rebuild enrollment—seemed to match my strengths and interests.

In an open forum attended by faculty and students, I fielded a wide range of questions about my background, leadership style, understanding of the challenges faced by the Seminary and visions for its future. As expected, a couple of the faculty raised hard questions about the Milwaukee meeting and my involvement in what some viewed as a move that could compromise the Episcopal full communion process. I explained that prior to the churchwide assembly, like many others, I was in a singular orbit around the full communion proposal. But given the intensity of negative response after *Called to Common Mission* was adopted, I and others had to shift our orbit around two focal points—ecumenical fervor and the unity of our own church. I went on to indicate that the way I responded amidst the crisis signaled how I would lead if called to head the Seminary—balancing the needs and perspectives of individuals and groups who would sometimes be in sharp conflict, while seeking to stay in relationship with those who personally disagreed with me.

Preaching at daily chapel on March 14 during the first week of Lent, the title for my homily was "A Defining Moment." I shared some of my personal defining moments, and invited listeners to reflect on those in their own lives. After exploring how Jesus' time in the wilderness after his baptism was a defining moment in his discerning God's call and claim on his life, I invited those present to consider their own callings.

> Could it be that right here in this quiet bucolic pastoral place, this small burgh in Pennsylvania, could it be that this is a defining place? That here, too, come crashing in all the forces of the universe? That here in these hallowed halls, whether student, faculty, or staff, you are caught in the dialectic tension between a theology of glory and theology of the cross? Between graduating from this place and going out to lord it over parishioners and a congregation, or to be their foot-washing leader? Between teaching by domination or intimidation and teaching by example and gentle, tender coaxing and frequent affirmations? Between either making or avoiding difficult administrative decisions in a cold and uncaring way, or guiding the seminary as a learning, even loving organization?

Following my campus visit, the search committee moved quickly to offer its enthusiastic recommendation to the board that I be hired as president. Unfortunately, the scheduled regular board meeting was several weeks away, creating an awkward pause in the process. Beyond it being uncomfortable for me to live in a state of uncertainty, the delay would create difficulty for the ELCA Office of the Presiding Bishop in making succession plans. Given those factors, George Anderson called the Seminary board chair and strongly urged that she call a special board meeting. That took place on April 6, 2000, and I immediately accepted.

By mutual agreement, we went public with simultaneous press releases in Gettysburg and Chicago to announce my election and acceptance. The board chair, Pastor Judith Mckee, said in her statement, "We are excited about the many gifts Pastor Michael Cooper-White brings to the office of president of Gettysburg Seminary, including a collegial way of working together with people, a breadth of knowledge of the ELCA, a depth of understanding of the issues facing the Church and the Seminary, a commitment to quality theological education, and above all a love for our Lord and His Church." Chair of the search committee, Pastor Kirk Bish, said he saw in me "a spirit of excitement about theological education and effective, competent and caring administrator, faculty chair and pastoral role model to the community."

Those releases, in which I expressed my delight at being called "to the ELCA's most historic seminary, whose best day is tomorrow," went out about noon. In the afternoon mail I received a copy of a memorandum issued by the Seminary's chief financial officer to the finance committee and board. It began with the question, "What does the date February 23, 2003, represent? On that date the unrestricted funds will be fully depleted." The startling communication went on to forecast that by that juncture the seminary would have a "projected deficit exceeding $1 million per year." In short, his financial models predicted that if dramatic actions were not taken, the seminary was on the fast track to bankruptcy. After reading that memo I said to myself, "Well, I knew this was going to be challenging, but now I realize it will be even more so than I realized!" While I had received and studied the seminary's most recent financial reports, as I would learn from experience, those are very complex documents that even CPA's unfamiliar with academic institution's finances may puzzle over and fail to fully understand. In my interviews with the search committee, there were vague references to some financial challenges on the horizon, especially those related to ongoing fund-raising for a $5.2 million rehabilitation of the seminary's main classroom building and administrative center that was underway and behind schedule. Probing a bit further after receiving the discouraging memo, I learned the school had fallen into "deficit spending," whereby for several years, expenses had exceeded income by several hundred thousand dollars. It appeared that with a couple of exceptions among board members and the CFO, most of the school's leaders were unconcerned. They saw the "bottom line" on the balance sheet continue to move upward due to a period of remarkable stock market growth, which yielded net endowment value increase despite tapping into it to meet current budget shortfalls.

Upon discovering the true financial picture of the seminary, I realized I would not have the luxury of a relatively "business as usual" entry into the presidency. While I would not formally take office until August 1, when my predecessor's term officially concluded, I felt I had to take some preliminary steps to address the looming financial crisis. I consulted with the presiding bishop and with the ELCA's savvy Executive for Administration, Robert Bacher, both of whom were supportive and encouraged me to begin getting involved as soon as possible. In conversations with board officers, I sensed a growing awareness on their part, but also deep reluctance to consider making the tough decisions required to bring the budget into balance. In a later period when severe belt-tightening was required, and most board members were again reluctant to face harsh measures, I characterized the stance as giving me the mandate: "Do major surgery, but don't draw any blood!"

My eyes were opened further to the real state of things at the seminary when, at my request, I attended the May 2000 board meeting as an observer/guest. When the time came for the treasurer's report, the CFO rehearsed the harsh realities outlined in his April memorandum. The current year income and expense statement confirmed that the trend of "deficit spending" was accelerating rather than diminishing. After his report concluded, there were no questions or discussion. Next came a session with the seminary's auditors, who had requested to meet with the board to issue a warning that the pattern of deficit spending had the institution on a short road to bankruptcy. After those reports from the CFO and auditors, the board took a coffee break. When it resumed a half-hour later, the next agenda item taken up was a recommendation from the faculty and a board committee that a search be launched for a faculty position vacated recently by a Bible scholar's departure for another institution. Again, with no discussion, the board voted unanimously to launch the search. I thought to myself, "They've just decided to dig the hole deeper without any discussion whether there might be cost-saving alternatives."

As the meeting proceeded, I learned the worst was still to come in my eye-opening session with the board. They went into confidential executive session for a meeting with attorneys representing the school in an EEOC (Equal Employment Opportunity Commission) complaint. I learned that in a recent faculty search process, a male candidate was chosen and one of the female candidates for the position alleged gender discrimination. Following an initial determination that she failed to make a credible case, the EEOC reversed itself with no explanation and signaled its sense that she had indeed been wronged. Recognizing that an ongoing investigation and potential litigation would drag on and not be resolved before I took office, I steeled myself to take on yet another challenge during my first months in office.

Additionally, while on campus for the board meeting, I was apprised by the outgoing president of a delicate personnel matter. It was the first of several situations I would face over the years when the conduct of faculty, staff, students, or others created conflict and required difficult decisions. Suffice it to say, they were among the most challenging and painful aspects of my presidency. I also hasten to add that Gettysburg Seminary was by no means unique in facing these difficult manifestations of human shortcomings. Contrary to the unrealistic expectations of many, people in churches and church-related institutions are not immune to all manner of unkindness, unfairness, abuse of others, and occasionally even criminal behavior. Leaders of any seminary or divinity school will face challenging student- and personnel-related matters from time to time.

To make long stories short, I will summarize the outcomes of the challenging situations I faced as a neophyte president. In the case of the financial crisis, I called for a meeting with key board leaders some weeks prior to beginning my tenure as president. While still considering the best moves to make, I told them I felt we had to seriously consider aborting the faculty search and take other cost-cutting measures immediately. Beyond the intrinsic value of realizing savings wherever possible, I wanted to signal that it was truly a new day, and I would not tolerate ongoing "deficit spending" that threatened the institution's long-term fiscal viability. I outlined a budget review process that would begin over the summer even before I took office, and initiated explorations with the CFO about how best to manage the expected two-plus million-dollar debt that would remain when the Valentine Hall construction project was completed. I had discovered no plans were in place beyond "hope for raising more" and "taking out of the endowment" whatever amount remained due to contractors. I persuaded key leaders that donors would be more likely to help retire debt than rebuild a raided endowment. With just a one-page note I signed, we received a $2.25 million low-interest loan from a local bank (Those were the days!), kept the endowment whole, and redoubled robust fund-raising activities. With a projected budget deficit of approximately $500,000 (approved by the board), trustees and the CFO believed it would take several years to bring things into balance. Through some across-the-board administrative cost reductions, abandoning the faculty search, and other measures, by the middle of my first year we adopted a revised budget with expenditures equal to projected income. My taking in hand the financial crisis seemed to establish confidence in my leadership. After several years of achieving balanced budgets, in one of my annual review sessions, trustee Bishop Ralph Dunkin of the West Virginia/Western Maryland Synod (and a seminary classmate) quipped that my tombstone would read: "He balanced the budget!"

Regarding the EEOC complaint, things proceeded with blustery letters and threats to sue from the complainant's attorney. In another inexplicable turn of events, a few months into my presidency, yet another communication was received from the EEOC, once again reversing their earlier determination. The letter stated the EEOC would take no further action, but recognized the complainant's right to sue the Seminary should she choose. "How's that for a mixed message?" we asked our attorneys. Apparently recognizing her case was weak, the complainant never followed through on her threats of litigation. Months after the EEOC's final determination, she requested to meet with me. While initially hesitant (and discouraged by legal counsel), I consented to a meeting on the condition that I be accompanied by the dean. When we met, she indicated that if the seminary would reimburse her legal fees (about $30,000), we would hear no more from her. Convinced there had in fact been no discriminatory behavior on the part of my predecessor or colleagues, I stated that we would not meet her demands. I assured her we bore no ill will, and hoped she would find opportunities to pursue a long and rewarding career in some institution. That was the last communication we ever had with the individual.

Finally, concerning the difficult personnel matter I inherited, I understood that I was being tested to determine the extent to which I could make tough decisions, which in some cases might require employee or student dismissal for inappropriate and abusive conduct. I sought to clearly communicate my expectations for appropriate behaviors, and how I would respond when institutional policies or commonly accepted ethical standards were violated.

A Grand Inauguration

Following my election and acceptance of the call to serve at Gettysburg, planning began for my formal inauguration. Board members and others initially expected to hold a stand-alone event in the fall of 2000. At my suggestion, it was decided to hold my inauguration in conjunction with the annual Luther Colloquy held the last week in October. With a history of decades, that event, which brought to campus renowned Luther and Reformation scholars from around the world as speakers, typically drew hundreds of alumni/ae and others in addition to the student body. Given expectations for a crowd that would exceed the Seminary chapel's seating capacity, the inaugural celebration on October 25, 2000, was held at the larger chapel of Gettysburg College, just down the hill from the Seminary. A banquet following the inaugural ceremony was also held at the College in its spacious student union auditorium.

In a show of continuing strong support for the Seminary by the synods of the ELCA's Region 8, all eight bishops from throughout Pennsylvania, Maryland, Delaware, West Virginia, and the District of Columbia were present and marched in the procession along with the board, faculty, students, staff, and representatives of dozens of academic institutions. My former boss, ELCA Presiding Bishop George Anderson, issued a "charge" for me to expand the Seminary's role and influence in the life of the church and society.

With ELCA Presiding Bishop H. George Anderson at my inauguration

Immediately following my election in the spring, and throughout the early months in office, I had struggled to craft an inaugural address that would not only set a tone for my leadership but cast a vision for the school's future. I studied demographic and ecclesiastical trends in the region, discovering Pennsylvania was among areas of the country experiencing a dramatic downturn in church attendance and membership. Realizing that many of the Lutheran churches in decline were being led by Gettysburg graduates, I wanted my inaugural address to challenge the faculty and entire Seminary community to ponder how we might better prepare students for the challenges they would face in their ministries. In my preparation and research, I also read the inaugural speeches of my eleven predecessors, which were invaluable in gaining a better sense of the institution's history.

The Seminary's recently adopted new vision statement stated:

> Bearing witness at the crossroads of history and hope,
> the Lutheran Theological Seminary at Gettysburg
> proclaims Jesus Christ to a restless world,
> by preparing students for faithful discipleship.

Building upon that compelling vision, I entitled my address "Gettysburg 2000: At the Crossroads of History and Hope." In an attempt to make it easier to remember, I decided to employ an acrostic, spelling out the town's and Seminary's name, attaching envisioned emphases and institutional values to each letter. I described the two-word themes as "Road signs that combine in a kind of ecclesial and pedagogical Burma Shave" message, referencing road marker advertisements that used to border highways throughout America pitching a brand of shaving cream. In the inaugural, I called the Seminary to a future marked by:

> **G**odly gospeling
> **E**vangelical ecumenism
> **T**rinitarian theology
> **T**houghtful training
> **Y**outhful yearning
> **S**criptural spirituality
> **B**ounteous beauty
> **U**rban urgency
> **R**ural rhythms
> **G**oing global

Following the ceremony, after I removed my academic robe and made a quick stop at the bathroom in the college chapel, a man I had not met before quipped, "I appreciated the address, and I'm sure glad you're not the president of the Massachusetts Institute of Technology or we would have been here all night!"

The grand colloquy and inaugural day ended back on the Seminary campus with a service of Holy Communion, at which my good friend and leader in the Conference of Bishops, Bishop April Ulring Larson from Wisconsin preached a powerful sermon. It had indeed been a joyous day and made especially so by the presence of Pam and our three children, my parents and brother Dave, and many friends who traveled from Chicago and elsewhere to join in the celebrations.

Our family at inaugural reception

Some Early Victories and Good Years for "P-Squared"

I have described above my unfamiliarity with the academic world upon accepting the seminary presidency. Just three months after my taking office, the institution faced its decennial accreditation visit by a team representing the two agencies that confer academic imprimatur to theological schools—the Association of Theological Schools (ATS) in the U.S. and Canada, and the Middle States Commission on Higher Education (MSCHE), the regional accrediting body for all schools of higher education in the northeast. While I understood to some degree the importance of accreditation, I felt ill-prepared for the role of being the primary host of the intensive three days of scrutiny by some of higher education's most seasoned professionals. I have quipped on occasion about that first experience with the process, "I was so naïve as to be asking, 'What's this accreditation business and why should I worry about it?'"

Following the visit, the school received full reaccreditation for a ten-year period from both agencies. That ringing endorsement gave a lift to morale. I credited the outstanding preparatory work by the Seminary's dean, Norma Wood, and a small team of faculty and staff colleagues.

While I had barely climbed into the saddle, among strengths cited in the accrediting team's report was that the school had a new and forward-looking president! While overall affirming, the accreditation report also required that the seminary produce a comprehensive strategic plan within one year, which had to include specific steps to stabilize financially. I welcomed that external driver, which gave me added leverage to marshal all constituencies of the institution in planning. Looking back on that initial chapter of my presidency, I often stated that the accreditors helped us accomplish in one year what under other circumstances might have taken several years.

The strategic plan, which was entitled "Directions for the Decade," picked up on themes sounded in my inaugural address, especially the need to better equip graduates for community outreach and reviving stagnant or dying congregations. The first among principles set forth to guide the school during the first decade of the twenty-first century called us to, "develop public theologians and mission leaders." It cast a vision for curricular review to ensure that, in addition to traditional subjects like Bible, church history, theology, preaching etc., a seminary education would strengthen students' leadership and administrative capacities.

> The Church of the early twenty-first century is in need of leaders who, in addition to serving congregations and other ministries, carry the Gospel into public arenas. Outreach-oriented pastors and other rostered leaders working in partnership with the laity can lead the church in evangelism and witness, reversing trends of membership decline and marginalization in many places. Every dimension of the seminary's curriculum and program will attempt to foster future leaders of courage and commitment who can articulate the Gospel in a missionary context.

Our strategic plan was strongly affirmed by the accreditors. We adopted a realistic balanced budget and achieved it. Within about three years, fund-raising results had enabled us to pay off the bulk of the Valentine Hall debt. The stock market had rebounded from a moderate recession and was yielding modest growth in the school's endowment. In part due to expanded and reenergized staff in our Admissions Office, enrollment grew by fifty percent during my first three years. We were at full capacity in student housing, and faculty members were beginning to complain about large class sizes! In the expectation of continuing expansion, the board appointed a Growth Management Task Force to plan ways to welcome even larger numbers of students. Things were really humming along and my annual reviews by the board were affirming. In a number of ways, those early years were a kind of golden era of my presidency.

Early on in my time at the seminary, students would ask, "What shall we call you"? Their awkwardness came in part from the fact that unlike most other faculty I did not have a Ph.D. and could not therefore be rightly called "Dr. Cooper-White." Our school never adopted the informality commonplace elsewhere where faculty and staff are addressed by their first names. Students who had military backgrounds would sometimes address me as "Mr. President." I would quip in response, "That's alright, but if you start to salute me you've gone too far!" Since I am clergy and wanted to serve as a role model for those preparing for ministry, I suggested in my second year that rather than Mr. President they might try Pastor President. That stuck for the remainder of my time, and still to this day some alumni/ae address me by that title when we meet on occasion. As those things do, the title soon received its shorthand version of "P-squared." The mathematical formula began to appear in various student descriptions and was even carved into a Halloween pumpkin proudly presented by a group of students one year. Things were less awkward after 2003 when, to my surprise, Susquehanna University conferred an honorary doctorate. While then I could more legitimately be called "doctor" by those who so chose, I never pretended to hold a "real" terminal degree. The year of my retirement, Gettysburg College added a second honorary degree, at the initiation of my friend, President Janet Riggs.

September 2001: A Week Bookended by Celebration and Horror

Prior to my arrival, plans had begun for the celebration of the Seminary's 175th anniversary the first weekend of September in 2001. At noontime on September 5th, the Seminary community gathered on campus and then marched down the hill to the site of LTSG's original founding at a building later converted to a large home owned by good friends of the Seminary, David and Jane English. On their spacious lawns we recalled how things all began in the fall of 1826. Later in the day a celebratory convocation and Communion service were held in the Seminary's chapel, the Church of the Abiding Presence. My sermon for the occasion was entitled, "All Must Be Fulfilled," in which I rehearsed critical junctures in the school's history and expressed my confidence that God was guiding us into an unknown future.

An historical collection of brief biographies of nineteen luminaries associated with the Seminary had been published for the occasion. In my foreword to *Witness at the Crossroads*, I wrote:

> We have before us in this volume stories of nineteen saintly sight-lifters. Herein chronicled are the godly lives and servant ministries of lay and ordained Lutherans who all in one way or another were associated with this "school of the prophets," the Lutheran Theological Seminary at Gettysburg.
>
> Dear companion in the journey of the spirit, you hold a treasure in your hands. Nineteen servant-saintly lives are offered as examples of faithful response to the call of the Holy One. After you have sampled here and there, or read the volume in its entirety, I know you will join me in saying, "Thanks to those who labored long and hard to present us with these compelling stories of witness at the crossroads!"

An evening banquet was held south of Gettysburg at the large Eisenhower Conference Center, bringing together about 450 alumni/ae and Gettysburg community leaders, in addition to the faculty, board and many students. Mark Hanson had just been elected a month before as the ELCA's new presiding bishop. Though not yet officially installed, Hanson readily agreed to come, and we eagerly awaited his arrival at the banquet. And we waited. And we waited. An airport pick-up by a seminary staff member's spouse somehow misfired. Hanson ended up taking a taxi from the Baltimore airport to Gettysburg with a confused driver who wandered around much of Central Pennsylvania before finally delivering the bishop-elect as dinner was concluding and folks were getting restless! In his remarks, Hanson said:

> It is a great honor to join the chorus of voices throughout this church who this day are saying, "Thanks be to God for the marvelous seminary and for Gettysburg's 175 years of preparing leaders for Christ's church." What a fitting place and occasion for a newly called presiding bishop to bring his first public greeting! Not only because Gettysburg is the oldest and most historic of our seminaries, but because you have placed this seminary at the crossroads of history and hope. That is precisely where I believe the entire ELCA stands today. Therefore, the ELCA needs a strong and vibrant Seminary to provide leadership to the wider church.

Less than a week after the pinnacle celebratory anniversary event, we were plunged into one of the most fearful events in our nation's history.

The Day the World Changed: 9/11/01

When on the seminary campus, I often began my workday at the office far ahead of the regular business hour of 8:30 a.m. when the staff arrived. But sometimes I lingered at the president's residence a bit later reading or doing some work in my home office. That was the case on September 11, 2001. When I sauntered into the office around 8:45, my assistant, Carol Troyer, asked, "Do you know what's going on in the world"? Since I hadn't had television on at home, I did not know that our nation was under attack. By the time I got to a television in the Valentine Hall coffee shop, the first passenger airplane commandeered by terrorists already had crashed into New York City's World Trade Center. Along with millions around the world, I watched aghast as then United Flight 175 crashed into the second tower. A former military intelligence officer who was one of our students, said in a barely audible voice, "That's Osama bin Laden."

While I had experienced other natural disasters—a major earthquake and the Oakland hills fire in the Bay Area—nothing compared to the events unfolding on what we all now simply refer to as 9/11. The moment I wondered if we should consider evacuation of the campus was when United Flight 93 crashed at Shanksville, Pennsylvania, less than 100 miles to our west. I was aware that the Camp David presidential retreat and Site R, the "Underground Pentagon" were just a few miles southwest of Gettysburg in Maryland's Catoctin Mountains. I also recognized that Gettysburg itself is an iconic site known around the world, and if the four attacks already mounted were just the first wave of a widespread assault on important American sites, we too might be in some terrorists' crosshairs.

Given that we had no plans for campus-wide evacuation, and the likelihood of an attack was probably relatively minor, I decided against any extreme measures. After trying to hold a couple of scheduled meetings, we realized everyone's attention needed to shift to caring for members of the community who were in varying stages of shock and personal anxiety. The husband of a student worked in the Pentagon, and she was unable to reach him for several hours. Others had family or friends in New York. One of our graduates from the previous spring was the brand-new pastor in Shanksville, where he later reported some teenagers approached him and asked, "Is the world ending, pastor"? As the noon chapel hour approached, I wondered if the student scheduled to preside and preach would be up to the task. I offered support to Laurie Carson, who said she felt she could lead the community as planned. And lead us in prayer and lament she did! It was one of my proudest moments as president to observe a student rise to the occasion. We had a couple of faculty members away at conferences when all air traffic was halted for several days. Staying in touch with them and their families was important. Students and staff separated from their families needed a special measure of support, and several of us spent hours just wandering around various places on campus to be available as needed.

It was also, of course, a frightening day for us as a family. Pamela was speaking at a chaplain's breakfast in the Philadelphia area when word came of the attacks. Afraid that that area could also be a target, she rushed to Macrina's school and peeked in the window of her classroom. Puzzled at spying her mom, Macrina asked, "Mom, what are you doing here?" The teachers and administrators at Springside School had decided it was best not to alarm the students by sharing the horrible news in the early hours of the crisis. But soon, since older students had cell phones, word was out schoolwide, as it was all around the world. In addition to caring for our daughter alone while I needed to remain in Gettysburg, Pam joined in ministering to the distraught Philadelphia seminary community. And like so many, of course, we were frightened for our many friends in New York and Washington.

For over a dozen years, I wrote a biweekly reflection on our seminary website entitled, "From the Gettysburg P.O." Its double entendre was to stand for both "post office" and "president's office." In my September 19 entry, I thought it was important to sound a rebalancing note to the hyper-patriotic outpouring that seemed to be pitting America against the rest of the world (a widespread sentiment that would resurge to a startling degree fifteen years later when Donald Trump was elected president). So, I wrote and published the following:

In Terror's Aftermath: God Bless the *World*

> Like people everywhere, we at the Lutheran Theological Seminary at Gettysburg watched in shock and horror the images on television as the World Trade Center and Pentagon were

attacked and burned. We are especially mindful of our graduates, staff and students who minister to many affected directly or indirectly by the tragedies in New York, Washington, and western Pennsylvania.

Now, in terror's aftermath, may come even greater challenges for us who are called to public ministries. One of the challenges will be sober discernment as our political leaders and the body politic seek broad consensus about the nature of appropriate response to the terrorism that did not end with the death of 19 mass murderers on board four aircraft.

Everywhere—on homes and businesses, billboards, and roadside flashing signals—are signs that declare, "God Bless America." Indeed, we may and must pray that God will be with our nation in the days ahead. But we dare not let appropriate patriotism (the love of country) slide down the slippery slope into a blatant nationalism that demonizes entire nations or cultural groups. To give in to hatred or desires to strike out blindly against some generic enemy would be to play by the rules of those hate-filled terrorists who in broad daylight attacked like thieves in the night. As our Secretary of State, Colin Powell, has reminded us, many who died at "ground zero" in the *World Trade Center* were not U.S. citizens. They came from some sixty other countries. The attack was against civilization and humanity, not just America.

So, in our prayers and public ministries, may we who are people of faith implore the Almighty and declare with certainty, God bless the *world*. As religious leaders, both clergy and laity, may our prayer be: "Oh God, continue to grant healing and hope to all who suffer and grieve. As citizens, help us discern appropriate steps for prudent containment of terrorist acts and intentions. Guard us especially against prejudice and lashing out at persons who look or sound like they might be our enemies. In this season of uncertainty, grant us strength and courage. Bless the world. Bless the whole world! Amen."

In many ways, life has never returned to the way it was before September 11th. Heightened security everywhere restricts access to public spaces. Added screening measures make airline travel more challenging. Anti-immigrant sentiments were fueled by fear of "those others" who were assumed to be enemies, especially Muslims. In my own preaching, as I made the rounds of congregations representing the Seminary, I tried to sound bridge-building themes and remind people that "God so loves *the world*," not just the United States of America. It was encouraging that many colleagues, including our students, were committed to the ministry of reconciliation, calming fears, and signaling hope for the future.

Leading in Wider Arenas

Heads of institutions often are tapped for leadership roles beyond those exercised within their schools or other organizations. With so many challenges at the Seminary, during my early years, I deliberately kept my focus close to home and avoided getting swept in "extra-curricular" roles. But a couple of responsibilities could not be escaped. Most time-consuming was serving simultaneously as seminary president and Executive Director of the Eastern Cluster of Lutheran Seminaries. The Cluster had been formed just prior to my becoming president, and included the three eastern ELCA seminaries, Gettysburg, Philadelphia, and Southern (in Columbia, South Carolina). Clusters were formed as a result of the ELCA's "Study of Theological Education," which was launched shortly after the church merger was completed in 1988. The study's purpose was to address a question unresolved as three predecessor church bodies came together to form the ELCA: "How many seminaries does the 'new church' need, and where should they be located?" Early in that study process, it became apparent that each of the eight schools had its circle of fierce loyalists, and any attempts to close or merge one or more would be met with a political firestorm. As a result, when the study task force reported to the whole church in 1993 and again in 1995, among the recommendations was that the eight seminaries would form three "clusters" that would realize economic savings and enhance the collective offer of quality education and leadership formation beyond what any were capable of on their own.

As might be imagined, implementing this mandate did not come easily in the face of institutions with long histories, tenured faculties largely resistant to significant changes perceived to erode their autonomy, and fiercely loyal alumni/ae cadres. Happily, however, the one cluster that really "worked" for about fifteen years was our Eastern Cluster. In its founding, a few wise leaders with extensive experience in governance recognized that incorporating as a separate entity could give the Cluster some "teeth" and a unique identity that would transcend those of the individual schools. To enhance each school's ownership of the Cluster, it was decided that the presidents would rotate and serve for two-year periods as executive director overseeing any programs the cluster would carry out. These steps gave credibility to the Eastern Cluster never gained by the other two, and enabled it over the course of its life to garner more than $6 million in grants and external funding for Cluster-sponsored programs.

One of the first projects undertaken by the Cluster was the creation of "One Library Under Three Roofs." With advances in technology, it was possible to create a common online catalogue, making readily available to faculty and students all library resources housed on the three campuses. A jointly sponsored Doctor of Ministry degree involved all three faculties, as did an annual diaconal ministry formation event on the Gettysburg campus. During my first stint as executive director, a multi-million-dollar grant was secured from the Lilly Endowment, enabling the Cluster to launch a nationwide effort to stimulate interest in church vocations. Those and other joint programs helped the schools deepen partnerships, and to some degree, overcome the competitive and even contentious relationships that had existed, particularly between Gettysburg and Philadelphia.

During my presidential tenure, I also served twice as chairman of the ELCA seminary presidents' group that met regularly. Serving in that role drew me into other churchwide responsibilities like attending the meetings of the Conference of Bishops and ELCA Church Council. By virtue of my long tenure (by 2015 I had more time in office than the other seven ELCA presidents combined!), I was often called upon to be the spokesperson for the seminaries in a variety of ELCA and ecumenical circles. While the informal nature of our meetings did not include recording official "minutes," I took it upon myself to write detailed "meeting notes," which captured the discussions and decisions at meetings of the seminary presidents throughout my tenure. Those are preserved in the ELCA archives for future historians who may be interested in one of the most dramatic periods of transition in U.S. Lutheran theological education.

"Human Factors" Most Challenging and Rewarding

While I found my early years at the Seminary fulfilling in many ways, there were also a number of challenging situations that caused some dark nights of the soul. As noted above, contrary to unrealistic perceptions in some quarters that seminaries are "angel factories" populated by always-holy people, theological schools are human communities that experience the same personal and relational struggles as all others. Over the course of my years at Gettysburg, the "human factors" were always the most difficult aspect of the job. A number of faculty divorces strained collegial relationships, and befuddled some students who held their professors on pedestals. While relatively few, instances of inappropriate behavior or incompetence on the part of staff members required me to make difficult decisions to reprimand or dismiss individuals.

Then, too, as in any educational institution, there were a small number of students over the years who caused us considerable difficulty. While some minor offenses could be overlooked, or treated with a light touch, a few threatened the safety and well-being of individuals or the entire campus community. After the dean and I removed a firearm from a student housing unit, fearing its owner might harm himself or others, I discovered we had no policy precluding possession of weapons. Unwilling to await a prolonged round of debates, as is almost inevitable in adopting any policy by widespread consultation in an academic institution, I simply decreed a ban on firearms, upsetting a few staff and board members who felt I had exceeded my authority. When it came up at a board meeting, I stated forcefully, "I will never allow the safety of the inhabitants of this campus to be compromised, and that's the end of this discussion." It was.

In 2003, Dr. Norma Wood completed her four-year term as Dean of the Seminary. I have said on many occasions that I doubt I would have accepted the call to serve as president had Norma not been the dean. I first came to know this gifted woman in my student days, when Norma had served as a part-time instructor in pastoral care and counseling. Her institutional knowledge after three decades at the school, the confidence she elicited on the part of faculty colleagues, and the respect in which she was held in broad ecclesial and academic circles was without parallel. Coming to the presidency without background in academia, I relied upon Norma in so many ways as guide and mentor. I knew that naming a successor dean would be a challenge.

As a search for the next dean was launched, we cast the net far and wide, attracting a large pool of candidates eager to be considered for the role. A search committee, which I chaired, considered applicants with a wide range of academic and administrative credentials. But as the process continued, it became clear to me and some others that the strongest candidate was right in our midst. Theology and ethics professor, Dr. Robin Steinke, was a "second career" ordained minister who held a doctorate in theology from Cambridge University in Britain. Since her "first career" had been as a corporate executive, it was clear her administrative capabilities were strong. Robin quickly gained the confidence of the Seminary community in her new role, and served a dozen years as dean, until she left Gettysburg to become president of the ELCA's largest seminary, Luther in St. Paul.

Soon after Norma retired and Robin became dean, we needed to conduct a search for a professor to fill Dr. Wood's faculty position in pastoral care and counseling. Pam and I were aware that, since she was already a widely respected pastoral theologian, it was possible she would be nominated for the position. While we had determined her being faculty at the school where I was president would be challenging for us as a couple, and for the Seminary, support for her candidacy on the part of several Gettysburg faculty raised my hopes it might be workable. We both, of course, felt the pull to live in one location again. Pam and I had further discussions in which she agreed to enter into further discernment about the possibility, and she also had a conversation with Robin as Gettysburg's dean. In the end, as Pam was about to be promoted to full professor at Philadelphia and was also serving in a vibrant part-time parish ministry, she felt that she needed to stay in that call. Also in the mix was the reality that Macrina, just entering her teenage years, had a circle of close friends and was in an excellent school in Philadelphia that she didn't want to leave. Nevertheless, when Pam made the final decision to foreclose the possibility, I felt a good measure of disappointment. Suffice it to say, this was challenging for us as a couple. Like so many dual career couples, we struggled to balance what was best for each of us individually with our commitment to our marriage and family. That mutual commitment saw us through that challenging time and others as we navigated our "commuter marriage" for more than a quarter century.

The greatest challenge during what I regard as the first extended "chapter" of my leadership at the Seminary came when, once again, major budget reductions were required to avoid risking the school's financial stability. At the January 2006 board meeting, I informed the directors that I would be initiating another comprehensive budget review process like the one I launched upon assuming the presidency. In communicating to seminary employees that the process would be challenging and probably require downsizing of staff, I did not sugarcoat the severity of our financial situation. Despite what I felt was a high level of transparency, the measures I ultimately imposed to bring the budget into balance were met with shock, disbelief, and widespread anger.

To achieve expenditure reductions upward of twenty percent, I knew that personnel reductions had to include some at the higher salary levels. The most troublesome for many to accept, including some board members, was my decision to eliminate the chief financial officer's position and lodge fiscal oversight in the hands of a very competent controller. Multiple additional staff changes were required, and other popular staff members' positions were eliminated. While tempted to defer the decisions until summertime when the campus would be quiet and virtually void of students, I accepted counsel that so doing would appear to be cowardly and I should face the music during the spring term.

Except for my "final chapter," when there was widespread sharp criticism surrounding the Gettysburg-Philadelphia consolidation process and my leadership in it, the 2006 "restructuring" as it came to be widely described, was the most difficult and lonely time in my presidency. In addition to internal criticism, questioning of my leadership came from some alumni, clergy and even my own bishop and synod, whose governing council wrote a sharply critical letter to the Seminary board. While stopping short of calling for my firing, its intent was obvious in signaling to the board it needed to rein in an irresponsible and insensitive president. The board also received a letter signed by a dozen-and-a-half clergy calling for my dismissal, and many trustees' telephone and email traffic was ablaze with criticism and calls for my head to roll.

After announcing the restructuring and staffing decisions, I knew that the spring 2006 board meeting would be challenging. But I was taken aback at the intensity on the part of some directors. Since we were dealing with matters of personnel, the board went into a confidential executive session, which lasted over three hours! Some members of the board seemed to have the need to go around and around on what an awful situation had been created, how the Seminary's reputation had been damaged, its future seriously jeopardized etc. I attempted to listen carefully and non-defensively. But finally, I'd had enough. "Look," I said, moving my eyes from person to person around the twenty-eight-member governing body, "these are good decisions; they were mine to make, and I made them to ensure the future of this institution." I was willing to be fired, but I would not cede the authority of the presidential office nor allow a couple of board members to bully me. Shortly afterwards, the executive session was adjourned and my most challenging board meeting concluded. Upon returning to my office, John Spangler said something to the effect of, "That must have been tough." I responded, "Well, I took a few punches in the ring, but it never came close to a knockdown!"

Both at that time and now with many years of distance from the events of that difficult season, I occasionally continue to engage in self-examination about my decisions. Could it have been done in a less painful way? Perhaps. It may have been the better call to await summer so dismissed employees would not have had to face a full campus during their last days. Perhaps I should have consulted more extensively with the board, though its size and range of views made achieving broad consensus unlikely. Could I have been more politically savvy in timing and preparing a broader group to bear the shock with me? Probably, though as is always the case, the wider a circle "in the know" becomes, the greater the chance for a premature leak that undoes the best laid plans for careful communication. As time moved along, the unrest surrounding the restructuring subsided, and I began to hear more voices privately affirming the difficult choices I had made. In later years, the fact that Gettysburg was rare among seminaries in consistently maintaining balanced budgets was recognized broadly.

During Sabbatical, Near Miss in High Profile Election

Following more than six intense years at the helm of the seminary, and in the aftermath of all the turmoil experienced in the previous year, I eagerly looked forward to a planned sabbatical that the board had encouraged me to take. At the same time, as I studied the histories at other schools where presidents encountered difficult reentries (and in some cases were eased out) following sabbaticals, I was wary of being out of the picture entirely for an extended period. Accordingly, I recommended that the board not follow a common practice of designating an "acting president" during my sabbatical. I assured the board that in the era of modern technology, I would be readily accessible by email or telephone should my weighing in on critical matters be deemed necessary. I also announced plans to return to campus every two to three weeks for brief check-ins, so that my ongoing leadership would not be in question. In my communications I referred to my "semi-sabbatical" as another way of sending a signal I would not be totally out of the picture.

In that same timeframe of early 2007, I began to hear that, as the ELCA prepared to elect a new churchwide secretary at its biennial assembly in August, my name was being discussed in broad circles. I understood that by virtue of having served as chief staff person for the Conference of Bishops and executive assistant to the presiding bishop, I was known widely throughout the church. While by no means feeling my work at Gettysburg was completed, I nevertheless felt I should be open to the possibility of serving in the second-highest office of the ELCA. Even as I loved my work at the seminary, the prospect of returning to Chicago and a position of wide influence nationally and even internationally held its appeal.

The Evangelical Lutheran Church in America has one of the most unusual methods of electing bishops and churchwide officers. Unlike most other church bodies, which have a more typical nominating and candidate vetting process, the ELCA elects those who serve in its highest offices by what's known as the "ecclesiastical ballot." That means simply that there are no pre-nominated candidates and anyone who meets the broad qualifications for an office can emerge in a highly democratic process. By contrast to the presiding bishop's and synodical bishops' elections, when only ordained pastors can be elected, any member of the church can be elected secretary. So, there were upwards of five million potential candidates for that office when 1000 voting members came together in Chicago for the 2007 churchwide assembly! On the first ballot, voters can write the name of any individual, and then the candidate list is narrowed ballot by ballot until someone is finally elected by majority vote. As the assembly neared, I was told by many that I was among a half-dozen or so thought most likely to emerge as serious candidates for the office. I had even received a formal visit from the national chair of Lutherans Concerned, a group strongly promoting full inclusion of gay and lesbian persons in the church's life, encouraging me and assuring me I was their preferred nominee.

Some weeks prior to the assembly, however, a troubling conversation took place. Presiding Bishop Mark Hanson and I had worked together when I was staff for the Conference of Bishops and he was the bishop of the Saint Paul Area Synod. We had collaborated especially closely in conjunction with the crisis surrounding the Called to Common Mission impasse and the Milwaukee meeting described above. Following his election as presiding bishop, Mark had even requested that I meet with him to consult regarding key staffing decisions and how he might achieve a strong launch of his administration. But apparently more than I realized, I had rankled Hanson and his staff at the previous churchwide assembly in 2005, when I introduced a simple resolution of appreciation to churchwide staff members whose positions were being eliminated by budget cuts and reorganization. When it became apparent to me that many in the assembly were unaware of the coming layoffs, I felt the church needed to issue people losing their jobs a word of thanks for their service. After I spoke to the matter in the assembly, Hanson was so frustrated he blurted out, "Oh, no you don't!" Later in the assembly he offered a public apology to me for his outburst. But it was clear that he remained offended, and in our 2007 conversation he signaled his reservations about how well we could work together should I be elected secretary. I continued to feel the church had a right to determine who could best serve in the secretary's office and was not scared off by that awkward exchange.

Having observed many elections by that unpredictable process of the ecclesiastical ballot, I knew as I arrived at Chicago for the assembly that anything could happen. When the results of the first ballot were announced, I had the most votes, but only 170 or so of the total nearly 1000. The big surprise that developed was that a layman from the west coast was gaining steam. Additionally, one of the outgoing secretary's assistants gained votes ballot by ballot, apparently convincing many voters his experience in the office was a strong qualification. On the final ballot, David Swartling, an attorney serving as lay vice president of a west coast synod, was elected and I ended up third following Secretary Lowell Almen's assistant. Despite not emerging victorious in the election, I received a great deal of affirmation during and following the assembly. After the finalists' brief addresses to the assembly, Bishop April Larson, the ELCA's first female bishop, handed me a note sharing her view that mine had been the best speech ever made at a churchwide assembly. Another synod bishop, Margaret Payne of the New England Synod, wrote to me after the assembly offering thanks for my openness to serve as ELCA Secretary. She suggested that she felt some had chosen not to vote for me in the secretary's election because they felt the seminary needed my continuing leadership. Her letter also said, "It seems that the assembly somehow was leaning toward a lay person for the office, regardless of the credentials and gifts of the ordained candidates."

In the weeks that followed the assembly, when there was the typical "post-game debriefing," I learned that Bishop Payne's instincts were on the mark. Many of the synodical vice presidents, all of whom are lay persons, had caucused and become excited at the prospect that the secretary's office would be filled by one of their own. Also, what seemed to have been a promise of solid support from those advocating for full inclusion of the LGBTQ community, began to erode as many voters learned that Swartling's advocacy would be as strong as mine. For the record, I want to conclude this segment with affirmation for the church's choice in that 2007 election. David Swartling proved to be an outstanding secretary for the ELCA. By virtue of his professional experience as an attorney, he undoubtedly was more effective in some areas than I could have been. In the years of his service, I enjoyed many good conversations with him and his wife Barbara, and always found them to be persons of extraordinary grace, humility, and commitment to the whole church.

While feeling a measure of disappointment as we drove home from Chicago, I also had a sense of renewed calling to serve the Seminary in the years ahead. At the encouragement of my board chair and John Spangler, I issued a written communication to the Seminary community, emphasizing that my openness to the secretary's position signaled no dissatisfaction in my current position. During the remainder of the semi-sabbatical, I finished a manuscript for my second book, *The Comeback God*, and enjoyed that project, and especially spending more time with Pam and Macrina in Philadelphia and at our get-away house on a small lake in the Poconos.

— 11 —

Seminary in an Era of Historic Transformation

As I SETTLED BACK into seminary life after the turmoil of the administrative and governance restructuring and the possibility of a call as a churchwide officer, I hoped for a period of relative stability if not tranquility. But it was not to be so. By late 2007 there were signs on the economic horizon that a major recession was looming. In March 2008 the greatest economic downturn since the Great Depression of the 1930's descended upon the nation. A dramatic collapse of stock values resulted in plummeting institutional endowments and individual investment portfolios. Donors to charitable causes of all types grew anxious and began to close their wallets.

When the seminary board met in April of 2008, as anxiety was building across the nation and around the world, I expressed confidence that we would weather the turbulent economic times. In my heart, I was worried that we would have to undergo another round of painful budget reductions to ride the growing recession. And I was concerned about possible embarrassment that would result if we fell far short of an ambitious revised goal for our *Crossroads* fund-raising campaign. Two years before, the board had approved a five-year $12 million campaign to address some pressing needs that could not be absorbed by annual budgets. By January of 2008, less than half-way through the campaign period of working synod-by-synod in our region, commitments had exceeded

$11 million. So, the board confidently doubled the goal to $25 million. Within weeks the economic crisis came on like a tsunami! I feared the campaign would languish, there would be a sense of defeat, and loss of confidence in me and our Development department's leadership. Happily, within another two years, and well before the economy had fully recovered, we had raised over $24 million in the campaign, and were well along the way toward ambitious goals established for a new Seminary Ridge Museum project (more to follow on that). Achieving those results under such trying circumstances gave a boost to morale and seemed to fortify solid confidence in my ability to maintain a steady hand at the helm amid troubling waters.

Economic Crisis Forced All Seminaries to "Get Real"

Within the vast lore from the Evangelical Lutheran Church in America's (ELCA) early years is an encounter between the first presiding bishop and presidents of the ELCA-affiliated colleges and universities. As the "new church" found itself in serious financial deficit during its early years, Bishop Herbert Chilstrom faced many groups who were angry about funding cuts. At a meeting with the college presidents, he told these chief executives of mostly well-funded and heavily endowed institutions the larger church would no longer be providing them with financial subsidies. "It's time to get real," Chilstrom told the presidents politely but firmly.

By the end of the century's first decade, we who served as chief stewards of the ELCA's eight seminaries did not need an external authority to tell us it was time for us also to "get real" in terms of extreme financial stresses. As occurred in almost every mainline denomination in the U.S., the ELCA had experienced declining church attendance year after year. In all corners of the church, a majority of congregations were shrinking in membership. More congregations were closing than new ones being created. Local churches passed along a diminishing proportion of their income to larger church agencies and institutions.

When I began my ordained ministry in the mid-1970's congregations were sharing around fifteen percent of their income with the larger church; by 2010 that figure had shrunk to around five or six percent. In my student days at Gettysburg, eighty percent of the budget was provided by the school's supporting synods and national church. During my presidency three decades later, only twenty percent came from the larger church. Tuition costs mushroomed, fundraising (development) efforts were expanded dramatically, and schools scrambled to attract legacy gifts that would build endowments as permanent income-generating sources. But we simply could not keep up with the escalating fiscal challenges. Annual audits revealed alarming deficit spending trends in most of the schools. Endowments were being tapped to fill gaps in current income and avoid even more dire tuition increases. It was apparent that my austere budget-cutting days were not over if we were to buck the trend, continue achieving balanced budgets, and preserve our endowment.

Fortunately, in our small-town locale, we did not bear some of the burdens of the schools located in more urban centers, where construction and maintenance costs, as well as security measures, added substantial expenses. I also acknowledge that we maintained fiscal stability by continuing to shrink the work force. Eliminating the positions of faithful and dedicated staff members disrupted their lives and caused widespread angst. The faculty was reduced by one-third during my years, and administrative staff cuts meant fewer people were expected to take on added workloads.

While in the early years of the 2000's, enrollments remained relatively strong at the ELCA seminaries (and both Gettysburg and Philadelphia saw quite dramatic increases for several years), that trend took a rather precipitous nosedive beginning around 2012. Within just a few years, overall enrollments declined significantly. That larger trend was mirrored at both schools in the northeast, to the point that during my last years at Gettysburg we plummeted to fewer than half the number of students enrolled just a few years before.

As we seminary presidents analyzed these enrollment trends, coupled with the growing budget deficits, aging infrastructures, and other challenges, we collectively began to call upon ELCA executives responsible for relating to theological education for assistance in planning. Though we were reluctant to admit it to one another or even ourselves in some cases, it appeared that the very survival of some schools was at issue. In January of 2009 a meeting I referred to as a "Seminary Summit" was held in Chicago. It included presidents and board chairs of all eight schools, along with a few others chosen for their expertise, including LTSG Dean Robin Steinke. While acknowledging that all the schools faced uncertain economic futures, there was continuing denial of the severity in some and optimism that the economic recession would turn around in time so that radical moves could be avoided. At that consultation and subsequent presidents' meetings, it became clear to me that while some of my colleagues recognized things could not continue on the same trajectory, their boards clung fiercely to institutional autonomy and had limited capacity to imagine a systemic new future for ELCA theological education.

I experienced growing frustration at the churchwide hand-wringing that was not leading us into new configurations. On several occasions I suggested to our ELCA churchwide leaders responsible for theological education that the presiding bishop and they could exert significantly more leverage. Their tepid response was typical of institutions faced with crisis—a task force was charged to engage in further study. The ELCA Church Council (governing board) formed a Theological Education Advisory Committee (TEAC), whose co-chair was Robin Steinke (soon to leave Gettysburg and serve as president at Luther Seminary). TEAC engaged a financial firm, Baker Tilly, to conduct a comprehensive audit of all eight schools and make recommendations. It dramatized the school-by-school and systemic unsustainability given enrollment and financial trends. Among possible solutions offered in the consultants' report was a recommendation that seminaries give serious consideration to new partnerships, including mergers with one another or other compatible institutions.

The first to make a bold move to ensure continuing theological education in the southeast was Southern Seminary, which announced in 2011 that it would merge and become a department or "divinity school" of Lenoir Rhyne University, a Lutheran undergraduate institution. While that ensured Southern's survival as an "embedded school,"[1] it led to the rapid dissolution of the Eastern Cluster of Lutheran Seminaries. Southern's new president's stance went beyond disinterest to outright hostility toward the Cluster. As a result, the entity that had brought about $6 million in external grants, and enabled significant joint programming for fifteen years, was virtually dismantled by 2015. But Southern's move was a harbinger of things to come in the years ahead.

---

1. In the world of North American theological education, currently about sixty percent of 280 seminaries are "free-standing" (independently incorporated and autonomously governed by their own boards). The remainder are referred to as "embedded schools," or graduate departments of larger universities. They typically have advisory boards and are led by deans, but the ultimate decision-makers are university boards and presidents.

Amidst Economic Crisis, Advancing on the Ridge

As I look back upon the middle years of my presidency at Gettysburg, I find it quite stunning that even amidst a severe economic crisis, rather than stepping back in retreat we were advancing in one of the most ambitious projects of the school's nearly two centuries. Prior to my arrival in 2000, my predecessor and other leaders had caught a vision of making Gettysburg Seminary a much more public place by leveraging its unique location and historic properties. With the promise of a planning grant from the Pennsylvania state government, thanks to an ELCA member with ties to the Seminary who was state treasurer at the time, a separate corporate entity was formed in 1999, the Seminary Ridge Historic Preservation Foundation (SRHPF). Its formation was necessary since the seminary itself—a non-profit entity whose sole purpose was religious education—would not be eligible for state or federal funds, whereas the new corporation with the sole purpose of historic preservation could land such major funding.

While the initial grant of $250,000 was substantial, it was exhausted within a few years by the studies required to begin contemplating the total rehabilitation of the Seminary's most famous structure, Schmucker Hall or "Old Dorm." The building stood at the epicenter of the first day of the battle of Gettysburg, and then, in the battle's aftermath, served as one of its largest field hospitals for soldiers from both north and south. By any civil war historian's assessment, it is one of the most iconic structures or "artifacts" of the entire American civil war. But due to the seminary's financial constraints during and after World War II, by the 1950's the building had fallen into such a state of disrepair that it could no longer be occupied as a dormitory or classroom building. At one point, the seminary board adopted a preliminary vote to demolish the historic edifice. Fortunately, before that could occur, external parties became involved, and the building then served for four decades as home to the local historical society of Adams County.

When the state grant was gone, the SRHPF board lost momentum and it seemed as though the grand vision planted a few years earlier would never be realized. As often happens when things reach such a stage of lethargy or disappointment, leadership change was needed to regroup and explore new pathways forward. A key in that regard was my agreement when a few board members and others suggested we needed to take SRHPF leadership "in house" among Seminary staff and, as gracefully as possible, dismiss a small group of volunteers who seemed paralyzed. About the same time, I received an invitation to breakfast from a well-known local pediatrician.

In 2006, Dr. Bradley Hoch was serving as chairman of the Adams County Historical Society (ACHS). While I had become acquainted with Brad in that capacity, we did not know each other well, so I was surprised to be invited to breakfast at his home. Also invited were Em Cole, the Seminary's new Vice President for Advancement, whom Brad had come to know through other civic organizations in which the two participated, and Wayne Motts, executive director of the ACHS. At one point during the course of the breakfast, Brad leaned back in his chair and said, "I want to share a vision with you." Over the next few minutes, he laid out a detailed plan, including sketches, for the rehabilitation of Schmucker Hall and its conversion into a first-rate museum. Brad envisioned that the "Voices of History" project would interpret the history of the first day of the Gettysburg battle, the Seminary's role and that of religion, together with Old Dorm's use as the largest field hospital on the battlefield. A bit taken aback following Brad's presentation, my initial reaction was simply, "It's a great vision, Brad, and it looks very challenging."

My assessment proved correct—a challenge it was indeed! Initially doubtful that the funds could be raised, I proceeded cautiously in introducing the possibility to the Seminary board and faculty. Being the fiscal conservative that I am, I could not see my way to authorize expenditure of the Seminary's limited resources on such a risky proposition. Fortunately, Brad, Em, and my executive assistant, John Spangler, had bolder spirits and kept leaning on me to get behind a full-throttle exploration of options. A breakthrough came when Brad led the ACHS in making a commitment to form a partnership and join the Seminary in funding exploratory efforts by a Harrisburg consulting and lobbying firm, Delta Development. Through Delta's efforts, alongside personal contacts with key local and Pennsylvania leaders and legislators on the part of Em, Brad, and John, applications were submitted for multi-million-dollar grants from Pennsylvania government sources.

U.S. Presidential Visit Offered Additional Encouragement

In the fall of 2008, I was sitting in my office one day when a call came from a renowned professor at Gettysburg College. Civil War historian and Lincoln scholar Gabor Boritt greeted me and asked, "Michael, what are you doing tomorrow? Would you have time to greet the president"? First thinking he had in mind the college interim president, Janet Riggs, whom I already knew, I then asked, "Gabor, do you mean *the* president, as in U.S. president"? "Yes, exactly," was his response! "I want both my presidents (college and seminary) to greet the Bushes," Gabor concluded. While I was no fan of George W. Bush, I determined that proper respect for the office required my joining President Riggs and local officials in greeting the President of the United States.

As his second term in the White House was nearing its conclusion, the president and First Lady Laura Bush held a reunion with his Texas gubernatorial staff at Camp David just across the Maryland border. Apparently, somewhat spur of the moment, a decision was made that the group would tour the Gettysburg battlefield and recently opened stunning new Visitors' Center. Dr. Boritt's books had been read by Bush adviser Karl Rove, who asked him to conduct the tour for the president, first lady, and Bush's current and former aides. What we imagined would be a simple meet-and-greet turned into an actual conversation with the Bushes, who expressed amazement at the public/private partnerships that had developed in Gettysburg during the previous decade. "We learned from what you've done here in Gettysburg," Bush said, indicating that it gave impetus to the administration's funneling additional funds into the Save America's Treasures historic preservation efforts. Going beyond her husband's comments, Laura Bush said, "We'd like to support your efforts." Thinking she meant following Bush's retirement the following January, we were surprised when she said, "We'll invite you to the White House before we leave." During the conversation, I was also able to brief the president on our plans to create the Seminary Ridge Museum. I explained that on the heels of opening the new Visitors' Center and renovated Wills House (where Lincoln slept the night before his famous speech), the Seminary Ridge Museum would complete a multi-year plan developed by a dozen community groups and governmental agencies working together through an umbrella agency called *Main Street Gettysburg*.

On the evening of November 19, 2008, Gettysburg's Remembrance Day (the anniversary of Abraham Lincoln's iconic Gettysburg Address), a group of about three dozen supporters of Gettysburg's historic preservation efforts were hosted by the Bushes in a private reception at the White House. On our way to the event, just days after Barack Obama's election as president, Pam quipped, "Right event, wrong White House!"

After clearing the stringent security checks, we were given a private tour, catnip for the historians among us, which included famous Civil War scholar, Professor James McPherson of Princeton. After mingling with the other guests, and chatting with our congressional representative, Todd Platts, we joined the line for personal greetings from the Bushes. In our exchange with the president and first lady, we spoke primarily of our common experience having daughters who studied at Yale. As we started to move on, "W" jovially slapped Pam on the back, so hard she had to hop-step forward. Next, we were ushered into the Red Room for the customary photo with the Bushes. Pam and I went to stand together on one side of the presidential couple. "W" suddenly grabbed her hand and whisked her over by his side since the protocol is for a couple to flank the president and first lady. As he did so, he said, "Come 'ere, babe!" I saw Pam smiling through gritted teeth, and thought to myself, "The president of the United States just called my feminist spouse a babe, and we need to just grin and bear it. If we cause a ruckus, we'll be unceremoniously ushered out by the Secret Service!"

As the group gathered following the individual photos, in his unscripted remarks, Bush lived up to his reputation of sometimes sounding a bit clueless. "Yep," he said, "Lincoln sure gave a great speech there in Gettysburg." Pam and I avoided looking at each other, for fear of laughing out loud, and I thought to myself, "Indeed so—the most famous oration in U.S. history." Given the overall impact of the Bush administration, causing further income inequality, and favoring the rich, and especially his launching the Gulf War that resulted in the deaths of tens of thousands for no good reason, we have been reluctant to reveal our participation in a small intimate gathering at the White House. But it happened, and the story needs to be included here for the record. Although her parents proudly hung in their living room a copy of the photo we gave them, Pam absolutely refuses to display the signed original in our home!

Museum Project a Team Effort All the Way

Over the course of a seven-year period, the Seminary and Historical Society succeeded in converting Schmucker Hall to a world-class, award-winning museum. Given its powerful witness, the Seminary Ridge Museum was added by the Museums of Conscience organization to its international list of sites worthy of visitation for their moral and social impact. With total costs upwards of $16 million—for complete rehabilitation (resulting in the 180-year-old building achieving LEED eco-friendly status), museum interpretive installations, parking, and other site development—the project was completed with only $3.5 million of long-term debt. More than $10 million was realized from federal and state grants coupled with a complicated "tax credit structure" that Cole stewarded, which required every ounce of his legal expertise and diplomatic skills in relating to bank executives and attorneys. Many highly regarded attorneys, accountants, and investment professionals on our boards, and in other ways connected to the Seminary, could only marvel at the complexity of the process involving over a dozen governmental entities along with PNC Bank's international corporate offices.

Another key player at critical junctures (such as when a mistake by the Seminary's auditors one year created the threat of losing millions and required submission of a hundred-page "private letter ruling" to the Internal Revenue Service) was Dr. Marty Stevens. At my invitation, Stevens had come to the Seminary some years earlier in a combined role as registrar and part-time Bible instructor. A so-called "second career" pastor, whose initial occupation was as a CPA in banking, Stevens brought an incredible skillset to LTSG. Already doing two jobs, when the Seminary lost its chief financial officer to another agency, Stevens stepped in on a temporary basis initially, but then filled the CFO role for several years during the highly complicated Schmucker Hall rehab and museum-creation process. On many occasions I said light-heartedly but also in all sincerity to the Seminary board and others, "I think there are only two people on the planet—Em Cole and Marty Stevens—who fully understand this complex 'structure' that contains the Seminary Ridge Museum."

I also must point with admiration to John Spangler as being "chief air traffic controller" at the epicenter throughout the construction and Museum start-up phases. Knowing that thousands of decisions would be required by us as "owners" of the project that involved dozens of subcontractors, government agencies and regulators, we appointed John and Brad Hoch as project managers for the SRHPF/Seminary and ACHS. They never missed a beat in their interfacing with all the entities and hundreds of individuals involved in bringing the project to completion on time and within budget. Given that Brad remained engaged full-time as senior partner in a large medical practice, John bore the brunt of the work on a daily basis. For a long time, his contributions went largely unrecognized. Upon his retirement in 2022, the Adams County

Commissioners responded enthusiastically to my suggestion that John be awarded a special public commendation for his efforts on behalf of the seminary, SRHPF, and ACHS. These key local leaders concurred with my assessment that without John's efforts, the Seminary Ridge Museum, which in addition to its intrinsic value further enhanced Gettysburg's lucrative tourist business, would not exist. The county's commendation also recognized John's leadership of the Seminary's eco-friendly "greening" measures, and his contributions in the wider community.

With my responsibilities as Seminary president, I grew increasingly comfortable with the museum-creation prospects, while remaining clear the massive project had to be structured to avoid threatening the Seminary's primary mission of theological education and preparing church leaders. After more than a decade of experience as a president, I had also observed colleagues in other schools get so caught up in managing major building and fund-raising projects that other aspects of their callings were neglected. I did not want my leadership to be similarly compromised. Accordingly, I resolved that my role would be one of high-level oversight, which was made possible by virtue of delegating responsibility and authority to Spangler, Cole and Stevens. I had total confidence in them, as well as Hoch and those with whom we contracted for the various phases of construction, museum design and build-out. We also were blessed that a nationally recognized leader in the museum world, Barbara Franco, was completing her work elsewhere and we were able to hire her as the museum's first executive director.

On July 1, 2013, thousands of Civil War enthusiasts had descended upon Gettysburg for the long-awaited three-day observance of the 150th anniversary of the pivotal battle of the American Civil War. The kick-off event for the entire celebration took place on the steps of Schmucker Hall as we held the official Grand Opening of the Seminary Ridge Museum (SRM). While President Obama had not accepted an invitation to come to Gettysburg for the 150th, the governor of the Commonwealth of Pennsylvania was on hand, together with one of our U.S. senators, congressman, state legislators, and dozens of local political and civic leaders. ELCA Presiding Bishop Mark Hanson, who had led a dedicatory prayer service on the west-facing "Peace Portico" the prior evening, joined us as well. As we conducted the ribbon-cutting on the eastern stairway that bright summer morning, I could only marvel at all that had transpired to create what I referred to in my brief remarks as "a gift to the Gettysburg community, to the nation and to the world."[2]

With the opening of the Seminary Ridge Museum, Gettysburg Seminary had moved into another chapter of its long and illustrious history. Together with our board, faculty, and others, I was hopeful that the momentum developed among our various constituencies around the Museum project would help reverse the decline in student enrollment, and also expand the seminary's donor pool. That would not prove to be the case.

With colleague John Spangler as Pennsylvania Governor Tom Corbett cuts ribbon at Seminary Ridge Museum Grand Opening: July 1, 2013

Other Developments in My Middle Years

The period from 2007 to 2014 constituted what might be regarded as the middle years of my seventeen-year presidency at Gettysburg. While the construction and launch of the Seminary Ridge Museum stands out as the Seminary's most significant public development of those years, much was going on internally and less visibly as well. In 2010–11 we went

---

2. The complete story of the Schmucker Hall renovation and creation of Seminary Ridge Museum is set forth in Bradley Hoch's 2022 publication, *To Save a National Treasure: Gettysburg's Schmucker Hall and Seminary Ridge Museum and Education Center 1950 to 2022*.

through the second decennial accreditation cycle on my watch, with a very positive outcome of an unqualified reaccreditation (with no "notations" citing serious problematic areas) for a ten-year period from both accrediting agencies. Major expansion of our academic offerings came by way of beginning to field more courses online and equipping the faculty for new pedagogical approaches.

Those years also brought joy as I hit my stride and became more involved in teaching. I led the senior seminars for students who had returned from their parish internships eager to reflect upon their learnings and sharpen skills in practical areas of leadership and administration. Similar courses were offered in summer sessions for groups involved in alternative pathways to ministry. Especially enjoyable were leading small groups of students in immersive study trips to Central America. Those trips enabled me to polish off my rusty Spanish and reconnect with the likes of El Salvador's heroic Lutheran Bishop Medardo Gomez.

With Salvadoran Bishop Gomez on one of our student study trips.

As occurs in any organization, colleagues moved in and out over those years, but we were blessed with continuity in key senior leadership positions. When he completed his service as board chair just as we needed a new Advancement vice president, I asked Glenn Ludwig to serve in that role. Under his leadership, our annual fund grew impressively, giving a renewed sense of the Seminary's ability to cultivate and maintain a broad network of financial support. A key change came in 2014 when, after serving as dean at Gettysburg for a dozen years, Dr. Robin Steinke was called to serve as president of the ELCA's largest seminary, Luther in St. Paul. Given the ongoing explorations of possible seminary reconfigurations, as well as seeing my own retirement on the horizon within a couple of years, I was reluctant to forge ahead in a search for a dean who would serve the standard four-year term. I consulted individually with each faculty member about naming an interim dean, and there was no strong consensus about an obvious internal candidate. Having observed her strong administrative skills and witnessed her fearless approach when difficult issues had to be faced, as well as her unflinching direct confrontation with me on occasion when she felt I was going down the wrong path, I asked Kristen Largen to fill the dean's office for a transitional period. Somewhat reluctantly, since she didn't feel particularly called to administrative work and was hesitant to give up time for her impressive publishing and scholarly work, Kristen accepted. Within a year, when it appeared dramatic changes were likely to occur before things would settle again, the board affirmed my recommendation to drop the "interim" and simply designate Largen as Dean of the Seminary for an unspecified term. As things would unfold, choosing Kristen was one of the best decisions I ever made, as her leadership in what was to follow was a key to its success. Her service as dean at Gettysburg undoubtedly also contributed to her being named president of her alma mater, Wartburg Seminary, in 2021.

The middle years of my presidency also brought significant changes in stewarding the seminary campus, as well as in its governance patterns. As noted, John Spangler's inspiration and dogged determination was key to forming a "Green Task Force" that gave attention to myriad ways in which the campus could be made more eco-friendly. We began monitoring our carbon footprint, installed composting facilities and low-flow water devices campus wide. In the most dramatic move, geothermal heating and cooling systems were installed for the chapel and Seminary Ridge Museum. In tandem with the Museum's development, and utilizing additional government funds acquired, we also installed a mile-long self-guided walking pathway that winds through the campus. Signposts along the way interpret for pathway pilgrims the history of both the civil war battle and Seminary.

In terms of governance, along with the staff restructuring into four administrative teams, and faculty governance restructuring early in Steinke's time as dean, we realigned the board into four governance committees that mirrored the staff pattern. Those changes were strongly endorsed by the board, which seemed to grow significantly in its oversight capacities. Also, another separate corporate entity was formed, the Gettysburg Seminary Endowment Foundation (GSEF), and we transferred the endowment's assets into that corporation, which had its own board of trustees. In addition to some intrinsic value of safeguarding assets in a separate corporate entity, this move expanded the circle of the seminary's governance partners and enabled us to appoint persons with investment expertise and proven or potential major giving capacity as well. As with the museum, Em Cole's leadership was critical in this endeavor, together with that of the one who served as GSEF chair throughout its life, Frank Leber, churchman extraordinaire and a senior partner in one of Harrisburg's most prestigious law firms.

As we experienced a steady decline in enrollment, which was mirrored at an almost identical pace in the other ELCA seminaries and more broadly in ATS circles, a "Seminary Futures" task force was appointed to seek creative new approaches that might attract students who could no longer commit to the traditional residential four-year degree model. More online and intensive on-campus courses were offered. We also increased funding for scholarships to make seminary more financially affordable. As was occurring widely in theological education, we explored options for reducing requirements and time-to-degree without watering down the quality of theological education and leadership formation. These explorations, which were going on almost everywhere, searched for what was described in shorthand as "shorter, faster, cheaper, and more accessible." Despite our best efforts, things did not seem to be turning around in terms of enrollment. Similarly, while our annual fund grew under Ludwig's leadership, church support from synods and churchwide coffers was flat or declining as their own revenues from congregations waned steadily.

A review of my annual reports to the board in those middle years of my presidency (submitted in October each year as required by the Seminary's bylaws), confirms that I was perennially raising the caution flag that we could not continue doing business as usual. Despite my repeated warnings, few seemed to fully grasp reality or gain a sense of urgency. At times I wondered if my own energy was flagging and thought perhaps the Seminary needed a new leader to experience a resurgence. But as I looked around at other schools, both ELCA and ecumenical, I saw many that had new and dynamic leaders but were in the same pattern of enrollment decline and on financially unsustainable trajectories. More and more, I was attempting to nudge the board in the direction of openness to radical changes. It helped in that regard that first Southern and then Pacific Lutheran (PLTS) Seminaries had merged into Lutheran universities. Wondering if that were at all an option for Gettysburg long-term, I initiated exploratory conversations with my colleague down the hill, Janet Riggs, president of Gettysburg College. While the relationship between the two institutions had always been cordial, and we had drawn closer in the years of Janet's presidency, she was firm that the college's identity was solid as undergraduate-only and they would not be interested in bringing the Seminary under their umbrella. We did commit to seeking ways to expand collaboration between the two schools.

So, if following the pathway taken by three of our peers (Trinity Seminary in Ohio soon followed suit with Southern and PLTS, merging into an ELCA university, Capital in Columbus) was not an option for Gettysburg, how would we find a way forward and guarantee the school's long-term sustainability? That was the question that loomed front and center for me as I entered what I expected to be the final chapter of my presidency somewhere around my fifteenth year in office.

ELCA Secretary's Office Beckons Again

Relative to seminaries of most other denominations, our ELCA schools continued to enjoy a relatively strong measure of support from the church body. Gettysburg's support from its regional synods (ELCA Region 8) was far and away the strongest, both in terms of finances and our being given access to synod assemblies, councils, and other key points of intersection. One expression of the seminaries' collective support from the denomination was the status of "advisory member" afforded to the eight seminary presidents each time the ELCA met in its national churchwide assembly. It was simply expected that we be present for the duration of these weeklong conventions held every two years.

As the 2013 assembly in Pittsburgh approached, I was relaxed and expected it might be my last time attending in any official capacity since I had begun to foresee retirement on the horizon. Two key officers were to be elected—presiding bishop and secretary, and important business would be conducted, but I had no responsibilities beyond attending sessions and hosting a reception for Gettysburg seminary alumni/ae as part of the all-seminary night held at each assembly.

It was widely assumed that the incumbent bishop, Mark Hanson, would be handily reelected. And whereas six years before, when there was not an incumbent running for secretary many people had urged me to be open, no such encouragement whatsoever came from any circles. I assumed Hanson had a short list of potential secretary candidates he was quietly circulating among some bishops and other influencers. And I was very sure I would not be on that list. To the surprise of many, the Pittsburgh assembly took an unexpected turn early in the balloting for bishop. Not only did Hanson not prevail on early ballots, but as voting continued, he began losing votes. A synod bishop from Ohio, Elizabeth Eaton, shot up following the first round of candidate speeches in which she offered brief punchy answers to questions, often not even taking up the full time allotted. It soon became apparent that the church was ready for a change, and Eaton was elected on the final ballot for bishop. Next came the secretary's election, in which I had only moderate interest given that I would not be in the mix.

To my surprise, when the first ballot for secretary was announced, I had received ten of the nearly 1000 votes on the ecclesiastical ballot. While no one had a huge number of votes, it was beyond imagining that I would emerge as a serious contender, as occurred six years before. Not wanting to appear in search of a new position, I determined to withdraw my name from further consideration. Then several things happened that caused me to reconsider. During the hour or so before the withdrawal deadline, I ran into my former boss, the church's first presiding bishop, Herb Chilstrom. "Herb," I said, "I'm sure there's no way I will be a serious candidate this time around." To my surprise he responded, "I think you should let it move forward and see what happens." Still unconvinced and wanting to avoid the embarrassment of receiving only a small percentage of votes, I headed toward the table where the withdrawal forms were being received. The next person I encountered was the new presiding bishop. "Liz," I said to my new bishop, "please know I'll do anything I can to support you in the challenging role." I was taken aback when, without missing a beat she responded, "What you can do for me is get elected secretary!" While I was still deliberating, another bishop approached me and nearly begged me to stay in the process. Since we had not been particularly close, and in fact I doubted he even knew me very well, I was puzzled at the urgency. "There's a person in the mix we're afraid could be elected and she'd be a disaster," he confided. While I was not interested in being a spoiler for a popular candidate (a synod vice president highly regarded among at least some of her peers), I weighed especially Bishop-elect Eaton's plea for me to stay in the process, so did not withdraw as planned.

On the second ballot my vote tally rose to forty-one. While still nowhere near the leading candidate, it appeared I could be among the seven finalists who would address the assembly. Given what had happened six years previously, when I felt unable to really connect with the body in such a large arena, I was anxious at that prospect.

Since we had in no way anticipated what was happening, Pam had not made plans to attend the assembly as she had in Chicago when it was clear I would be a serious contender for the church's second-highest office. In a round of phone calls we debated whether she should rush to Pittsburgh. Still unconvinced I would be a finalist, I encouraged her not to make a long drive on the Pennsylvania Turnpike. We agreed that in the off chance I would be elected, she could come for the installation ceremony on the final day of the assembly. I also called my seminary board chair, Jim Lakso, and assured him I was not eager to leave the seminary, but he should be prepared in the event things now out of my control would produce a surprising result.

Fortunately, our daughter-in-law Melissa Ramirez Cooper was at the assembly in her role as the ELCA's Director of Public Relations. Melissa had been offering her support during breaks, and we agreed to go off for a quiet dinner the night before the speeches. I confided in her my ambivalence about the possibility and my total lack of preparation since the developing momentum behind me was a complete surprise. In her wise and compassionate way, Melissa said simply, "Mike, you have to reach down deep inside yourself and discover what you want to say." During the hours after our dinner, I wrestled with what I might say and remained at a loss until the wee hours when I jotted some notes and went to bed where I tossed and turned until morning. One of the graces of the assembly planners was providing chaplains to pray with candidates for the various offices. As the seven finalists for secretary gathered in a room, the presence of those colleagues, both of whom I already knew well, was a gift. I felt a sense of calm and trust that whatever happened would be fine for me, and that I could hold my head high for once again being viewed as a serious candidate for such high office.

In my speech I said a bit about my background and told the story of being in El Salvador facing machine guns as Pamela and I accompanied Bishop Medardo Gomez on that fateful night near Panchimilama. I said my leadership style would be to accompany the new presiding bishop and other church leaders through thick and thin in the years ahead. When the third ballot was announced, my votes had risen to 160 and I was in third place. At that point I began to sense this could really happen. Prior to the fourth ballot, a Q&A session with the three finalists was held, in which again I felt I had been genuine and made good responses to the questions asked. I received good support from my seminary president colleagues as the hours ticked by until the penultimate ballot would be cast. Holding my breath as the results were announced, as I looked up at the tally on the screen, I knew the tide wasn't coming my way.

A bishop from the west coast who was ineligible by term limit to continue in office, but was not yet ready to retire, was in the lead over me by 388 to 282. While there were 242 votes in play (since the third candidate was dropped at that point) my experience watching many other ecclesiastical elections told me it's rare once a candidate has a commanding lead that things will turn around. A few hours later, when the final ballot was announced, indeed Bishop Chris Boerger was elected as the church's new secretary by 489 to 376. While I had received sixty percent of the votes in play, it was not enough to overcome Boerger's lead. The two of us stood together as the final ballot was taken and announced, and I was the first person after his wife to congratulate him upon his election. After the assembly applauded their new secretary, when Mark Hanson thanked me for being open to the call, the assembly again rose in a standing ovation.

Once again, as when David Swartling was elected, I have only good things to say about Boerger and his service over the ensuing six years. By virtue of his being a registered parliamentarian and experience as a long-term bishop, he was eminently qualified for the position and filled it faithfully and competently. As we would see each other in various venues, he occasionally confided that he thought I may have been the ultimate "winner" in the election. While having a high profile within the church, the secretary's office involves a lot of thankless administrative work, attention to details and minutiae that I could have done but would have found less fulfilling in many ways than the Seminary presidency.

In the "Monday morning quarterbacking" that inevitably follows a close election, I heard that once again there had been a fair amount of politicking going on behind the scenes. Robin Steinke overheard a bathroom conversation in which a group of women agreed that "Cooper-White already has a good job and Boerger is about to be unemployed." The extent to which that sentiment swayed some voters is impossible to assess, though I suspect it was a minor factor. More significantly, it became clear in the months after the assembly that a significant number of bishops had encouraged their synod's voting members to elect someone from their ranks. Having served as the bishops' chief staff person, I understood that dynamic. At least in those years, there was within the Conference of Bishops a degree of what could almost be called a bunker mentality. "Nobody but a bishop can really understand the burdens we bear," is how I would summarize that dynamic. One bishop confirmed my hunch in this regard and told me bluntly the bishops felt one of their own would best work with Eaton, who had been a synod bishop too.

As I drove back to Gettysburg on the Pennsylvania Turnpike following the assembly, I had a sense of peace and far less disappointment than experienced in Chicago six years before. I was also much more warmly welcomed home by many of my Seminary colleagues, who expressed relief I would continue at the helm for a while longer. I appreciated that I would be free to retire at a time of my choosing, whereas had I been elected secretary I would have had to remain in the saddle until age sixty-nine. I also felt there was the likelihood that the Seminary was soon coming to another significant crossroads moment, and I was eager to lead it into the next chapter. I could not imagine at that juncture how quickly and dramatically things would happen on that score.

— 12 —

Gettysburg's Surprising Final Chapter

IN THIS CHAPTER I will provide a somewhat detailed account of the final chapter of Gettysburg Seminary's 190-year history, which coincided with the conclusion of my seventeen-year presidency. Beyond being a key part of my life's story, and therefore relevant in this personal memoir, I do so in order that future historians who may compile a comprehensive history of the school will have the benefit of these reflections from the last president. Woven into the chapter is also a fairly extensive chronicle of events that led to the consolidation of Gettysburg with the Lutheran Theological Seminary at Philadelphia (LTSP), which resulted in the formation of the United Lutheran Seminary (ULS). To round out the picture, these inter-related historical strands must be viewed within the larger fabric of theological education in the ELCA and its predecessors. Moving beyond a mere factual recounting of events and actions by key players, I will also offer some personal interpretation of the multi-faceted dynamics at play in bringing together two historic Lutheran institutions. Finally, while I was blessed throughout my presidency with competent and committed partners, the senior staff team in my latter years at Gettysburg merits special mention, and I will make some comments about each member of our inner circle of leaders.

The Larger Picture and Longer View

On July 1, 2017, the United Lutheran Seminary came into being. The "new seminary" with campuses in Gettysburg and Philadelphia, Pennsylvania, resulted from a consolidation of two historic institutions—the Lutheran Theological Seminary at Gettysburg (LTSG) and the Lutheran Theological Seminary at Philadelphia (LTSP). Founded by Lutheran pioneer Samuel Simon Schmucker in 1826, the former was the oldest continuing Lutheran seminary in the Americas. By many accounts it has been the most historic U.S. Lutheran institution by virtue of the central role its campus played in the great Civil War battle of Gettysburg. The Philadelphia seminary was founded in 1864. A major impetus for its creation was theological controversy with positions espoused by Schmucker and others at Gettysburg. It too resided on a site of historical significance since the revolutionary war battle of Germantown was fought on ground that was to become its campus.

For over 150 years, there had been a range of relationships between the two Pennsylvania seminaries, from cordial and friendly, to competitive and downright oppositional. Within the larger context of American Lutheran theological education, perennial questions were raised about the necessity and efficiency of having two Lutheran seminaries within such close geographical proximity. Prior to 1918, the schools were affiliated with different Lutheran bodies, Gettysburg with the General Synod and Philadelphia with the General Council. But in that year, a merger consolidated several Lutheran synods, after which both schools were institutions of the United Lutheran Church (ULC). As a result, external pressures mounted for the two seminaries to merge and form a unified large-scale institution in the northeastern United States. But multiple attempts to force consolidation, on the part of the ULC and an even larger merged national church, the Lutheran Church in America (LCA), failed. Each time the prospects seemed hopeful, last-minute maneuvering on the part of one or both schools' boards and broader constituencies scuttled plans.

For those who had long envisioned uniting LTSP and LTSG, a promising era emerged in the 1960's as part of a comprehensive planning process conducted by the LCA's Board of Theological Education. With many among both constituencies optimistic that at last the two would join forces, potential sites for the merged new school's location were explored in New York, Philadelphia, Washington, D.C., and Baltimore.

Amidst the turbulent social ethos of the times, national church executives and planning councils determined that all seminaries should be located in urban areas adjacent to and in partnership with major universities. So, while Gettysburg had a spacious campus able to accommodate growth in a low-cost economic setting, it was deemed unacceptable by many in the LCA. The national church body's stance fueled the Philadelphia constituency's insistence on remaining in the City of Brotherly Love, albeit on a new site adjacent to the campus of the great University of Pennsylvania. Such a site was purchased and held for a number of years before finally being sold when it became clear no relocation would occur. While by no means anti-urban (in fact, LTSG produced a high percentage of urban pastors and national church executives with urban ministry responsibilities), the Gettysburg leadership was reluctant to abandon its strategic location that enabled it to serve both urban and rural constituencies. At one point, however, the LTSG board expressed openness for a newly merged seminary to be located in the nation's capital. Gettysburg's contacts with leaders of all denominational seminaries and university theology departments became a major catalyst in the formation of the Washington Theological Consortium in 1969, a vibrant ecumenical and now interfaith coalition that exists to this day.

As had occurred several times before, the process aimed at merger arrived at an impasse, and decisions were made by both boards to move forward with "maximum functional unity" between the two schools. But hopes for a unification rose quickly again when the Philadelphia board made a bold move and asked the Gettysburg board to share its president, Donald Heiges. The "joint administration" was thus initiated in 1964 and persisted for a half-dozen years until it was dissolved by the end of the decade. Shared programs were developed from time to time throughout the 1970's and 1980's, particularly in contextual or field education, and continuing education opportunities for clergy.

The next era in which pressures to join the two seminaries again surfaced came in the mid-1980's as a result of yet another national church merger process. As already noted, in 1982 decisions were taken at conventions of the American Lutheran Church (ALC), Association of Evangelical Lutheran Churches (AELC), and Lutheran Church in America (LCA) to unite and form the Evangelical Lutheran Church in America (ELCA). Throughout the several years leading up to its official start date of January 1, 1988, leaders of the merging churches struggled with the question of "number and location of seminaries." It was clear to both LTSP and

LTSG that the two Pennsylvania schools were at the bullseye of the target in this process. But once again, strong self-preservation impulses within both constituencies succeeded in fending off a forced merger. Leaders and fiercely loyal alumni/ae and donors of all eight seminaries of the merging churches prevailed in their lobbying efforts to stave off mergers, relocations, or other major moves. As the ELCA came into being, commitments were made to conduct a "Study of Theological Education" during its early years.

While the can was kicked down the road for another few years, leaders at LTSP and LTSG knew they were on notice that the new denomination was unlikely to extend unlimited patience for the "Pennsylvania seminary matter" to be resolved. Insofar as any such matters can be assessed, it was probably the case that anxiety ran highest among those in the Gettysburg constituency during the late 1980's and early years of the ELCA. Coming into the ELCA, Philadelphia's endowment was four times the size of Gettysburg's (approximately $24 million versus $6 million). A trend appeared to be emerging whereby especially younger seminarians preferred to study in an urban locale as opposed to Gettysburg's town-and-country context. Whereas both schools faced enormous physical plant maintenance issues, the situation was even more dire at Gettysburg, where the main classroom and administrative building, Valentine Hall, was fast becoming uninhabitable (with plaster literally falling on faculty members' and students' heads on occasion!)

ELCA Study Creates Clusters

As "The Study" (of theological education) proceeded during the ELCA's initial years, tensions mounted among the seminary leaders. Those who served as presidents in the late 1980's and early 90's spoke of challenging meetings in which they were at odds with each other and with the ELCA's Division for Ministry staff charged with leading the Study process. Several characterize those meetings with the quip that, "Nobody wanted to go to the bathroom for fear you'd come back and your seminary would have been closed or merged while you were out of the room!"

By 1993, when a preliminary progress report was presented to the ELCA Churchwide Assembly in Kansas City, it was becoming apparent to those who had hoped for seminary consolidations and/or closures that the forces advocating maintenance of the status quo would prevail. An arrangement forged at the beginning of the ELCA whereby both Pennsylvania seminaries were supported by and reported to all fifteen synods in their combined regions, was dissolved. From then on, Gettysburg received financial support only from the eight synods of the ELCA's Region 8, and Philadelphia was the officially designated seminary for Region 7. Along with decoupling joint financial support, the new arrangement reconfigured the boards so that LTSP would no longer have Region 8 representatives, nor would LTSG benefit from trustees elected by Region 7 synods.[1] Those actions seemed to signal a reinforcement of the status quo and abandonment of efforts for all the northeastern synods to "own" both seminaries.

In what many throughout the ELCA viewed as caving to pressures from the seminaries and their constituencies, the Study task force ultimately made no recommendations for change in the eight-school "number and location" question. Instead, as noted previously, they recommended, and the church in assembly adopted, policy to mandate the "clustering" of the existing schools as a means to achieve greater efficiencies and expand degree and continuing education offerings. The Study also recommended that schools be designated nationwide as centers of specialization, and that other schools avoid replicating programs unique to each school. Gettysburg offered to serve as the Center for Diaconal Ministry Formation,[2] and to fortify its Town and Country Church Institute (TCCI). Philadelphia promised to maximize the offering of its Urban Theological Institute (UTI), as well as offer advanced degrees (Doctor of Ministry and Ph.D.), with the other Cluster schools collaborating. While embraced initially by the schools, the Study's call to honor such school-specific programs was soon disregarded. As seminaries scrambled for more students and financial support, some replicated other schools' programs that seemed to be proving successful. For example, when it became

---

1. The ELCA Region 7 consisted of synods in eastern Pennsylvania, New York, and New England. Region 8 included the rest of Pennsylvania west of the Susquehanna River, West Virginia, Delaware, Maryland, and the District of Columbia.

2. A Study of Ministry was also conducted in the ELCA's early years. The most controversial issues surrounded "lay ministries," i.e., types of public ministry carried out by persons who were not ordained clergy. Several variations in how lay ministries were structured in the predecessor church bodies were combined into an official roster, whose non-ordained members were called Diaconal Ministers. Subsequent Churchwide Assembly action determined that as of January 1, 2017, such professional lay workers would be called deacons, and ones who had previously been "consecrated," as well as new inductees would be regarded as ordained Ministers of Word and Service. Pastors, including bishops, are ordained Ministers of Word and Sacrament.

evident that Gettysburg's diaconal preparation degree was gaining steam, with a quarter or more of our students in that track, other schools began to offer their own programs.

Much of the same kind of jockeying for survival that had ensued throughout the Study process continued as cluster formation proceeded. One seminary's president resistant to change proposed that his school be regarded as a "cluster of one!" There was much head-scratching over the initial proposed structure whereby Southern Seminary in Columbia, SC was to be paired with Trinity in Columbus, Ohio. The joke in some circles was that the only things the two schools had in common were similar sounding names of their home cities. In the end, Southern was paired with the two Pennsylvania schools in what came to be known as The Eastern Cluster of Lutheran Seminaries (ECLS). By comparison with the other two clusters—Western Mission and Covenant—the ECLS lived out the vision of shared programming at a high level for nearly two decades. The three schools' presidents enjoyed strong collegial relations and rotated serving two-year terms as the cluster's executive director in addition to their local school responsibilities. Collaborative degree and lifelong learning programs were developed; the three libraries were merged electronically, affording students and faculties on the three campuses full access to all the resources held by the schools; and more than $6 million in grants from foundations was received to support vocational discernment, youth theological education, and other programs.

Given the three schools' locations, with Southern being 550 miles to the south of Pennsylvania, it was probably inevitable that a higher level of ECLS collaboration began to evolve between Gettysburg and Philadelphia in some areas. Initially developed by Philadelphia with a grant from the Lilly Endowment, a popular "Theological Education with Youth" (TEY) program evolved into a shared effort. At one point, the two schools hired a shared faculty person, though the arrangement proved unworkable and was discontinued after one year. Given that Pamela was a member of the Philadelphia faculty, and she and Macrina lived primarily in a campus home there, I came to know that community quite well. Similarly, since LTSP's president, Phil Krey and I had been classmates at Gettysburg in our student days, he knew the history and several LTSG faculty. Periodically, we two presidents held exploratory conversations about the possibilities for a higher level of cooperation that might eventually evolve into full consolidation. A major obstacle in that regard, however, was the growing disparity in the financial state of the two schools. LTSP ran significant annual deficits most years and had to fill the gap by depleting its endowment. Its financial strains were compounded with construction of an expensive, large classroom and administrative building, the Brossman Center. The school had experienced enrollment growth for several years, and leaders were convinced that student numbers and tuition dollars would only increase if they had more adequate facilities. Unfortunately, the Brossman Center's construction coincided with the beginning of a dramatic downturn in seminary enrollments. Furthermore, the tide was turning from residential education to online learning, which requires minimal campus facilities. In addition, LTSP's capital campaign fell far short of goals, resulting in the need to borrow approximately $10 million for the Brossman Center.

Due to the disparity between the schools' fiscal status, accordingly, leaders at Gettysburg were extremely reluctant to contemplate merger or other forms of a shared future with Philadelphia. When I would quietly raise with some key Gettysburg board leaders the prospect of institutional realignment, their immediate reaction was, "We don't want to take on Philadelphia's debt and financial problems." In addition to the financial issues, an ongoing challenge was posed by a competitive spirit between faculties, students, and alumni/ae that sometimes rose to unhealthy levels. We at Gettysburg chafed at what seemed to us an attitude of superiority on the part of some at Philadelphia. Upon hearing that one LTSP professor described Gettysburg as the "Sunday School seminary out in the country" in a class session, I sent an email urging reconsideration of that assessment. Another myth, voiced often in Philadelphia circles, was, "We train scholars and Gettysburg prepares good pastors." In fact, by virtue of generous endowments that could be used only to offer graduate study fellowships for its alumni/ae, Gettysburg probably supplied more candidates for academic posts over the years.

As had occurred several times over nearly a century, it seemed the two schools had drawn closer for a few years (raising hopes among some that this time courtship would lead to marriage), only to pull back and continue on separate pathways. At Gettysburg, where there was growing embrace of the concept of "public theology" (which was also a major theme in LTSP's articulation of its mission) a new opportunity presented itself near the end of 21st century's first decade. The creation of the Seminary Ridge Museum, described in the previous chapter, was a centerpiece for this focus on public outreach and witness.

LTSP Financial Crisis Spurs Renewed Explorations

While understandably reluctant to reveal its true fiscal state, by 2012 or so, LTSP was in a very challenging financial position. Annual audits, which must be shared with state and federal Departments of Education, caused interventions that required costly "letters of credit" for LTSP to continue receiving federal student loan funds. The school was in arrears on loan payments to the ELCA's Mission Investment Fund that carried the mortgage on the learning center. After the economic collapse and its unremitting draining to meet deficits, the Philadelphia endowment was severely "under water" (meaning the values of many donor-restricted funds had fallen below original contributions). In desperation, LTSP's board transferred some of its physical property into the separately incorporated endowment to raise the overall value. As would be revealed a few years later, unfortunately, the properties were overvalued and thus afforded a false sense of security that the school could overcome its severe financial challenges.

Some leaders at LTSP did grasp reality and recognized that things could not go on much longer on the same trajectory. Phil Krey suggested that we explore possible collaboration with Lancaster Seminary in a potential three-way partnership. Once again, however, a series of cordial meetings over a couple of years led nowhere. Next for LTSP, the possibility that Palmer Seminary (an evangelical school affiliated with Eastern University in suburban Philadelphia) would relocate to the LTSP campus held out hope for an infusion of additional income, shared faculty, and other measures that would lead to financial sustainability. On the cusp of sealing the deal, to LTSP leaders' great frustration, Palmer backed away, apparently feeling it would lose its institutional identity. While not stated publicly, it was also felt the more theologically conservative Palmer was anxious about the ELCA's decision to ordain LGBTQ persons, which was soundly embraced by the Philadelphia faculty and leadership.

Soon, yet another possibility emerged in Philadelphia's quest for a new future. Conversations between Krey and the dean of Yale Divinity School yielded an offer from the latter to locate a portion of LTSP's operation on Yale's campus in New Haven in exchange for receiving net proceeds from the sale of assets in Philadelphia. Given that only four LTSP professors would be guaranteed positions at Yale, when the Philadelphia faculty learned of the proposal, strenuous objections arose.

After fifteen years as Philadelphia's president, Phil Krey announced his resignation in 2014. When that news became public, I strongly urged Gettysburg's board to engage in a new round of conversations with their counterparts at Philadelphia. Additionally, I signaled to my board's key leaders that should a joint presidency or even merger make sense, I would readily step aside in order to pave the way toward a new future for Lutheran theological education in the northeastern U.S. And since I feared that my involvement in these exploratory conversations could be perceived as a "Gettysburg takeover attempt" by some in the Philadelphia constituency during their vulnerable transition time without a president, I indicated I would not attend meetings.

During the course of the summer of 2014, meetings of both boards' officers, though generally cordial, proved inconclusive. The Gettysburg officers reported to me that at one meeting, when a very financially astute LTSG director said he had concerns about Philadelphia's financial status and handed LTSP's most recent audit to their board chair, she quietly pushed it back across the table and said, "We're not going to talk about that!" The continuing apparent denial about the school's dire fiscal condition caused great reluctance among LTSG's directors to consider any radical reconfiguration that could jeopardize our own future. Nevertheless, the officers lifted up the vision of "Two Seminaries with One Faculty and One Administration" and developed a brief proposal to submit to both boards.

At the fall 2014 LTSG board meeting, that vision garnered lukewarm response at best, in part because Philadelphia was moving forward in its presidential search. Some of the Gettysburg board members felt that if their counterparts to the east were serious about such unified leadership, it didn't make sense for Philadelphia to lock itself into a new presidency. I reminded them that the call at Philadelphia was for a defined brief period, probably intended to coincide with my anticipated retirement, which by then was on the horizon. During one of the summer meetings, the LTSP officers had suggested that LTSG's board ask for my resignation as president so that the possibility of calling one president for both schools could be explored immediately. I stated unequivocally I would do so if the LTSG officers deemed it in the best interests of theological education's and the two schools' futures. But my board leaders were quite insistent in opposing that option. They indicated they felt the schools would both benefit from my experience, fiscal restraint, historical knowledge, and relationships with synodical and churchwide leaders during a period of transition.

A New Day Dawns in the Northeast

LTSP's presidential search resulted in the selection of David Lose, who had been a faculty member and dean at Luther Seminary in Minnesota. While he was an alumnus of LTSP, his father, uncles and other family members were all enthusiastic LTSG alumni, which he was quick to point out in every conversation with Gettysburg's leaders. Early in his presidency, he began to signal his high regard for both schools and his commitment to fortify our partnership in whatever form that might occur. Following Lose's appointment as LTSP president, the two of us began to get acquainted in a series of conversations as well as at meetings of all eight ELCA seminary presidents. We expressed mutual commitment to continue building bridges between the two Pennsylvania seminaries. Lose's public transparency regarding LTSP's financial condition was refreshing and signaled a new day had arrived. We discussed the possibility of moving gradually to a shared faculty and perhaps even a new form of shared administration, as the boards' officers had suggested.

To my surprise and genuine delight, in the fall of 2015 I received an email from David Lose in which he proposed a "thought experiment." David wrote, "What if, rather than a more gradual evolutionary process of increased cooperation, we instead proposed to our boards a bold recommendation to consider full institutional union"? I immediately responded that I considered his overture an answer to my prayers. Shortly, we two presidents began a series of meetings in which we imagined this new future and how it might come about. I readily embraced David's suggestion that rather than a typical "merger" we propose to both boards the closure of both existing institutions and reopening of a "new school." While by no means desiring to erase or diminish the rich legacy of both seminaries, we felt that such a paradigm would signal a new day in theological education, and also give powerful testimony to the fact that an often-contentious relationship had once and for all been healed.

Following confidential conversations with both our board chairs, who signaled openness to the idea, in December of 2015 we convened a ten-person meeting at the Lower Susquehanna Synod office in Harrisburg, PA. Present were presidents and deans, board chairs, and two additional key leaders from both schools. To David's and my surprise, the receptivity exceeded our expectations, leading to a proposal for consolidation into a "new school" that was presented at simultaneous meetings of both boards in January of 2016. In Harrisburg and at subsequent meetings, I helped frame the conversation by pointing out that transformative change almost always results from both push- and pull-factors. That is, organizations usually do not make bold changes unless they are either forced by unsustainable current trends or drawn forward by a compelling new vision. Such was the case for each of the Pennsylvania seminaries at that juncture. Both had experienced dramatic enrollment downturns, with combined student bodies less than half what they had been a decade before. LTSG's total enrollment had declined from nearly 300 to 138 and FTE (full-time equivalent) from 160 to eighty, with projections for 2016–17 of sixty-nine. With an employee FTE of fifty-five, I quipped to the board, "That's a higher ratio than infant daycare!"

While LTSG's careful fiscal stewarding had preserved enough unrestricted endowment to see us through several more years, I could not justify recommending continuation on the same pathway. I admit to being sorely tempted to simply continue business as usual for a few more years, quietly retire, and leave coping with the inevitable hard decisions to my successor. But I felt the "push" factors needed to be acknowledged, and I could not in good conscience shy away from the tough decisions I felt needed to occur on my watch.

So, a commitment to not avoid the challenge of ensuring long-term sustainability and the new overture from Lose constituted the "pull" dynamics, which, coupled with the push factors compelled me to move forward in fully considering the potential benefits and possible pitfalls of creating a new entity out of the two historic seminaries. The benefits seemed quite apparent. A unified faculty could draw the strongest members from both and be reduced ("right-sized") to the current student enrollment and budgetary limitations. Given Gettysburg's location, despite good efforts, we had failed to attract persons of color as faculty. Philadelphia's diversity in faculty and the student body would bring to a combined school the multicultural milieu that had eluded us. Administrative costs would be reduced significantly without the need for duplication in all offices and functional areas. And the very concept of a "new school," with creative pedagogical approaches and expanded online and other distant learning offerings, would have strong appeal to prospective seminarians.

From Gettysburg's vantage point, the biggest hurdle, as noted, was Philadelphia's precarious financial situation. But early in the exploratory due diligence process, Lose and others at LTSP assured us that portions of its property were primed for sale and development, and the proceeds would more than eliminate its approximate debt of $13 million and replenish funds "borrowed" from the endowment. Given my knowledge of what had occurred at other seminaries with valuable urban properties, these assurances, based upon LTSP's consultations with real estate experts in greater Philadelphia, seemed realistic. Those reassurances notwithstanding, I could neither be personally comfortable nor recommend to the Gettysburg board that we proceed without guarantees that in a worst-case scenario the new entity would not be saddled with unresolved Philadelphia debt or endowment shortfalls. In consultation with our joint legal counsel (Given the high level of trust we felt had been established, there did not appear to be compelling reasons for each school to have its own attorneys.), it was determined that a "merger" would not construct the firewall needed to shield the new entity from the LTSP encumbrances. That fact, together with a surprise development thrown our way a few months into the process by the Pennsylvania Department of Education, caused us to hit the pause button.

While both our accrediting bodies (the Association of Theological Schools or ATS and the Middle States Commission on Higher Education or MSCHE) had given positive signals about the plan to close both schools and reopen as a "new school," the PA Department ruled that the resulting entity would not be fully licensed at the outset. Among other ramifications, the "new school" would not be eligible to administer federal student loans, which would devastate our ability to attract students. At that critical juncture, our legal counsel and the education department advised that a preferable pathway would be for one school to close and transfer its assets and students into the other, which would guarantee continuity of full accreditation and licensure. With little debate, it was determined that Gettysburg would be the ongoing entity. In addition to the financial complications at Philadelphia, Gettysburg had the oldest charter, which would be retained, and also had unqualified accreditation for several more years that would accrue to the new venture, whereas Philadelphia was on a short leash with the accreditors due to its financial condition.

To build the protective firewall, on which I insisted, a further variation evolved. The pathway to the new venture would be a "consolidation" rather than merger. Philadelphia transferred its assets into the Gettysburg corporation, but while LTSP closed as a school as of July 1, 2017, its corporate entity continued as the "owner" of property and holder of the related debt. Insofar as it was possible, that configuration guaranteed the success of the new school, and would free its administration from getting caught up in coping with the complicated real estate matters at Philadelphia.

A Strategic Approach Based Upon Historical Analyses

Having carefully studied the history of at least a half-dozen prior attempts to merge the two Pennsylvania seminaries, I approached the consolidation process with some key convictions. To succeed, I was convinced, the process had to move quickly and decisively. Also, it had to be driven administratively and by the governing boards, since faculty members' understandable self-interest to preserve their jobs would generate resistance, especially among recent alumni/ae who revered their professors. All previous attempts faltered when those who proposed bold moves unrealistically expected and awaited widespread faculty and constituent support.

To have a prayer of success, I was convinced, we would also have to demythologize broadly held perceptions that Gettysburg and Philadelphia seminaries had significantly different missions and radically disparate cultures. The extent to which those perceptions permeated the church is attested by the autobiography of the first ELCA presiding bishop, Herbert Chilstrom. In *A Journey of Grace*, my former boss wrote of the state of theological education: "We had learned in our predecessor churches that merging seminaries simply would not work. Philadelphia and Gettysburg may have been only a couple of hours distant from each other but were also on different planets."[3] For some time, I had challenged that assessment and questioned widely held assumptions. "Can you tell me how our missions are really that different? If you walk into an ELCA congregation on a Sunday morning and listen to the sermon, can you really tell from which seminary the pastor graduated? If Philadelphia is the 'urban seminary,' how is it that an entire generation of LCA and ELCA urban ministry leaders influenced by Professor Bertha Paullsen and others graduated from Gettysburg?" Through such probing questions I tried to help doubters reassess their prejudices and consider the merits of joining forces for the sake of sustaining a strong, unified ELCA seminary in the northeast. I will never know the extent to which those efforts contributed to a new day of openness to go where past generations had been unable to go.

Another conviction I held going into the process was that we could not look for strong leadership from the ELCA churchwide offices. Perhaps wisely, since attempts to exert influence from external authorities often causes internal resistance, the partners in Chicago signaled that

---

3. Herbert W. Chilstrom, *A Journey of Grace: The Formation of a Leader and a Church* (Minneapolis: University Lutheran Press 2011), p. 579.

seminary reconfigurations would have to emerge locally. Despite my sense it was futile, we asked the churchwide organization for a grant of $100,000 to help defray some of the costs of the consolidation. My prediction held true, and no financial support was received. What we did not count on was resistance from the church's presiding bishop. As already noted, among recommendations from the ELCA's Theological Education Advisory Committee (TEAC), was that seminaries should explore merger options. In light of that, we were puzzled when Elizabeth Eaton publicly criticized our plans.

In early December of 2015, even before we met with a small circle of our schools' leaders, we held a confidential conversation with the ELCA's director of theological education and the executive for administration, the presiding bishop's right-hand person. At the conclusion of that telephone call, we specifically asked if we should personally converse with the bishop. We were told that would be unnecessary since her staff would keep her fully apprised of our plans. A few months later, I met in Chicago with Bishop Eaton and our supporting synodical bishops. David Lose was unavailable for that meeting so I was alone in an embarrassing moment when Eaton sharply criticized us for going off on our own and not informing her. I responded forthrightly to set the record straight, after which she acknowledged that there had been a failure to communicate within her office. While her stance remains an enigma to me, my speculation is that she was holding out for a larger merger involving several of the seminaries and felt we had preempted that grand design by moving forward as the two Pennsylvania schools. Despite her initial resistance, when I retired, Bishop Eaton sent a gracious letter, which included commending me for my part in helping form the United Lutheran Seminary!

Fortunately, with one exception, the fifteen bishops of our supporting synods lent their endorsement to the consolidation. Prominent among them was my own bishop, Jim Dunlop, whose commitment to Gettysburg and then ULS was solid. To be sure, some hard questions were asked in a few of the synod assemblies in the spring of 2016 when we had gone public with consolidation plans. But several synods adopted resolutions of support and commendation for our bold attempt to achieve a sustainable reconfiguration of theological education in the northeast. We responded with a comprehensive outline of the rationale for consolidation to the West Virginia-Western Maryland Synod, where strong reservations had been voiced.

With the course to the future carefully charted, and a good measure of support from key constituent groups, both boards gave final nods of approval at joint and separate meetings in the summer and fall of 2016. David Lose and I were present at both boards' meetings and also began making other appearances on both campuses to signal our strong partnership and "being on the same page" in all important matters. Key staff from both schools began to meet and identify all the issues that would need to be settled in the unification process. The self-appointed joint working group that had been meeting for months was converted into a formal Transition Team appointed by both boards.

Heavy Turbulence at Warp Speed

The workload throughout 2016 and the first half of 2017 was enormous as we had to keep both existing schools fully functioning while building the foundations for the unified new entity to be launch-ready on July 1, 2017. While most kept silent their reservations to avoid discouraging us, several (perhaps most?) board members harbored serious doubts that we could accomplish the consolidation on the announced timeline. Some began to refer to the timeline requiring impossible "warp speed," referring to a term bandied about in space travel fantasy literature and movies. That we met the timeline and accomplished the myriad tasks involved was due to the hard work of many people, but especially our seasoned and competent Gettysburg administrative team. With the exception of the dean, our Philadelphia counterparts were relatively new in their positions and had not developed relationships broadly within the constituencies. Also, by late 2016, David Lose had been called to serve as senior pastor of a Minneapolis mega-church. While his official start-up was delayed until summer, he began to be drawn into things there immediately. And since his family had relocated to Minnesota, in addition to his keeping up a busy travel schedule as a popular speaker, he was frequently absent from the Philadelphia campus and not as fully engaged in the latter phases of the consolidation.

Not unexpectedly, the most difficult aspects of the consolidation involved the "human factors." We knew from its earliest phases that, much as we would try to soften adverse impacts for employees of both schools, there was simply no way to accomplish the transformative change required without causing disruption and hardship for some individuals. Even prior to formation of the Transition Team, in the initial phase of the process we formed a working group charged with attending to support for faculty and staff. They gathered folks on both campuses to hear their concerns, communicate as much information as possible, and offer measures of support. Severance policies differed greatly between the two schools, with Gettysburg having much more generous provisions for any who would not be offered positions in the new school. Accordingly, Philadelphia's policies were amended to bring them into conformity and honor our commitment to treat all employees of both schools the same. Provisions were made to ensure extended medical insurance coverage for any employees whose employment would end upon start-up of United Lutheran.

By and large, with a few exceptions, administrative employee anxiety at the two schools seemed to be held in check as the months rolled along. People kept doing their work, though a few at each campus sought and were offered positions elsewhere. The heaviest turbulence in the entire transition process came in the summer of 2016, when faculty transition offers were made at the strong encouragement of legal counsel. We had hoped that several faculty members who were eligible for retirement would exercise that option. When that did not prove to be the case, the boards determined tenure would not carry over into ULS. To achieve an appropriate student/faculty ratio, and realize necessary personnel cost reductions, we simply could not guarantee positions to all the tenured professors. Under the conditions of the transition offer, those who accepted voluntary retirement would receive generous severance payments. Others were offered non-tenured contractual positions with ULS for a two- to three-year period, during which the nature of long-term faculty permanency (a new form of tenure) would be determined.

The decision to suspend tenure created anger and resentment on the part of the majority of faculty members. At one point, they hired an attorney to challenge the boards' rights to move ahead with the consolidation. Their efforts did not prevail, but the unhappiness among faculty rippled out broadly into both schools' constituencies, with alumni/ae who felt their beloved professors were being treated poorly up in arms. Fairly widespread social media traffic was sometimes disrespectful if not disdainful of David Lose and me, as well as both boards.

An additional complicating factor on this score was the nature of the consolidation. As noted, Philadelphia closed as a school and its students, degrees, programs transferred into the Gettysburg corporation. Legal counsel concluded that pathway meant that if tenure were preserved, it would apply only to the former Gettysburg faculty, since Philadelphia's employees' jobs would all end on June 30, 2017. The prospect of that scenario, favoring LTSG's professors at the expense of LTSP's faculty members, was untenable. This unforeseen factor further confirmed the necessity of ending tenure for both faculties. While a lesser factor, we also held hopes that the way we were approaching the consolidation might carve new territory in ELCA and broader theological circles. For all its benefits, particularly the safeguarding of academic freedom, faculty tenure was becoming increasingly problematic in terms of making it all but impossible for schools to restructure and reduce costs before being forced into the dire status of financial exigency or declaring bankruptcy. In 2016, a statement on the challenges in theological education was issued by all eight of us ELCA seminary presidents. It was made available at the Churchwide Assembly, where it received some attention in forum discussions. Regarding tenured faculty, the statement included:

> We acknowledge a sharp dilemma in our network of theological education. We both need to find ways to provide long term, continued support for our faculty members who are called to teaching ministries and need to consider the ways that tenure as presently configured may reduce the ability for seminaries to act fluidly within a changing context. Together, we will look at models of faculty support that seek to achieve greater flexibility and a redefinition of tenure in order for our seminaries to be fully responsive to the changing theological landscape, while honoring academic freedom and meeting accreditation standards.

We felt this collective stance might help ease any sense that the LTSG and LTSP faculty were being "targeted" unfairly in the temporary removal of tenure. That did not prove to be the case. None of the other schools took any steps to revisit their traditional definitions of tenure.

As often occurs when tensions are running high, we also failed to recognize how a seemingly minor matter would take on symbolic freight beyond the intended result. Draft severance documents included a standard non-disparagement clause, which stipulates that in exchange for end-of-service compensation a former employee agrees not to cast aspersions against her/his former employer. The majority of faculty members reacted to that as a "gag order," which they felt would violate their academic freedom and clergy members' ordination vows. Despite reassurances on my part and that of others leading the consolidation process that was not the intent, this remained a source of anger for many faculty members. During the first year following the start-up of ULS, continuing pressures from faculty resulted in the new school's board simply reestablishing tenure as it had been and granting to all who had held that status in LTSP and LTSG.

On Toward the Finish Line

In the spring of 2017, David Lose and I preached in chapel services on the other school's campus. My sermon at Philadelphia on April 27 was entitled "Step by Step in Love." Knowing there were strong feelings among some on both campuses that David and I were unsympathetic toward those whose lives were being disrupted, I attempted to acknowledge the pain and affirm the good will that was also being demonstrated by many. In my introduction I said:

> To be among you at this particular moment when we seem on the cusp of overcoming and healing the residue of 150 years of history since there was a parting of the ways during the tumultuous years of the great Civil War brings a measure of humility and gratitude that is simply hard to quantify or express. Let me say, both personally and on behalf of the entire Gettysburg Seminary community: Philadelphia, LTSP, Mt. Airy, Lutheran (the school was widely known by each of those monikers), we believe that we need to be together moving forward.

I went on to make the claim that the coming together of two schools that had often been at odds and in competition gave powerful testimony to the possibility for churchly and societal unity in a time of division. And I also acknowledged the challenges of becoming a truly *united* seminary would be formidable.

> It is a natural tendency to separate, divide and distinguish. We and they. Our kind and the others. Our tribe and those other folk. Red states and blue. . . . But we are all we. All who trust in God and embrace the gospel are one community.
>
> In the months ahead there is much that we have cherished which in measures greater or smaller will forever be left behind. There will be for us all a sense of loss, a measure of anxiety mixed with relief, for some a good bit of anger that what we have loved so long cannot simply continue forever. The road ahead will not always be easy.

But as we now seek to blend together the finest traditions of two great theological institutions with a combined history of nearly three and a half centuries, can we do so with a generous measure of careful listening to one another?

I concluded with a plea to embrace what I felt strongly was "our calling this day and in the days ahead." "It is there in the gospel, plain and simple, short and sweet: 'I give you a new commandment, that you love one another.'"

As we neared the consolidation completion date of July 1, 2017, by virtue of the fact I was president of the continuing corporate entity, I had to oversee all the personnel matters leading up to the launch of United Lutheran Seminary (ULS). Contracts for faculty and staff being retained were prepared and presented, and many were met with questions and objections or requests for modifications. Separation agreements were also issued to the small number of faculty and staff who chose to enter retirement or were not being offered positions in ULS.

My executive and administrative assistants, John Spangler and Elizabeth Meighan, did commendable work on both campuses in fielding employee questions and anxieties. They developed budgetary and staffing projections for the initial ULS work force, and Elizabeth also took the lead in developing personnel policies and an employee handbook.

Who Will Be the ULS President?

Once the decision was made to create a "new Lutheran seminary" out of the two existing schools, a key question for many on both campuses and broadly within the respective constituencies was, "Who will lead it"? I had already signaled my intent to retire, since I would be turning sixty-seven in the summer of 2017 as the new entity was launched. Younger by nearly two decades, David Lose was by no means in a similar position. Many, including several bishops in the regions supporting LTSP and LTSG, began to encourage him to be open to serving as the first ULS president. I was among those who felt that David was uniquely positioned and well-qualified for the position. His family legacy with multiple generations of Loses among the Gettysburg alumni coupled with his being an alumnus and briefly president at Philadelphia, together with his national stature as preacher, widely-sought-after speaker and writer would, I felt, give ULS the high-profile leader it needed for a strong launch.

But by late 2016 David became convinced he did not feel called to the position. Shortly thereafter, as noted above, he was called to serve as senior pastor of the largest congregation in the ELCA, enabling his return to Minnesota, which had come to feel like home for the Loses during his years as professor and dean at Luther Seminary in St. Paul. With David out of the picture, and no obvious internal candidates at either LTSP or LTSG, it became evident that the presidential search would be wide open. David and I were clear that we needed to distance ourselves from the search process, lest there be any perceptions we were trying to pick our successor. But, since we knew our trustees and colleagues perhaps better than anyone, we did offer suggestions for who might be appointed to the presidential search committee. And we were assured it was not inappropriate for us to nominate candidates we knew from our extensive networks in the church and world of theological education. I strongly encouraged (and ultimately nominated) two colleagues, Kristin Largen and John Spangler, but both chose not to be open to the call. David shared with me that he recommended a former colleague at Luther Seminary, a Presbyterian pastor and professor who had moved to a school in Michigan.

While the faculties' input to the presidential search committee had recommended the search be limited to Lutherans, the board (and by this time the LTSG board had been reconstituted as the first ULS board by adding former LTSP trustees) overruled that and indicated that members of ELCA full communion partner churches would also be deemed eligible. So, when the new LTSG/ULS board chair provided a courtesy advance notice about the search committee's selection of Lose's nominee, the Rev. Dr. Theresa Latini, a Presbyterian minister, I was not totally surprised that she had been chosen.

One of the Finest Teams Anywhere

With the legal consolidation process all but completed, and a president-elect chosen at the board's April 2017 meeting, I could breathe a sigh of relief and enjoy a wonderful retirement banquet. That balmy beautiful April evening, as a glorious springtime sunset gave way to growing darkness, I was keenly aware that the sun was setting on not only my tenure, but the unique and unrepeatable team spirit that was the key to all that had been accomplished, and at the center of creating a new future for the

United Lutheran Seminary. My concluding comments, which some may have regarded as emanating from a clergyperson's requisite demeanor of false humility, were genuine and heartfelt.

While many had celebrated and praised progress and accomplishments during the Cooper-White years at Gettysburg, I knew that none of what had occurred was a result of my efforts apart from those of colleagues. In the final months at the seminary, on many occasions when words of praise were directed my way, I told the unvarnished truth: My most important contribution was to assemble and encourage one of the finest leadership teams that existed anywhere in the world of higher education. As best I could, I attempted to undergird their creativity, provide as many resources as could be mustered, and stay out of their way. I never had reason to question the integrity or doubt the judgment of any member of the senior administrative team.

In retrospect, when mistakes were made, they were more often mine than those of colleagues. When criticisms came or attacks were made, I tried to shield and support colleagues with a simple statement that I believe is integral to the role of a chief executive: "At the end of the day, everything that happens at Gettysburg Seminary is my responsibility. They deserve all the credit for the wonderful things that have happened. I take all the blame for things that didn't go right." At the risk of downplaying and failing to give proper due to earlier incumbents in the senior administrative leadership roles, for the permanent record I want to offer some brief comments about each member of Gettysburg Seminary's last executive team.

For nearly a quarter century, Ms. Carol Troyer served ably in the president's office as administrative assistant, and in the latter years, also personnel officer whose responsibilities included oversight of our campus maintenance team. As Carol was planning her retirement, I feared that any successor would fall short in fulfilling the breadth of responsibilities lodged in that position. We had other good candidates, but one stood out in terms of experience, qualifications, and upbeat spirit. So, rather than limping along during my final years as president, we forged ahead with the capable and spirited leadership of Ms. Elizabeth Meighan. A graduate of Gettysburg College and active member of a Lutheran congregation pastored by one of my seminary classmates, with prior work experience in schools and at a highly sensitive military installation, Elizabeth adapted immediately to the unique school/church/educational institution environment that is a seminary community. Barely two years into the position, Elizabeth readily embraced the added work required by the consolidation. Together with John Spangler, Elizabeth was the key player in building the administrative foundations, creating and posting position descriptions, recruiting and interviewing candidates, and facilitating all the personnel processes. The results speak for themselves. On July 1, 2017, the United Lutheran Seminary was ready for launch. A side-benefit of Elizabeth's coming aboard was the fact that she was married to Marty Qually, one of Adams County's three governing commissioners. That relationship further strengthened the Seminary's community connection, and Marty and Elizabeth soon became good friends with many of us. It was a source of great sadness to me—and a fair measure of anger—that Elizabeth was not retained on staff by United's first president.

As occurs in the course of a long presidency spanning almost two decades, over the years there were several incumbents in some of the senior staff positions. As I noted for the board in my final time with them in April 2017, during the Gettysburg years I worked with five Directors of Admission and six Chief Development Officers. Each in turn brought the right gifts at the right time. In some cases, I thought colleagues left those positions just as they were really coming into their prime years of effectiveness. But as I was quick to quip when asked why someone was leaving or upon hearing dismay at their decision to accept a new position or call elsewhere, "I try never to stand in the way of the Holy Spirit!" I also recognized that the common pattern in higher education for incumbents in those demanding offices averaged two to four years.

Following decisions by the fourth incumbents in both Admissions and Development or Advancement departments to accept calls to parish ministry, I determined not to conduct broad-based searches but rather turn to two individuals whose gifts, skills and passions for the Seminary's mission had already been demonstrated in full measure. This was in keeping with my general rule, which is not universally accepted by others; that if you already know who you want for a key position, it's unfair to raise hopes on the part of other potential candidates. Along with knowing who I was convinced could best serve in those positions, I was aware it would take a special commitment to risk accepting a call to serve with a president who was obviously in the final stages of service.

In the case of the Admissions Director position, experience both at Gettysburg and elsewhere suggested that, all things being equal, having an alumus/a in the role is ideal. Who better can speak to potential enrollees about the school than one who has experienced it as a student?

I felt that my being an alumnus of LTSG was an asset to my presidency in this regard, whereas colleague presidents who had no prior experience with a school spoke of the challenges of stepping in without any sense of its history and ethos. Given the downturn in enrollment at all ELCA seminaries, and Gettysburg's growing difficulty in attracting younger students (often referred to as the "millennial" generation), I deemed it wise to take a rather bold and somewhat controversial step. I invited a graduating senior with no ministerial experience other than a one-year internship to serve as our Admissions director.

I had reviewed the internship experience of Lauren Muratore, a young woman from greater Baltimore, who boldly embraced placement in a large congregation in Lincoln, Nebraska. During her senior year, I was deeply impressed as I heard Lauren preach and observed her interactions with her peers. Initially stunned when then-Dean Robin Steinke and I asked her to consider the position, Lauren came to embrace it as her call. Her bishop supported a request, which required approval of the entire ELCA Conference of Bishops, that she be granted an exception to a rule in our polity which requires that a first ministry be in a congregation. So, it was my privilege to preach at the service of ordination for Lauren and three of her peers in the Delaware-Maryland Synod, and then later to preach for her installation at the seminary.

As predicted, Lauren proved herself adept at relating to prospective seminarians who were still in college or their twenties. But she was no less pastoral and effective in gaining the confidence of those who had long been referred to as "second career" or in some cases "older students." Together with a couple of board members, and with my strong support as well as that of the faculty and our other team leaders, Lauren was a sparkplug in igniting a movement to declare the seminary as a "Reconciling in Christ," school, formally labeling us as a place of welcome and hospitality for LGBTQ students. While modest in their results in terms of numbers, Lauren's efforts in this regard helped the Seminary become a more inclusive and diverse community.

When the decision to form United Seminary was made, Lauren committed herself to forge a strong partnership with her Philadelphia counterpart. Their combined efforts, bolstered by the announcement of generous increased scholarships, resulted in the "new school" launching with a significantly larger entering class than had been the combined totals for several prior years. As was the case for Elizabeth and John Spangler, Lauren also worked gracefully and uncomplainingly under unnecessary pressures caused by a couple of colleagues at the sister school who constantly tried to undermine her efforts. As the months wound down toward the launch of United Lutheran, Lauren discerned that her calling was to parish ministry, and she excitedly accepted a call to serve in a two-pronged urban ministry in Baltimore city. A few years later, she moved to Augustana Lutheran Church in Washington, D.C., where, as noted in Chapter 5, I had served briefly decades before. It was a special joy when she asked me to do some consulting with the parish as they engaged in some planning and problem-solving.

In another key search process, which I determined to limit to a "targeted search," I invited the Rev. Glenn Ludwig to consider serving as the Seminary's vice president for advancement. Glenn, a widely known and highly regarded parish pastor, who had served a quarter century in a prominent Baltimore area parish, was chair of the Seminary's Board of Directors for the maximum three terms (six years). While I was blessed with strong board chairs throughout my presidency, Glenn was in a category of his own in terms of guiding the board as it made some of the most significant and risky decisions ever encountered by Gettysburg's governing body. In the course of the board's weighing the potentially high-risk investment in creating the Seminary Ridge Museum, for example, over and over again, Glenn's calm and confident leadership enabled board members to engage in careful deliberations, after which solid decisions were made and implemented. Shortly after the conclusion of his service in that key role, our Advancement vice president, Kathleen Reed, accepted a call to a prestigious parish on the fringe of Harvard University. I soon invited Glenn to lunch in nearby Harrisburg, Pennsylvania. At some point during the meal, I looked him in the eyes and made a short but compelling statement: "Glenn, I know who I want as our next Vice President of Advancement; and it's you!" Following a few days of the requisite "prayerful discernment," (which in his case meant largely gaining the support of his spouse Stella, who had been hoping he might actually settle into retirement), Glenn enthusiastically accepted the position.

Given the unrelenting financial challenges faced by the Seminary, including the need to avoid further steep tuition increases, and with flat or declining "church support" from our regional synods and the churchwide expression of the ELCA, board members and I recognized the need to grow our annual fund contributions from generous donors. In our budget-building, a deficit loomed on the near horizon and threatened to compromise a principle I had established early in my tenure: that

Gettysburg Seminary doesn't do deficit budgets! I swallowed hard as we adopted a budget for the FY 2014–15, which called for a significant increase in donor giving. Since we had never exceeded a half-million dollars in unrestricted giving, the goal of a twenty-five percent increase seemed unrealistic. I was glad to be proven wrong! With Glenn's leadership, that vital income stream grew by over sixty percent in a two-year period, a record few organizations could boast.

Beyond his outstanding leadership in our fund- and friend-raising (the latter greatly enhanced by virtue of Glenn's reputation in regional and even national church circles), he took on the role as "point person" for a new leadership development program funded by a generous grant from the Lilly Endowment. This Senior Pastors' Training Institute was the first of its kind, and the incarnation of a vision I held since my days as chief staff for the ELCA Conference of Bishops. Over the years, I had listened as bishops throughout our church, and in ecumenical circles as well, lamented the dearth of pastoral candidates with the skillset and aptitude to serve as heads of staff in large corporate-sized congregations. Since Glenn had himself been so effective in such a role for over a quarter century, he was well-suited to spearhead this program. Together with an advisory group of seasoned veteran senior pastors, he organized a series of intensive seminars for clergy nominated by their bishops, who regarded them as potential future lead pastors. The program proved highly popular and continued with Glenn's leadership for more than a decade.

As Glenn crossed the threshold into his 70's, and we were in the waning days of my presidency, he and I sought to identify and position the next generation of leadership in this critical leadership arena. The Rev. Dr. Angela Zimmann, a seminary alumna who had earned a Ph.D. in homiletics, was serving in a challenging international mission, which included assisting the president of the Lutheran World Federation. Learning of Angela's and her family's possible return to the U.S., I phoned her in Jerusalem and invited her to consider joining our Advancement staff, and also offering some courses in preaching. During her first couple of years with us, she quickly proved her adeptness at fund-raising and executive leadership. So, when Glenn and Angela proposed a kind of role reversal, whereby she would become Vice President of Advancement and Glenn would focus more on his work as president of the Gettysburg Seminary Endowment Foundation, I readily said, "Let's do it!"

Angela proved as capable as we expected in leading the Advancement effort during the remainder of LTSG's life. Her dedication to the fledgling new institution would prove even more invaluable as she ended up becoming the Advancement team leader when ULS's initial vice president for Advancement was named chief operating officer. Following departure of the first ULS interim president in 2020, Angela also served ULS effectively in that role for several months. After helping current ULS President Guy Erwin in his early years in office, Angela accepted a position leading the Advancement work at Wilson College in Chambersburg, PA.

For an institutional chief executive, there is perhaps no greater vulnerability than in the area of financial management. Unless one is a CPA, a president must depend upon the competence and skills of an incumbent in finance to maintain fiscal integrity. This is a critical area, as ineptitude for even a few weeks can leave an institution highly vulnerable. I discovered this late in my tenure when we hired an individual who came with impressive credentials and strong recommendations to succeed Marty Stevens, who wanted to focus more on her teaching and scholarly work. After a few months, it came to light that our new CFO was falling further and further behind in fiscal management. We breathed a sigh of relief when he announced he was moving to another position. Fortunately, when I pleaded for her help, Marty Stevens briefly stepped back in to help us out, after which I promoted our recently hired controller to the lead spot. A person of deep faith, Jennifer Byers was a strong team player who was well-received by administrative colleagues as well as faculty and the staff of the Seminary Ridge Museum, for whom the Seminary continued providing financial services. In the consolidation process, Jennifer grew increasingly uncomfortable with the cross-campus tensions and resistance to her leadership by some of the Philadelphia colleagues. Despite my encouragement to be open to the ULS position, she decided to accept a position closer to her home in York, Pennsylvania. We have remained in contact following my retirement, and I am grateful for her friendship.

Noted previously was my decision to ask Kristin Largen to serve as interim dean, which evolved into dropping the "interim" label after she proved herself such a good leader in that critical role. Since joining the faculty in 2006, Kristin had demonstrated that, in addition to being a first-rate scholar and teacher, she was an effective leader. I especially appreciated her honesty and forthrightness in challenging me on some occasions when she thought I was making a poor decision. In asking Kristin to serve as dean, I knew she would bring the same competence and integrity to the office as had her predecessors, Norma Wood and

Robin Steinke. And I was confident we would enjoy mutual respect, which certainly proved to be the case.

In the earliest stages of exploring possible consolidation with Philadelphia, I had no hesitation in engaging in confidential discussions with Kristin. She raised all appropriate questions, but quickly embraced the same conviction I had come to, that joining the schools held the best prospect for ELCA theological education's future in the northeast. Once a decision was made to bring the schools together, Kristin became a fearless champion for the venture. Empathetic in the face of faculty and staff colleagues' anxiety, she also set limits, and when necessary, could say, "We need to move on." During the transition, Kristin was the "point person" for curriculum design, faculty planning, and a host of other tasks. Her Philadelphia counterpart, Dean Kirin Sebastian, has a very collegial spirit, and the two worked well together. She was a stalwart supporter of and personal confidant for me, especially when we hit some of the low points in the process.

Kristin's gifts were recognized far beyond the seminary. As her cutting-edge interfaith theological work began to circulate in wider circles, she received frequent speaking invitations throughout the U.S. and internationally. Nearer to home, when Gettysburg College's longtime chaplain retired, President Janet Riggs was eager to explore with me the possibility of Kristin's serving part-time as college chaplain and associate dean for spiritual life. She accepted that role and began serving at the college when the ULS consolidation took effect. It was a joy when, in 2020, Kristin was elected president of her alma mater, Wartburg Seminary. During her first year, I was honored to serve as her executive coach.

I have left for last in this series of tributes the one who was closest of all for the entire duration of my presidency. When I became president in 2000, Pastor John Spangler was serving in a part-time role as communications director. I immediately recognized his wide-ranging skills and gifts, as well as his calm and unflappable demeanor. As the years passed, the scope of John's leadership and influence just kept growing and expanding. His ultimate title of Executive Assistant to the President hopefully conveyed the scope of influence as my chief of staff. On occasion I would comment to board members and fellow presidents that I believed in all sincerity the Seminary could withstand my departure or retirement easier than should John choose to leave. From my perspective, John and I enjoyed the kind of symbiotic relationship I experienced with George Anderson when I was the latter's executive assistant. John often thought of things needing attention before I did and could serve occasionally as my ghost writer for public statements. That he and his family (John is married to Dr. Maria Erling, noted church history professor at LTSG and ULS) lived just two blocks from the seminary meant he was always ready at hand and on the scene in times of crisis or when we had to make early morning decisions about closing or staying open amidst a snowstorm. We became friends as families, and Pamela and I continue to enjoy the exceptional hospitality in the Erling-Spangler home.

As noted previously, John played a key role in the creation of the Seminary Ridge Museum and overall campus management. Beyond the depth of his technical expertise in construction-related matters, and his deep commitment to environmental stewardship, John has a keen appreciation for the arts. Together with his assistant Katy Giebenhain, John staffed a seminary fine arts committee that brought a series of first-rate art exhibits to our campus. He also supported one of the Seminary's primary public outreach programs, *Music Gettysburg!*, which sponsors fifteen or more concerts annually by a wide range of regionally and nationally known soloists and ensembles, including the U.S. Air Force chorus. Above all his other gifts and abilities, John was a consummate diplomat in relating to the broad range of the seminary's constituents. Internally, he was the "go-to guy" for staff, often quietly helping resolve tensions and absorbing anxiety in times of crisis.

Throughout my years at "the crossroads of history and hope," it was truly a blessing to serve alongside these and other gifted colleagues. I simply was surrounded by what I regard as the finest team in all theological education!

— 13 —

Endgame: Historic Seminary's Last President

MUCH OF MY TIME during the final weeks of the presidency was taken up preparing for the transition, transferring important records to the archives, and saying farewell to friends and colleagues, some of whom had been coworkers the entire seventeen years I was in office. While we had been slowly working at the move-out from the Lewars House (president's residence) on campus for several months, its final clearance of our personal effects also required considerable time and emotional energy. We wanted to make the house available well ahead of my term's end for painting and other changes that a new president might request; and we achieved that goal and vacated early in the spring.

I found myself surprised at the emotions that sometimes overcame me. Every drawer held a memory! We had come to love the stately mansion with its amazing views of the Gettysburg battlefield, often graced by what must be among the world's finest sunsets! I reflected on the hundreds of occasions when we welcomed students, faculty and staff, board members, alumni/ae, donors, public officials, friends and family members, and others to our home. When we arrived in 2000, we had resolved that Lewars House be a place of hospitality. Over the course of our years, literally thousands of people spent time in our home at receptions, dinners, parties, and other special events. While we had already occupied a lovely home on a scenic property in the countryside (which Pam calls our "forever house"), and by then also had a spacious Manhattan apartment provided by Pam's professorship at Union Seminary, I knew I would miss Lewars House.

A Glorious Retirement Banquet

Even as they were attending to all the ULS transition-related matters, while simultaneously keeping LTSG running smoothly to its very end, staff colleagues joined Pamela and Ms. Leslie Hobbs in planning a lavish retirement banquet, at which I was honored on April 21, 2017. Elizabeth Meighan deserves special mention for all her work in planning the banquet, while simultaneously overseeing the preparation of Lewars House for its new occupants. Ms. Hobb's participation in planning for this amazing gathering was especially gratifying in that she had chaired the synod committee that supported me as a seminarian forty-five years before, and then also served as a member of the presidential search committee when I was interviewed in early 2000.

No one could hope for a more festive and gracious farewell event than the retirement banquet on April 21st! It was a beautiful spring Friday evening, which afforded nearly 200 guests the opportunity to enjoy the outdoor patio during the cocktail hour at Sidney's fine dining establishment just a mile west of the Seminary on the Lincoln Highway (U.S. Route 30). All our children, their partners, and our three granddaughters (at the time) were able to join us, affording all one last gathering in the Lewars' House and on the Seminary campus. Following a sumptuous dinner in Sidney's beautifully decorated main dining area, a program of over an hour featured a parade of "tributes" that blended humorous and serious short speeches by the board chair, community leaders, staff colleagues, my bishop, LTSP President Lose, and family members. There were comments on my years in parish ministry, my work as urban coalition director and assistant to two synodical bishops, and my years at the churchwide offices in Chicago .The most extended comments were by colleagues, current and former board chairs, and others on the seventeen-year chapter in which I served as the last president of the historic Lutheran Theological Seminary at Gettysburg.

The board chair announced that the trustees had acted to name me President Emeritus of United Lutheran Seminary, named the newest building (a student and visiting faculty residence) in my honor, and launched a fund-raising appeal to create the Michael Cooper-White Endowed Chair of Leadership, for which a lead gift of $600,000 had been contributed by the Delaware-Maryland Synod. A presidential portrait was unveiled, that hangs in the Gettysburg library of ULS. The mayor of Gettysburg presented me with a key to the city; President Lose with the rarely bestowed Henry Melchior Muhlenberg medallion conferred by the LTSP board; Adams county officials with a formal declaration of appreciation; and our children and granddaughters with a lovely leather folder embossed with the name of the consulting group we formed, The Gettysburg Group. Written expressions of appreciation and citations were received from the governor, Pennsylvania's senators, our congressman, and others. Dozens of letters and notes were compiled in a book of tributes, including from current and former ELCA presiding and synod bishops, current and former student leaders, faculty colleagues, board members, colleague seminary presidents and a host of others. Unable to be present, Gettysburg College's president sent a letter, which shared the news that our sister institution would be conferring my second honorary doctorate (the first having come years before from Susquehanna University) at its May commencement.

Glenn Ludwig was a gracious emcee for the festive evening. Having served as board chair and Advancement vice president, Glenn and I had a unique relationship. "First he was my boss and now I'm his," was the way I often described it. John Spangler's tribute noted that mine was the longest Gettysburg presidency in a century. His light-hearted comments recalled many events over the years, including my almost always showing up somewhere on campus with a shovel after a big snowstorm. On a more serious note, John lifted up our joint efforts to expand the Seminary's public influence and impact, including my service on the Gettysburg 150th planning committee. John concluded his remarks, "By now, you should get a picture of the type of leader Michael has been. Hands on. High expectations with self-effacing tone. Prudent spender. A collegial art critic. Patient with staff. Willing to take risks, and support staff when they do, and always a champion of justice. Taking a stand at critical times; and teaching us all with your abundant orientation of gratitude."

An airplane piñata was included in the décor, and a poster-sized photo of me leaning on my airplane was superimposed on the official portrait as it was unveiled, to the delight of all present. For a moment, some (including Pamela) were convinced that a last-minute decision had been made to actually substitute the casual shot for the formal portrait.

Family members in turn each commented on our life together as the Cooper-White clan. Their tributes were most gratifying of all as one-by-one Pam and each of our three children spoke from the heart about our family life together. Pam was also thanked for her many contributions to the Seminary community over the years. She was presented with a framed reproduction of her favorite historic painting of the Seminary and surrounding vistas in its early years (which has a prominent place in our dining room today).

After the various tributes, it was my time to simply say some words of appreciation and offer a concluding benediction. As one of the most memorable and treasured evenings of my life was drawing to a close, I was able to express my profound thanks for the privilege of serving as the last president of my beloved alma mater, often called "the school for the prophets" located on Gettysburg's "glorious hill." In my remarks, I repeated the statement I had uttered seventeen years before in accepting the call to the Seminary presidency: "I see Gettysburg (about to become with Philadelphia "United") Seminary as the ELCA's oldest and most historic seminary, whose best day is tomorrow." I concluded with a quote from Abraham Lincoln's farewell address to his neighbors and fellow citizens in Springfield, Illinois, as he prepared to move to the White House and assume the U.S. presidency: "During all this time, I have received nothing but kindness at your hands."

Final Round Serving as the Seminary's Public Face

One of a chief executive's key roles is to serve as the public face of an organization or institution. In the case of denominational seminaries, a key constituency is "the church" as understood in its broadest sense. In the ELCA, beyond individual donors, seminaries are financially supported by congregations, synods and the churchwide organization. As noted previously, Gettysburg received its primary support from churches in much of Pennsylvania, Maryland, Delaware, West Virginia and the District of Columbia, the ELCA's Region 8. With eight synods, many of them clustering on two or three spring weekends, it was impossible for me to personally appear at each. Most years I could attend three or four, and my staff colleagues, together with board members, presented the seminary report at others.

As we reviewed the calendar for the 2017 synodical assemblies, I wanted to give priority to an appearance in my home synod of Lower Susquehanna. This synod, on whose clergy roster I had served throughout the seminary presidency years, led the entire ELCA in seminary financial support, giving far in excess of their recommended "fair share." Its bishop, the Rev. James Dunlop, had graduated in the early years of my tenure, and I wanted to publicly acknowledge his strong support, and his leadership of the Transition Team. Since that assembly fell the same weekend that I was due to be in Minneapolis for David Lose's installation as senior pastor of Mt. Olivet Lutheran Church, I had to rush off to catch a plane shortly after my appearance early in the agenda. Following my report to the assembly, I was surprised when the bishop presented me with a painting by a local artist. Following his very kind verbal tribute to my presidency, the synod rose in an extended standing ovation. That meant a great deal to me, especially since, when I had taken progressive stands on certain issues, I faced sharp criticism and even personal attacks from some conservative clergy and congregations in the synod.

The following week, my last public appearance representing Gettysburg Seminary (and also the emerging United Lutheran Seminary) was at the Southwestern Pennsylvania Synod assembly held at Pennsylvania's California University. There too, Bishop Kurt Kusserow, who had become a good friend, offered kind words of appreciation for my years of leadership at the Seminary. It was also gratifying that the final chapter concluded in the synod whose former leaders had played such key roles in my journey. Long-time synod secretary, the Rev. Kirk Bish, had chaired the presidential search committee and served as a board member and officer throughout much of my presidency. The synodical vice president, Mr. Brandon James, had served as the seminary board treasurer, a GSEF trustee and one of our strongest cheerleaders. And the synod's former bishop, the Rev. Donald McCoid, had chaired the seminary board during a time of challenging transition. Having the opportunity to personally and publicly thank these great friends and coworkers was one more step in my coming to closure on an amazing chapter of my life and ministry.

In those final synod assembly addresses, I sought to sound chords of gratitude for the grand legacy of Gettysburg Seminary and to project hopefulness for the new seminary about to be born. I announced that United Lutheran Seminary would continue offering full scholarships to all ELCA full-time students, as we had already initiated at both LTSG and

LTSP. Echoing a theme I had introduced the previous year, I invited our thousands of supporters to dream of what the future might hold:

> Imagine a seminary like that! A seminary that offers full tuition scholarships to all full-time students; a seminary on the cutting edge of innovative curricula preparing leaders for the church of the 21st century; a seminary committed to providing greater access for more students in an era when our ELCA faces a growing crisis in the shortage of clergy; a seminary saving $3 million per year compared to the joint budgets of its two predecessors; a seminary carrying forth the grand legacies of what's gone on at Gettysburg for 190 years and in Philadelphia for 153. This United Lutheran Seminary will come into being on July 1st at the stroke of midnight, at the precise midpoint of the 500th anniversary year of the great Reformation. God is doing a new thing! And we're part of it!

Sharing Some Insights and Learnings

A study by the American Council on Education in 2016 revealed that higher education presidencies in the early 2000's lasted an average of about six years. By the time I concluded my seventeen-year service, only a handful of the 270-plus presidents of schools in the Association of Theological Schools (ATS) had served tenures of my duration. Accordingly, as one of the "old timers" in theological education leadership, on occasion in my final months I was asked what I had learned that might be of value to other chief executives.

At my last meeting with the ELCA seminary presidents I offered seven insights in a piece entitled "Looking Back from the End of the Road." This piece was disseminated broadly in publications of both the ATS and In Trust, an organization funded primarily by the Lilly Endowment to offer resources and consultation for seminaries and divinity schools. During my final year in office, I was also asked to join with other colleagues in a presentation at an ATS-sponsored event on "searching for sustainability in a volatile environment." It afforded me the opportunity to reflect on the series of challenges we had faced and difficult decisions that resulted in Gettysburg's maintaining one of the strongest fiscal positions among seminaries.

Another opportunity to look back over the sweep of my presidency was afforded by the local Gettysburg newspaper editor when Alex Hayes scheduled an hour-long interview in my office. His front-page retrospective article was generous in recounting major events and accomplishments of "the Cooper-White" years.

Preserving a Grand Legacy and Preparing for the Handoff

Grasping the reality that the historic Gettysburg Seminary was coming to an end, and that I was its last president, I recognized that future historians might have particularly keen interest in some of my papers, correspondence, and other artifacts. Accordingly, I spent considerable time in reviewing files, with an eye to transferring key documents, my chapel sermons, and other materials to the archives. Since I had served as secretary for the Transition Team that laid the groundwork for the United Lutheran Seminary, I also gave close attention to preserving the history of that eighteen-month journey. Minutes of meetings, email exchanges between David Lose and me, correspondence with our attorney, accreditors, state and federal education departments, and other documents were organized in files and binders.

During the months leading up to the launch of United Lutheran Seminary, David Lose and I sought to prepare the way for the one who would succeed us as the first president of the consolidated school. In conversations and public events, I described it this way: "While we don't want to tie the hands of our successor, we also don't want to say to that person, 'Here's your Boeing 747, new captain, and by the way, you have no crew to help you get if off the ground!'" In other words, we wanted to identify and encourage key leaders from both seminaries who could commit to at least a transitional period of service, helping the new president get established and ensuring United Lutheran Seminary a strong launch.

In a series of extended telephone conference calls involving President-elect Latini, and board chair, Rev. Elise Brown, the two of us attempted to accomplish a hand-off and knowledge transfer to our successor. We briefed them on key pending matters, the status of senior staff, and issues that would require their immediate attention. I supplemented those verbal briefings by compiling an extensive transition manual that provided more expansive explanations and background documents for the new president. Whether or not that proved helpful is unknown, as it was never acknowledged.

Given staff transitions in the financial operations area, with the absence of a chief financial officer on both campuses, it became apparent that no one was monitoring cash flow and projecting fiscal needs for the first few months of United Lutheran Seminary's operations. Given that David Lose had accumulated vacation time and concluded his work at Philadelphia some weeks before July 1, it fell to me to take steps that would avert a crisis, which Latini would otherwise inherit immediately upon taking office. Among other things, I was worried that there would be insufficient cash to meet payroll over the summer months, when income typically is low. As more accurate information was received on the state of the Philadelphia endowment, it also became apparent that it had very low liquidity and could not supply much for United Lutheran's start-up operations. Additionally, we learned that things were not very far along by way of staging portions of the Philadelphia campus for sale, a key to repaying the debt.

Working with the board chair and president of the Gettysburg Seminary Endowment Foundation (GSEF), I called for a special meeting to authorize release of up to an additional $1 million for temporary cash flow. Over the strong objections of a handful of the trustees, this emergency measure was adopted by the GSEF trustees. The GSEF board also determined that this emergency release of additional funds was a "loan" that obligated the board of United Lutheran to repay within the first years of ULS's life. When GSEF officers asked legal counsel to draft a Memorandum of Understanding documenting matters related to these financial transactions, as they felt required to do in fulfilling their fiduciary responsibility, they were sharply reprimanded by the new president and board chair for overreaching.

A Final Farewell to a Historic Institution

Given all the time required tending to last-minute administrative matters and covering the final synod assemblies, I had limited opportunities to simply wander around campus and personally thank each colleague for our years together. My last week in office I issued a final written communication to all Seminary personnel, hoping thereby to convey my deep appreciation to these women and men who had kept the place running so well.

> Dear colleagues, this will be my final written communication to you as president. While I will have opportunity these last days

in office to express a personal word of thanks to many, some are away from campus this week, and so a brief note seems in order. Pamela and I look forward to joining in the "Wake, Awake!" festivities on Friday evening as we say a final farewell to Gettysburg Seminary and greet the dawning of the United Lutheran Seminary.

My first "epistle" to the Seminary, distributed August 1, 2000, concluded: *In the months and years ahead, the seminary will have many opportunities and experience many challenges. . . . Together we are the community of those called to serve in this place. Please know that you are in my prayers and my heart as I begin my ministry among you!*

These past years have indeed been ones of many opportunities and challenges. To all I express my profound gratitude for the privilege of serving among you. As we think back upon our seventeen years on Seminary Ridge, Pamela and I are grateful for all the colleagues and friends with whom we have shared a portion of life's journey.

For all that has been and all that is to come, we say a resounding, "Thanks be to God."! And please know that you are in my prayers and my heart as I conclude my ministry among you!

With the office vacated of all my personal effects, on Friday June 30, I tended to a few final matters, handed over to the personnel officer my keys and Seminary credit card, removed my nameplate outside my door, and headed home for a few hours. Pamela and I had invited the senior staff team and their spouses to our country home for a leisurely dinner, during which we reminisced about all we had shared over the years. This provided an opportunity for me to thank these coworkers, about whom I had often stated publicly, "They are more important to the life of the seminary than I am." As noted previously, we had assembled one of the finest administrative leadership teams to be found in higher education. With a mixture of sadness and satisfaction, we gathered around table for a final time, and I offered a toast to these wonderful friends who made my final years as president so rewarding and gratifying.

As evening fell, we returned to campus for the "Wake, Awake!" events planned by a small team headed by our worship professor, Dr. Mark Oldenburg. Events included processing to key spots on campus where longtime Seminary servants recounted vignettes that had occurred in the various locales. One of the final stops was at Lewars House where Dr. Kris Stuempfle, (by then a dean at Gettysburg College) recounted memories of growing up in the house when her father served as the Seminary's tenth president in the late 1970's and throughout the 1980's. Kris held up an old wooden tennis racquet, which, she said, reminded her both of Herman Stuempfle's prowess on the campus tennis court, as well as its use to swat the occasional bats that appeared from time to time during every president's tenure in the home!

Then, Pam and I spoke briefly of our memories hosting so many guests during dinners and receptions held throughout our seventeen-year occupancy of the historic mansion named for its most famous occupant, prolific author Elsie Singmaster Lewars. Following the viewing of fireworks from down the hill (sponsored by the local fire company in conjunction with their annual fundraising fair), the stalwart "Wake, Awake!" participants who had lasted until the late hour convened in the Seminary Chapel (the Church of the Abiding Presence) for a brief worship service. Together, we marked the passing into history of the Lutheran Theological Seminary at Gettysburg and welcomed into existence the United Lutheran Seminary.

In our prayers just before the stroke of midnight, we gave thanks "for all who have been a part of the ministry of this seminary throughout its life." We sang the seminary hymn, "Serene Upon Her Hill-top" that had been sung for generations since its composition by Elsie Singmaster Lewars:. It concludes:

> In love her children gather,
> upon her wooded hills,
> and with the oil of wisdom,
> their lamps again they fill.
> O, may they ever find her,
> when seeking here they come,
> a fount of life and blessings,
> their mother and their home.

Then, as the beloved historic institution's life came to a close, and my service as its final chief steward concluded, it was my privilege to pronounce the final blessing. It was an emotional evening to be sure. As I recall, I made a final pass through my office corridor, and as we passed by, we bid farewell to the presidential home we had occupied for seventeen years. Pam and I drove to our country home west of Gettysburg, and I prepared to begin a new chapter of life.

— 14 —

An Active Retirement

As my seventeen-year presidency at the Seminary, and career of four decades in active ordained ministry drew to a close, I was surprised at the relative low drama of it all. Imagining in advance that I would feel a great measure of relief upon relinquishing the weight of office, I found instead in the early days of my retirement a degree of what I can only call "unfinished business." I found myself wishing I could have seen through a number of developments that remained incomplete. More than I had anticipated, I missed the daily interactions with my colleagues, who had also become fast friends. While I felt it permissible to maintain occasional social contacts, I needed to minimize such encounters so my former colleagues could transfer their loyalty to the new president.

From talking with other new retirees, as well as reading a number of books and articles on this phase of life, I recognize that my experience is fairly typical. One does really "fall off a cliff" going from intense work weeks to the freedom described as every day being Saturday. Overnight, an inflow of dozens of emails and phone calls trickles to a handful. The daily hundreds of exchanges with close colleagues evaporate and one spends a great deal more time alone. While never terribly status conscious, I admit to missing a degree of prestige afforded to one who bears the title of president.

Enjoying International and U.S. Travel

It was a wonderful gift that Pamela and I had planned extensive international travel in the weeks immediately following my official retirement. The week after I concluded my seminary service, we departed for a ten-day intensive experience in Israel/Palestine. Pamela had been invited to serve as keynoter for the third annual gathering of the newly formed International Association for Spiritual Care. A pre-conference tour hosted by the interfaith Rossing Center for Dialogue and Education in Jerusalem and environs was a powerful experience. When we had mentioned this upcoming travel to our children a few months before, Macrina stated her desire to accompany us. Experiencing my first "Holy Land" trip with the two women closest to me in the world provided a marvelous opportunity to put things in perspective about my career and the recent endgame at the Seminary.

A few weeks later, Pam and I again boarded international flights for a delightful week-long visit in Vienna and Budapest. Pam had made good friends in both places during her Fulbright fellowship sabbatical in Vienna and a subsequent student tour that included Hungary, which she led while still teaching at Columbia Seminary. Being whisked around these two great European cities by local hosts, enjoying leisurely dinners in some of Austria's finest restaurants, and imbibing generously in the fine wines of Europe helped me begin the process of easing into the new phase of life commonly referred to as "retirement."

When offered the opportunity for a no-cost second Holy Land pilgrimage (thanks to our friend and United Seminary Alumni Director Martin Zimmann) in January 2018, we jumped at the chance! That trip was a more typical Christian-led pilgrimage of "following in the footsteps of Jesus," and took us to many places we had preached about over the years—Galilee, the Jordan river, the Dead Sea and so on. Over meals, and on our long bus rides, we enjoyed the companionship of longtime friends and made some new acquaintances in this group of clergy from around the nation as well. An overnight stay in the home of gracious Palestinian hosts was especially poignant as they shared their feelings about living under the thumb of the Israeli government.

During my second year of retirement, I had further opportunities to accompany Pam when her scholarly work took her to Europe and Scandinavia. Once again Macrina expressed interest in joining me as we rendezvoused with Pam in Vienna, where she had spent several weeks doing research. In what would be our last extended father-daughter time before her wedding, Macrina and I traveled by train to Prague and on to our ancestral island of Fehmarn, as noted in the first chapter. We met up with Pam in Berlin, and then spent a few more days in Vienna. In 2019, Pam was keynoter for a conference in Oslo, Norway and I again enjoyed traveling with her. It was interesting for me to visit the place so many of our Norwegian-heritage Minnesota neighbors referred to as "the old country."

Following my retirement, we divided our time between New York City, where Union Seminary provided us with a spacious Manhattan apartment overlooking a park, and our Orrtanna timber home with its commanding view of the Adams County orchard country west of Gettysburg. Given my flying, journalism work with the *Gettysburg Times*, and the need to tend our home and property, I spent most of my time in Pennsylvania, but enjoyed my many New York sojourns as well. Pam and I felt blessed to experience these diverse contexts and comfortable lifestyle.

In the spring of 2019, Pam was asked by Union Seminary President Serene Jones to become the storied institution's next academic dean. Thus began a three-year stint in which her workload increased to an unrelenting hectic pace. With her extensive experience as a senior executive, as well as being an outstanding academic, she flourished in the role and helped lead the school through a period of crises unforeseen when she accepted the deanship: a pandemic and period of intense political polarization and racial reckoning. In early 2020, what became a worldwide Coronavirus pandemic emerged in the U.S., ultimately taking more than one million lives. New York City was hit especially hard in the early days of the pandemic, and Union Seminary urged as many staff and students who could do so to relocate elsewhere. All in-person classes were suspended, and as dean, Pam had to help colleagues pivot to online teaching, at which few were adept. As if that crisis were not enough, in that same time frame the Union community was further traumatized in the aftermath of nationwide multiple acts of violence, including horrific murders, perpetrated upon Black citizens and other persons of color, by police in some cases. When a noose (symbol of lynching) was found in a maintenance closet on the Union campus, Pam and her colleagues arranged for counseling and other measures of support to a community in deep distress. Her heroic work as "the Covid Dean," in the words of President Jones, was recognized at her retirement banquet in the spring of 2023. Shortly thereafter, at commencement in May, it was announced the Union board had conferred the honor of naming her Professor and Dean Emerita.

The silver lining amidst the Covid-19 pandemic's peak months was Pam's working and living full-time in our Orrtanna home. After so many years of spending the majority of time apart, we cherished this prolonged period of daily togetherness, which also made us anticipate even more her retirement and that pattern becoming permanent. While most members of our family eventually joined the majority of Americans in contracting Covid, fortunately we did so after vaccines and boosters had been developed and mitigated the symptoms and duration.

More Hours and a New Rating in My Logbook

As I started to settle into the retirement lifestyle absent the constant demands and heavy schedules I had maintained for over four decades, there was ample time to begin pursuing some long-deferred interests. I stepped up my flying by taking on a couple of new students and by joining the Mid-Atlantic Soaring Association (M-ASA) at the nearby Fairfield, PA airport. Initially joining M-ASA for the opportunity to fly a pristine Piper Super Cub, the same kind of plane in which I learned to fly fifty years before, I was strongly encouraged to start flying gliders. Earning my commercial glider rating posed a far greater challenge than I had imagined. At the outset I thought that after a few flights, my piloting skills gained through nearly 2,000 hours in airplanes would enable an easy transition. It was only after months of dual instruction and dozens of flights that I was cut loose for solo flight, followed months later by a successful and memorable checkride in such turbulent conditions the examiner refused to go up for the standard second flight!

Joining M-ASA took me into a broader circle of fellow aviation enthusiasts, which led to new friendships and helped fill the void I felt in missing my former seminary and wider church colleagues. In addition to my glider lessons, I was soon qualified as a tow pilot flying the Piper aircraft that pull the gliders aloft. Also, recognizing my administrative background and writing abilities, the M-ASA president asked that I take over when the club's corporate secretary resigned. In that role I served as part of the club's leadership team.

While flying at M-ASA was a new adventure, my first year there also included the most traumatic moment in my fifty years of flying. On a turbulent windy spring day, we were launching from an airport near a Pennsylvania mountain range where "ridge soaring" was possible. After a delightful and exciting long glider flight along the ridges, I offered to share tow pilot duties so a fellow pilot could take a turn in a glider. After landing, when the Piper Pawnee had slowed almost to taxi speed, a strong gust of wind caused me to step hard on a rudder to counteract the sideways gust. As far as we can determine, in jabbing my foot on the rudder, I caught the top portion of the pedal, which applied the brake and caused the plane to nose over onto its propeller. Such incidents, of course, catch the attention of the Federal Aviation Administration (FAA). Following a review of the incident, and my previously spotless flying record, an FAA inspector conducting the obligatory "counseling" (in a five-minute phone call) concluded, "Try not to do it again." I assured him that was my intent! Determined not to let that mishap diminish my joy in flying, I "got back in the saddle" quickly and resumed flying the tow plane, gliders, and flight instructing in my Cessna 150. My M-ASA colleagues were very gracious, and as time went by, several of them also confessed to having accidents or incidents.

In my flight instructing, I have given priority to teaching young persons to fly. It is gratifying that at least three I have had a hand in instructing are now airline pilots, and a fourth is well on her way to flying the big jets. I am gratified they stay in touch and let me know as they attain new career goals. A flight student I helped gain his Private Pilot license while still in high school, Liam Dwyer, wrote in a thank you note: "In the wake of my first solo flight, I'd like to take the opportunity to seriously thank you for all the time and effort you've dedicated to teaching me how to fly. It's been an honor learning from you, and I look forward to continuing. It's been a lifelong dream of mine and you've made it a reality."

Evan Kerr also learned to fly with me while he was in high school. I hadn't heard from him in a while, so I recently sent a text asking about his career flying widebody jets with Delta Airlines. Five minutes later he responded, "I'm actually over the Atlantic right now flying back from Berlin on a Boeing 767." Reminiscing later about his first flight with me, he wrote, "Shortly after takeoff, Mike handed me the controls. That moment and one simple climbing turn has been engraved into my head permanently. Since that first flight with Mike, I've known that this was going to be a lifelong adventure."

Evan Kerr's first solo in 2014; now he flies B-767's for Delta Airlines.

Launching a Multi-Faceted Encore Career

As I contemplated the future during my last months in office, I felt that my experiences in and insights from the various calls held over the years could be of value to others. So, I determined to make myself available for occasional consulting as that might be requested. In a round of conversations with our family members, it surprised me that our "kids" were interested in making it a family business. We settled on *The Gettysburg Group* as our name, had a group photo taken at my retirement banquet, and prepared to start advertising our availability. In addition to Aaron, Melissa, Adam, and Macrina, I invited my close friend Eric Shafer and an LTSG/ULS board member Cheryl Williams, both of whom had extensive consulting experience, to join the group. While I took some initial steps in promoting the group, I soon discovered it would take considerable effort to really drum up much business. To my surprise, I also became heavily involved in other projects and retirement pursuits. So, thus far, The Gettysburg Group has been a group in name only. But I have been personally engaged in a handful of consulting projects, including conducting a seminary presidential review, executive coaching for a new president and leading a comprehensive administrative audit at her school, as well as a similar organizational climate assessment process at another school.

When she heard of my impending retirement, Union's Dean at the time, Dr. Mary Boys, asked that I consider a very part-time role as Director of Lutheran Formation. This modest position involved occasional gatherings with Union students who were in various degrees of exploring or developing their Lutheran identity. I was available to them for personal counsel and advice in their relationships with the synodical candidacy committees and accompanied them to annual gatherings with peers from the other northeastern divinity schools, Harvard, Yale, and Princeton. At Union I also taught a course in ELCA polity and history, and an advanced Doctor of Ministry course, "Leadership in Complex Systems," designed for chaplains in large hospital systems. It was enjoyable and rewarding getting to know a small circle of Union's bright and challenging students, and the Lutherans especially seemed to appreciate my support and encouragement.

In yet another unforeseen institutional connection, I was invited to serve as adjunct faculty in Eastern Mennonite University's (EMU) aviation management program at its satellite campus in Lancaster, Pennsylvania. This resulted from my serving with the FAA Safety Team at the request of its former manager, John Sibole, who went on to become the EMU program director. I enjoyed this experience teaching undergraduates in basic organizational theory and leadership but found a weekly four-hour evening class followed by a late-night drive home from Lancaster a bit exhausting.

Adding "Journalist" to My Resume

The biggest surprise that came my way right after leaving the Seminary was the opportunity to launch what I have called my "encore journalism career." Within weeks of retiring, I spotted an ad in our local *Gettysburg Times* newspaper for a part-time "correspondent." Since I knew the paper's managing editor, Alex Hayes, I sent off an email expressing interest in learning more about what the work would entail. Alex responded quickly and we met to discuss the possibility, after which he assigned me two regular "beats"—a school board and township board of supervisors.

Although I had done a lot of writing over my career, I had no experience or formal training in journalism. With a bit of coaching from Alex and other *Times* veterans, I adapted quickly to the style of writing required, which differs considerably from that in academic and ecclesiastical publications. As time went on, Alex began sending more and more assignments my way, including major feature stories, to the extent I often had front-page articles appearing a couple of times a week. I also began submitting regular brief personal reflections to the Saturday "Reporter's Notebook" page, as well as occasional op ed reflections on a range of topics. After a few months, I began receiving encouraging comments as I moved about the community. I was told I had developed "a following," and that many readers in the greater Gettysburg area appreciated my contributions. I enjoyed roaming around Adams County, seeing old friends, meeting new folks and sharing their stories, and contributing to local journalism, which I regard as more important now than ever.

Early in my work for the *Times*, I was assigned to cover a Republican caucus at which a candidate would be nominated to replace our Pennsylvania State Senator who had resigned. In that first encounter with Douglas Mastriano, I grasped that he was an ultra-rightist with an ego that knows no bounds. As time went on, I began following him closely, including viewing many of his long social media rants on evening Facebook chats. Growing increasingly concerned, particularly regarding his Christian nationalist perspectives, I began writing occasional op eds for the *Times*, as well as news stories covering campaign events when he announced his candidacy to become Pennsylvania' governor.

After one of the senator's "fireside chats," in which he encouraged people whose churches were closed during the Covid-19 pandemic to find a better church, and bastardized some of Martin Luther's perspectives to bolster his stance, I invited Lutheran clergy colleagues to marshal a joint response. A total of three dozen of us published an ad in the *Times* in which we challenged the senator's views. He went ballistic! While not specifically named, in his next Facebook diatribe I was described as "a hack." Covering a summer 2021 campaign event, I was physically intercepted and turned away by one of the senator's "bodyguards" as I approached him for an interview.

In a contested primary with multiple Republican candidates, Mastriano succeeded in garnering the nomination for the 2022 fall gubernatorial election, which he lost by a landslide of more than fifteen percent. I persist in being a watchdog of this man who, in my judgment, poses one of the greatest threats to American democracy and authentic public Christian witness. My tailing Mastriano resulted in his featuring prominently as a prime case study in Pamela's 2002 book, *The Psychology of Christian Nationalism*.

Watching ULS Implode: An Excruciating Time

I have always been of the conviction that when a leader leaves a post, she or he must be very careful not to intrude in the ongoing life of a community or organization. As I was winding up my days at Gettysburg, a few trustees and others suggested I might serve in some ongoing capacity. I insisted I would only accept any such roles at the express invitation of the current president. Since leaving the office of president, I have only occasionally returned to campus for a *Music Gettysburg!* concert or other public events, and a couple of faculty farewells at the invitation of an interim president. Since I was expressly invited, I attended the inaugurations of both the first two presidents, but have avoided graduations, alumni events, public lectures etc.

Within weeks of retiring, at social events around the community, I began to hear rumblings of dissatisfaction with the ULS first president. Her style was described as abrupt and aloof. Staff at Gettysburg felt she dismissed their perspectives in favor of two vice presidents and others on the Philadelphia campus. Except for Kristin Largen and Angela Zimmann, my former colleagues either resigned or were dismissed within the first few months. It was extremely painful to watch such shoddy treatment of talented and committed people.

The story of the unraveling of the presidency and Theresa Latini's dismissal by the board after just seven months is a complex one. Given that this book is my autobiography, this is not the place to share the details of that story. As noted in the Introduction, since no one appeared to be capturing it for history, I compiled an extensive chronology of events from publicly available documents and news reports. Given the sensitivities involved, however, including for many living individuals and the still-fragile "new institution," it is for the best that detailed history remain sequestered in sealed archives until some future time.

To summarize briefly, the early months of leadership at United Lutheran Seminary were described by many as "a disaster." Millions of dollars were squandered[1], to the ignorance of the board, which received no credible financial reports during the first two years of ULS's existence. The presidency ended abruptly following revelations the incumbent had omitted from her resume an earlier stint in which she headed an organization advocating "conversion" of gay and lesbian persons. As word spread on both LTBTQ-friendly campuses, there was a firestorm. Many accepted Latini's disavowal of her earlier views, but the failure to disclose her past eroded trust, and the fledgling presidency was doomed. The board was rent asunder, with its officers' resignations leaving a vacuum. After the first president's abrupt departure, when a capable interim president finally fired the husband-and-wife team of vice presidents David Lose had brought to Philadelphia, they sued ULS for wrongful dismissal. While the amounts of severance and settlements are confidential, undoubtedly, they contributed significantly to the staggering deficits incurred by ULS during its initial years.[2]

As I watched all this unfold, I was aghast at the pain caused to so many individuals I had come to love and admire. A few sought me out for personal support or my historical knowledge that might help avoid further chaos. It was also conveyed to me that some suspected I was somehow undermining the new president and her team. When my own bishop, who served briefly as acting president, said we could not be seen together in public I just shook my head. Making reference to the infamous Watergate furtive meetings of a reporter and high FBI official, who met by night, I said, "Bishop, I'm not going to meet you in an underground parking garage!" A low point for me was when David Lose

---

1. The ULS Self-Study prepared for its reaccreditation visits in 2021 stated: *The interim CFO's report to the board in September 2019 summarized the major problems within the financial services office during the seminary's first two years (Evidence: Board Sept 2019 CFO Report). Among the problems the interim CFO discovered: an improperly designed general ledger, leading to issues with fiscal year rollover balances; donations of permanently restricted funds were co-mingled in accounts with temporarily restricted funds; erroneous procedures resulted in overstatement of both income and expense.* That report documented that the initial total indebtedness of $17 million (including all LTSP external and endowment-related internal debt) had ballooned to more than $24 million.

2. The lawsuit is a matter of public record, but not details of the out-of-court settlement.

published a widely disseminated blog post suggesting that a great deal of the fault for the president's troubles lay with my former senior staff members. Nothing could have been farther from the truth. To a person, they were committed to serve the new president had she allowed.

Following a brief interlude in which Bishop Jim Dunlop was acting president, ULS was served for more than a year by Dr. Richard Green, a seasoned former college president, whose calming presence helped stabilize things. After another short interim period, in which Angela Zimmann continued rebuilding confidence, ULS called Rev. Dr. Guy Erwin, an ELCA bishop from California and former college professor. His positive, upbeat leadership has brought a measure of stability that suggests ULS can have a bright future. Additionally, the president's being a married gay Native American enhanced the ULS profile as a broadly inclusive, welcoming community. It also helped things greatly that, within the first year, a donor we had cultivated throughout my presidency, died and left ULS $33 million in her estate. That gave the fledgling united seminary breathing room and enabled ULS to offer full scholarships to all students, thereby strengthening its ability to rebuild enrollment amidst the increasingly competitive world of theological education.

On occasion I am asked if I had it to do over again, would I lead Gettysburg into the consolidation with Philadelphia. Yes, I continue to believe it was the best stewardship of resources for ELCA theological education in the northeast. I remain convinced there is a powerful lasting witness in two rival schools with 150 years of strained relationships coming together as a united entity. While its challenges remain considerable, with good leadership moving forward, I believe ULS has a promising future.

The Registry Put Me Back in a President's Office

Within my first year of retirement, I accompanied Pamela to the annual meeting of the American Academy of Religion (AAR), where she introduced me to Dr. Bill Nelsen, a senior consultant with *The Registry*. A former Lutheran college president and ELCA pastor, Nelsen was eager to explore my willingness to join the organization, which matches available retired presidents and other senior executives with interim positions in academic institutions. Nelsen and others were seeking to make *The Registry* gain more traction in theological education circles. As noted above, while he was still at ULS, I joined Richard Green in a *Registry* consulting assignment with Lancaster Seminary. Following completion of that assignment, Lancaster began a search for an interim president, and I was invited by *The Registry* to be a candidate. It became evident in the interviews that the school's faculty were wary of me, given their perceptions that I had not adequately supported faculty during the ULS consolidation process. While a bit disappointed in not being selected, I was also relieved to not enter even a short-term role where some were biased against me from the outset.

In the summer of 2022, Bill Nelsen called to ask if I would consider the interim presidency at Brite Divinity School, a progressive seminary in Fort Worth, Texas. For some time, I had been telling Pam and a few friends I felt "I may have another short chapter of leadership in me before retiring fully." This opportunity to lead a nationally recognized divinity school for a short period piqued my interest. The school needed a steady hand following the retirement of a president who had served two decades. There also were some issues to be resolved in terms of better communication, restoring board-faculty mutual respect, and helping the school in strategic planning and recovery from a nosedive in enrollment.

The greatest challenge by far as I entered the Brite interim was a health crisis that came as a "bolt out of the blue." In my second week in Fort Worth, a stomachache I had experienced sporadically for several months became more and more severe. Finally, I admitted myself to the nearest emergency room in the middle of the night. Following diagnostic tests, it was revealed I had another bowel obstruction similar to those that required two surgeries in my adolescence. Apparently, scar tissue from those earlier surgeries had twisted my small bowel in contortions that became a "case study" for the surgeons at Texas Health Harris Hospital in downtown Fort Worth. When I pleaded with the surgeon to postpone surgery until Pam could return from Vienna where she was wrapping up a research trip, he responded, "We're booking an operating room now and I want to personally do this surgery." I later discovered he was the huge medical center's chief of surgery. Following surgery, I endured a round of complications that brought me back on two other occasions, for a combined total of eighteen days of hospitalization.

The great blessing amidst the trauma of my prolonged medical ordeal was the love of family and friends I experienced. Since Pam was overseas, Aaron hopped on a plane in Chicago and arrived in Fort Worth the night my surgery was completed. Pam rushed back from Vienna and spent several weeks lovingly caring for me in the hospital and during recovery at home. Macrina and James drove from California shortly after my surgery, and Adam left his own family behind at Thanksgiving to spend several days caring for me when Pam had to attend a conference and return to care for things in Pennsylvania. From across the country came flowers, cards, texts, emails, and calls from dear friends assuring me of their love and prayers. It was also a gift that the Brite Board of Trustees chair, Dr. Stuart McDonald, is a prominent physician who practices at Harris Hospital. Every day he was making patient visits or responding to emergencies, he stopped by to check on me. I am also grateful to Brite's very capable and gracious Dean and Executive Vice President, Rev. Dr. Michael Miller, who stepped back in as acting president during my medical crisis. Following my final round of hospitalization, I returned to work remotely with reduced hours in the office. After a few weeks at that pace, I resumed full-time on-campus work after Thanksgiving.

As I finish work on the book, I remain in the final months of the interim assignment at Brite. While its leaders will render their own assessment, I feel it's gone well, and I have made some significant contributions. I blended well with other members of the administrative team and seem to have been appreciated by most of the faculty members. My tenure there has included development of a new strategic plan, working with the dean in several key personnel transitions, offering counsel to the presidential search team, and leading the effort to grant full scholarships to all students. In addition to easing the burden on students, that bold move resulted in a fall 2023 entering class more than double in number as compared to the past several years. While the stated goal of enhancing communication and a sense of "shared governance" was somewhat elusive and hard to measure, I think the state of board-faculty relations improved significantly. I hope my experience and insights have been of value to this fine institution. I will be watching from afar as the years go by at Brite, with gratitude for the brief time I was a fellow traveler in that community.

And Another Challenging Project

Shortly before the invitation to Brite was extended in mid-2022, I was asked to conduct a major project for the ELCA Churchwide Organization, a comprehensive audit of its Foundation's restricted funds, which had been without close oversight for several years. With multiple staff turnovers, the pandemic's interruption of work patterns, and another major ELCA restructuring, it was time for someone with the requisite skills to review 800 endowment funds to ensure their continuing use according to the original donors' intent. Since I had experience with endowment oversight as a seminary president and had participated in reviewing restricted funds to ensure their seamless transfer as the United Lutheran Seminary consolidation proceeded, I felt up to the task. Over the course of six months, including some evenings and weekends while serving Brite, I spent many hours reviewing the digital files, spot-checking payments to beneficiaries, and making recommendations regarding how fund usage could be adapted to new realities. The ELCA executives who commissioned me for the project seemed pleased with my work, and I was glad to offer some assistance to my denomination.

End Word: Summing It All Up (Thus Far!)

As noted in the introduction, beyond being a mere chronological recounting of life events, an autobiography or memoir seeks to answer that haunting question: What does it all mean? How can I briefly sum up a life of seven decades thus far? How does one take stock of a career in ministry? Some contend that ministry is not a "career" at all, but rather simply the daily exercise of a sacred calling or vocation. The very notion that one "makes progress" or "is promoted," as commonly understood in most occupations, is anathema to many in the profession of ministry. Indeed, its very characterization as "profession" remains contested. Whatever it involves, engaging oneself and others in the quest to grow closer to and be more faithful to God transcends the application of knowledge and skills according to a standard of care, the common definition of a "profession." In another sense, the fact that at the very heart of ministry is "profession" of what one is convinced is true and authentic, would suggest it is of all professions *the* most authentic.

Upon retirement or at other key milestones in professional life, it is natural for a practitioner to look back with self-assessment. Indeed, as Socrates' assertion that "the unexamined life is not worth living" suggests, self-reflection is not peripheral but central to meaning making. Psychologist Erik Erikson and others built upon this ancient insight in recognizing that, absent a search to integrate the whole of one's life in some measure, older persons will experience disillusionment and even despair. As I have had the luxury of time post-retirement to engage in more self-reflection and the search for integrity of which Erikson wrote, I have begun to discern the major themes in my life's symphony thus far.

They are interwoven with the values, habits and *weltanschaung* (world view) embedded in me since my early years.

While not a workaholic (I really can and do enjoy rest, recreation and "down time"), the work ethic I learned on a small dairy farm served me well in a series of demanding ministry contexts. When tempted to say of some task or long-term project, "It's too difficult and demanding or too prolonged a process," I would think of my Dad milking the cows morning and night, every day of every year for decades. I quipped in conversations on some occasions, "A cow's full udder is no respecter of the dairy farmer's desire for a day off, sick time or a vacation." Indeed, I recalled those days when Dad was sick as a dog, but since he had no fallback, got out of bed, and did his chores.

Similarly, the embedding in my memory of stories from Mom's and Dad's early years gave me a certain fortitude in the face of daunting challenges. Several times in their early years farming, a bumper crop of corn and grain was wiped out in minutes by a raging wind and hailstorm. "We'll just keep going," was their only possible response. I tried to emulate that fortitude when confronted by the life-threatening political situations in Chile and El Salvador, when facing the difficult pioneering start-ups at Angelica and the Bay Area Coalition, upon confronting several cycles of severe belt-tightening at the Seminary, and the final challenges of the consolidation.

My self-assessment renders a range of marks or grades. In some areas I think my performance was strong. In other areas of ministry, I would assign mediocre grades. Perhaps in a few, if not failure, a "barely passing" mark is merited. My strengths seemed to fall in areas of administration and "leadership," with complementary ability to be in some measure a "public theologian." As signaled in my first published little book, *On a Wing and a Prayer*, my avocation in the field of aviation created a theoretical framework for organizational leadership. Key themes from my pilot training informed my ecclesial leadership: Keeping one's head amidst crisis or emergency; paying attention to situational awareness, seeking always to make decisions based upon the big picture; and accepting responsibility (as "Pilot in Command") for all that goes on in the organizational system appeared to serve me well, especially in the final chapters as seminary president at Gettysburg. That I have been asked to serve as secretary in many groups over the years points to my eagerness to foster clear communication and distill complex matters into understandable summaries. That same ability to listen carefully, synthesize a variety of perspectives into cohesive common themes, and present them succinctly now serves me well in my journalistic endeavors.

Preaching and Teaching Were Special Joys

In my work with parish call committees during the coalition and synod staff years, all sought a minister who is a great preacher. I always pointed out that they would see a common pattern in candidate resumes presented to them. "No one ranks her- or himself as a poor or even mediocre preacher!" Most of us seem to think we're among the best! My own approach to preaching conformed with the Lutheran commitment to interpret scripture readings appointed for a given Sunday or other festival. I consistently attempted to find some new insight and allow the scriptures to speak to our current situation. My views about preaching are spelled out more clearly in Pamela's and my book, *Exploring Practices of Ministry*, for which I was primary author of the chapter on "Proclamation."

While she was a young pastor serving in North Dakota, Gettysburg graduate Sarah Voorhees took the time to send an email expressing gratitude for an ordination sermon sent to her by a recent graduate. Sarah wrote, "It reminded me that your preaching has been very important to me in my journey toward ministry." She quoted a passage from my sermon at the opening service of her senior year:

> Seek throughout all your days on this hill to become a bit bigger person. Dare to live big, to move beyond pettiness. Take seriously Jesus' words, "Do not be afraid." Of your assignments, the reading lists, your professors, your bishop, your candidacy committee. Respect them. Honor them for their ministries and their responsibilities. Do not be afraid. Look every challenge in the eye and simply do your best; usually it will be enough.

In preaching, I sought to strike a balance between the pastoral and prophetic—or as it's often described, letting the Word "comfort the afflicted and afflict the comfortable." While not a firebrand orator, I attempted to take on some of the tough issues that came along through the years—the proliferation of nuclear arms, anti-immigrant and racist attitudes and actions, economic injustice and the growing wealth gap, homophobia, anti-Muslim attitudes in the wake of September 11, 2001, as well as "local" issues that cropped up in each context of ministry. As a brash young pastor, preaching to a gathering of all the LCA bishops in San

Francisco, I drew some criticism about a sermon stating my conviction the church needed to go further in embracing gay and lesbian persons.

As Donald Trump began emerging on the scene as a presidential candidate, in a December 2015 seminary chapel sermon, "What Then Should We Do"? I said:

> Faced with a candidate for U.S. president who has gained a remarkable following, and who now advocates banning all sisters and brothers who call our common One God "Allah," what then shall we do? Get right back in the face of this in-your-face narcissist bully and say, "Go back to your tower in Manhattan and stay there for a long, long timeout." In other words, treat him as any good junior high school principal would deal with an adolescent whose hormones are out of control.

I went on in that sermon to address also the vexing issues of gun proliferation and climate change:

> Confronted by legislators at all levels of government too cowardly to take on the gun lobbyists as week after week fellow citizens bleed out in the streets or their homes or workplaces, what then shall we do? Tell them their platitudes to pray for the victims and their families are not enough; to move beyond the gross misinterpretations of the second amendment and enact the kind of gun regulation and reduction laws that most other nations have found sensible and salutary.
>
> Perplexed by the daunting challenges of an endangered environment, when for the first time in human history there is reason to fear whether our great-grandchildren will inhabit a livable planet, what should we do? Redouble our greening endeavors; walk and bicycle more; reduce our consumption; live in smaller and more energy-efficient places; continue to advocate for and support renewable energy alternatives.

Comparing myself to others, I never saw myself as a highly effective or engaging teacher. But as the years went by, I grew in confidence and enjoyment in that role too. My best training in pedagogy was when I prepared to become a flight instructor and had to pass an FAA exam in learning theory and related subjects. While to some degree, clergy are always teaching, the greatest opportunities for more formal classroom instruction presented themselves in my years at the Seminary. In my first couple of years, I team-taught a course in "Congregations as Systems" with Dean Norma Wood. After Norma retired, I reshaped that syllabus and regularly taught the senior seminar (entitled "Integrative Seminar") for the Master of Divinity students in their final year. I especially enjoyed that interaction with students who had gained some practical experience in parish internships and were hungry to hone skills in administration and leadership before going out on their own, most as solo practitioner leaders in small to midsize congregations.

I found that the relationship with students was among the most gratifying parts of being seminary president. Over the years, a number have offered kind expressions of appreciation for my approachability and interactions in the classroom and the more informal encounters that happened in a residential community. As he was about to graduate, in May 2008, Paul Wayne Benjamin wrote a letter to the chair of the Board of Directors "to express my heartfelt appreciation for the seminary's pastor-president, Michael Cooper-White." Benjamin wrote:

> The pastor-president has been an inspiration to me in my time at seminary. First, he greeted us very warmly during the prospective student weekends and that was one of the reasons I chose to attend Gettysburg. Second, he inquired about my back pain and progress during my illness the first semester. Third, he attended our wedding and offered prayerful support during my second year. Fourth, he attended our World AIDS \Day candlelight vigil on campus and joined us in prayer. Fifth, I have witnessed him cutting brush and doing yard work numerous times throughout the summer to keep our campus looking crisp and clean. Sixth, I have received great pleasure from reading his on-line column "From the PO" that affords me time to reflect theologically on our mission and ministry. And finally, I learned a great deal from his course in Church Administration and Leadership during my last semester here on the ridge."
>
> In none of the institutions I have attended and worked for have I found such inspirational leadership in the organization's president. Michael Cooper-White is an example and a model for ministry. I cannot tell you how much he has meant to me during my time at Gettysburg, especially when I know how very busy he is. Those acts of kindness that I listed may seem small to some folks, but in a rushed world where everyone is too busy for one another it means so much to me.

Gettysburg was fairly unique among institutions in its long tradition that, rather than inviting a distinguished guest to deliver a commencement address, that honor was reserved for the president. I was told when I arrived that the tradition was established decades previous after a couple of invited outside guests failed to connect with the seniors, or perhaps have any real grasp of theological education and seminary realities. At any rate, it was a privilege each year to craft a message I hope offered some encouragement and excitement to the graduates, and also expressed appreciation to them for all they had contributed during their student years.

Another annual highlight was the fall "LutherBowl" touch football tournament played on our campus, in the spacious fields right behind our house. Dating back to my student days, when the annual face-off was just between Gettysburg and Philadelphia, the playoff had grown to eight teams from ELCA and ecumenical partner schools. Carloads of student athletes converged every fall from as far away as Chicago. Entirely student-led and hosted, our only role as school administrators was to join the festivities and cheer on our local team (which, alas, in my seventeen years of cheering never won the championship!) At one point I did need to intervene after there were seven trips to the local emergency room on the Saturday of the playoffs. I insisted that thereafter trained referees were contracted to keep things in check and avoid future mayhem. A couple of years, I even joined the LTSG roster on game day and jumped into a game for a few plays at both offense and defense. Those and other traditions, where we as faculty and administrators joined in with students, were great fun and leave me with cherished memories.

I especially appreciated the love, concern and care shown by students during both high and low moments in our personal lives. Congratulatory applause was offered in chapel when I announced the birth of our granddaughters. Sympathy cards and flowers were presented when word spread first of my mother's and then father's death.

It All Comes Down to Faith

Beyond any sort of self-diagnostic assessment or weighing the votes of others who appear at the polls when one's success or failure is evaluated, lie the middle-of-the-night conversations with the Almighty. "Oh, dear God, have I been faithful to my unique calling? Recognizing I can never merit your love or grace, and don't need to because of your extraordinary mercy and compassion, I nevertheless ask in all humility, 'Have I been a good steward? Have I been on the right side of history? Done a bit more good than harm?'"

My theological convictions are clear: the answers to all of the above questions have no bearing whatsoever on my eternal salvation. God has taken care of that. Whatever happens when my earthly sojourn ends, I am confident with St. Paul that, nothing "in all creation will separate us from the love of God in Christ Jesus our Lord." (Romans 8:39) Nevertheless, the answers to those questions about faithfulness and effectiveness matter to me in a penultimate sense. When the final moments come, if I am aware enough to ask one last time, it will matter whether or not I personally conclude that I lived a *good life*. As I write now, I answer that question as follows: Yes, I have received unmerited gifts in extraordinary measure.

The degree of unearned privilege I have enjoyed as a white male in the latter half of the twentieth century should not be underestimated. That status and my social location afforded enormous advantages, by comparison to women, persons of color, and the millions without access to the resources made available to me. Added to those demographic realities is the fact that I was raised in an intact and largely harmonious family environment, with parents and siblings who loved and desired the best for me. I have enjoyed and benefited enormously from access to affordable quality education. Except for a ruptured appendix that nearly caused my death in my teens, and the bowel obstruction that required another emergency recent surgery, I have been fortunate to enjoy good health, undergirded by readily available medical care. To be sure, there have been annoying back aches, colds, flu bouts, and a relatively mild case of Covid-19. But I have been spared debilitating health crises that could have impeded my career and adversely impacted family life.

Divorce in my mid-thirties remains the greatest personal crisis of my life thus far. But again, I was fortunate that long-held taboos against clergy divorce had given way to a general climate of compassion and understanding. My bishop and boss, Stanley Olson, could not have been more supportive, signaling broadly that it was beyond question I would continue in the post as his assistant. Other colleagues and friends buoyed me up and helped me avert prolonged depression. Nevertheless, I endured the gut-wrenching experience of family separation, spending most of my time apart from my two beautiful young sons, Aaron and Adam. Despite the separation by distance when Doris remarried and moved to Nebraska while Pam and I remained in California, I am grateful that the boys and we maintained a close relationship. It has been a joy watching them grow into the fine men they are today.

I have said on occasion that the divorce and family break-up taught me more about the grace of God than any other experience of my life. As my marriage to Doris was ending, I expected to be single for a good long while. To my amazement, a new love emerged quickly, and sharing the journey with Pamela since the mid-1980's has brought joys beyond measure. Ours has never been a simple or uncomplicated relationship. In her words, by virtue of backgrounds (she the only child of a suburban Boston couple, educated at Boston and Harvard Universities; and I a farm boy from rural Minnesota with far less impressive academic pedigree) ours is a "cross-cultural marriage." Prolonged periods of living apart as we have navigated a commuter marriage the past quarter-century challenged our relationship, but ultimately strengthened the bonds of love. Most challenging were the years we served at rival "sister" institutions, the two Lutheran seminaries in Pennsylvania. But through all the ups and downs, our commitment to each other, our marriage and family has remained strong and unwavering.

We have long imagined coauthoring a book on how we and other couples in commuter marriages navigate the challenges of "living apart together." In our case, except for rare occasions when one or the other was absolutely unavailable, we have held nightly extended *Facetime* conversations. No matter how busy with our hectic schedules and many projects, we have held fast to being in touch on a daily basis in this way, as well as by frequent email and text exchanges. Grateful for the wonders of modern technology, we may have spent more "quality time" than many couples who live together uninterruptedly.

And Life Might Have Been Different

At this waystation, I can say that I have no regrets about the path my professional life has taken. And at the same time I acknowledge a wistfulness about a few "might have beens." I cannot imagine a fulfilling life that did not include years in ministry, preaching and public speaking, and leading historic but somewhat fragile organizations in times of great change. My portrait appears alongside some of the giants in American Lutheran history—at Angelica church in Los Angeles and in the library of Gettysburg (now a part of United) Lutheran Seminary. To be in a lineup that includes the likes of Segerhammar and Burke, Schmucker, Wentz, Heiges and Stuempfle is humbling indeed.

The wistfulness lies in wondering how things would have evolved if ministry had been my "second career" following a stint as an airline pilot, attorney, or other professional. Watching several young people I have taught to fly land airline careers after advanced training makes me wonder how things might have been had I received greater encouragement and been less risk-averse following college. Or had I followed the strong advice of college and seminary professors in pursuing an academic doctorate, would I have made greater lasting contributions?

At the end of the day, I am at peace. The overwhelming feeling is one of gratitude. This farm boy from a small midwestern community has traveled much of the world. I have addressed crowds small and large in churches and venues across the country. I have preached and taught in hundreds of congregations, including such renowned places as Washington's National Cathedral. I have rubbed shoulders with some of the finest teachers, scholars, writers, and ecclesial and public leaders of our time. Two outstanding Lutheran colleges—Susquehanna and Gettysburg—have conferred honorary doctorates. For twenty years, I was a trusted colleague and advisor to two synodical bishops and the ELCA's first two presiding bishops. During my Chicago years, I was also a partner with all sixty-five synodical bishops throughout the entire ELCA, and a peer among the senior executive leadership team called the Cabinet of Executives. While coming up short in the end, my emergence twice as a top candidate for the ELCA secretary's position was a measure of widespread recognition of and confidence in my ecclesiastical leadership abilities and administrative competency. Along the way, I was privileged to be a traveling companion with a handful of people I consider among the heroes of the faith in the twentieth and twenty-first century—Helmut Frenz and Medardo Gomez in particular.

During the Gettysburg years, mine was the privilege of working with and helping shape an outstanding faculty, recruiting competent staff, serving with dedicated board members, and an expansive network of alumni/ae and generous supporters. Opportunities for community leadership came my way as I joined other key local leaders in planning and preparing for the 150th anniversary commemoration of the great Battle of Gettysburg. The creation of the Seminary Ridge Museum drew me into circles that included local, state, and national leaders. At its dedication in

July 2013, we hosted the Governor of Pennsylvania, one of our Senators, and all regional and local political leaders.

And now in retirement, opportunities for a modest advisor role at Union Seminary, serving as Brite's Interim President, and teaching as adjunct faculty in Eastern Mennonite University's aviation degree program have allowed me to keep a foot in the world of academia. These roles have provided ongoing occasions to interact with a broad range of local, state, and even national leaders in various fields. My journalistic work with *The Gettysburg Times* enabled me to continue the joy of writing, stay abreast of life in the local community, and share in print the inspiring stories of some well-known as well as "ordinary folk" whose stories are worth telling. While limited due to my other involvements, the consulting assignments I accepted seemed to be appreciated by and helpful, especially to younger leaders.

The Greatest Blessings of All: Family and Friends

As I have come to grasp more fully how the world is wired, I have become more cautious in using the word "blessed" to describe my feelings of gratitude. The risk in suggesting that I have been blessed by God is to imply that others who have had less fortune and suffered difficult lives have not been so favored by the Almighty. I simply do not believe that. I can only entrust to mystery how some of God's beloved creatures have relatively easy lives and others' journeys are filled with pain, struggle, and oppression. At the same time, simply leaving it at "I've just been lucky" does not feel quite right either. But perhaps that is the more accurate conclusion. I *have* been incredibly fortunate. My life *has been* and *is* rich and full. Thus far, our immediate family members have been spared horrible diseases or other crises that plague so many. Our "kids" have chosen wisely in their life partners and brought us the delight of being grandparents. For three dozen years I have been married to an amazing, brilliant woman and delightful companion. Her stellar academic career, with prestigious positions at Philadelphia, Columbia (in Decatur, Georgia) and Union seminaries took us into lively centers of theological inquiry in exciting urban locales. Each provided a lovely faculty home, which we enjoyed in tandem with the Gettysburg president's residence and our sequential personal properties. Now in retirement, Pam and I are assured of adequate financial resources should we live another two or three decades.

Our three wonderful children, Aaron, Adam, and Macrina

But the greatest blessings, which I regard as totally unearned and unmerited gifts, are the members of our family and a broad network of friends who make life joyful. Each of our three children found wonderful spouses and have blessed us with a total of four granddaughters as of this writing. Aaron and Melissa Ramirez were married on August 28, 2004, in Chicago, and their daughter Marina, now an extraordinarily well-rounded teenager, was born October 27, 2009. Aaron and Melissa are both communication professionals, who have served a range of nonprofit organizations, including the ELCA churchwide organization. Adam married Sara Blazek on July 30, 2011, in Omaha, in the chapel at Boys Town, the world-famous organization where they met. Their wonderful daughters, Monica and Tatum, were born October 8, 2012, and September 6, 2016 respectively. Adam and Sara have both served in social work positions; she is currently teaching, and he now is an internal auditor at Creighton University. New York City's Cathedral of St. John the Divine was the setting for Macrina's marriage to James Dieffenbach on September 14, 2019. As I am completing the manuscript for this book, we were recently in Los Angeles for the birth of their beautiful first child, Ella, on July 10, 2023. Macrina works for the international tech giant *Meta* as a researcher, and James is an independent singer/songwriter. Over the years, joining in the celebrations of weddings, births, baptisms, birthday celebrations, graduations and other high moments of our immediate family has been such a joy. It has also been an unexpected gift in recent years to draw closer to my brother Dave and his wife Diane. Living less than a two-hour drive apart means we can "be there for each other" in ways that weren't the case for much of our adult lives. That feels especially important as we move along in life's final decades.

Our family: Macrina's and James' wedding at St. John the Divine Cathedral, NYC, in 2019; their daughter Ella was born in 2023.

As this autobiography is being completed in the fall of 2023, Pam has just joined the ranks of the retired. The prospect of our now living together full-time after our prolonged commuter marriage pattern is a happy one indeed! We look forward to spending more time in the places our family members reside. Also, given her international reputation as a leading scholar in the field of pastoral theology, and recent publication of a blockbuster timely new book on Christian Nationalism,[1] continuing public speaking invitations are likely to be forthcoming for Pam. I will likely tag along when possible, providing additional opportunities to enjoy interesting places and meet new people.

---

1. Pamela is the author of ten books, as well as dozens of articles and contributions to other publications. Her most recent book is *The Psychology of Christian Nationalism* (published 2022 by Fortress Press).

Looking Ahead at Crossroads to Come

Regardless of age, of course, none of us ever knows how much time awaits us before death. But hoping another decade or more awaits me, I conclude this book looking forward to what may lie up ahead. As noted, the interim presidency at Brite is currently in its final stages. While a "fully retired" status has its appeal, I sense there may be more opportunities for some part-time professional engagements. I would enjoy occasional consulting with parishes and other church and nonprofit organizations. As long as my health allows, I expect to continue flying, and perhaps flight instructing for a few more years. I am likely to resume some degree of journalism, if requested by the *Gettysburg Times* and other publications. There may be some major writing projects after this book that well up within me; about that we shall see.

For the immediate coming years, our plan is to continue enjoying our beloved Pennsylvania home. At some point it is likely that advanced aging and health conditions will suggest the wisdom of our final years spent in a retirement community with progressive stages of care. Of course, the possibility of major illness or disease or even sudden death does grow as one advances in age. Having witnessed the diminution of one's world and growth of health-related struggles in all four of our parents, I am not sure I aspire to reach my parents' respective ages of ninety-two and one hundred. But if allowed to approach those milestones, I may well feel differently about the matter! Time will tell.

As I contemplate my life's final phase, I also reflect upon the larger context in which we find ourselves at this juncture in history. More optimistic than pessimistic, I am nevertheless deeply concerned about the future of our nation and the world, and how life will be for our children, grandkids, and future generations. The list is long of current crises that are likely to grow worse in the coming years and decades. Climate crisis, continuing racism and other widespread oppressive attitudes and actions, the growing trend of violent deaths, gun proliferation, and the profound political polarization in our country do not portend well for a more "peaceable kingdom" in the coming years.

Despite the foregoing, at this crossroads, in the year of 2023, my seventy-fourth on the planet, I conclude this reflection on my life thus far with an overwhelming sense of gratitude. I am profoundly thankful for the roads opened to me thus far and those who have traveled these ways with me, above all my life partner now for half the journey, Pamela. One cannot ask for a richer life than ours. I am grateful to God for having called me along a pathway described now for 2000 years as the Christian way. The longer I live and the more I study and reflect, I am increasingly convinced that God equally calls others along different pathways. But the Christian road has been and will remain mine. And I believe when this life's journey ends, God will embrace me at that crossroads too. And then we shall see what lies up ahead . . .

www.ingramcontent.com/pod-product-compliance
Lightning Source LLC
Chambersburg PA
CBHW062003220426
43662CB00010B/1216